BUDDHIST PEACEWORK
CREATING CULTURES OF PEACE

Edited by

DAVID W. CHAPPELL

Wisdom Publications • Boston

published in association with
Boston Research Center for the 21st Century

Wisdom Publications
199 Elm Street
Somerville, MA 02144 USA

Library of Congress Cataloging-in-Publication Data
Buddhist peacework: creating cultures of peace / edited by David W Chappell.
   p. cm.
   Includes bibliographical references.
   ISBN 0-86171-167-X (alk. paper)
   1. Peace—Religious aspects—Buddhism. 2. Buddhism—Social aspects
  I. Chappell, David W., 1940–
  BQ4570.P4 B836 1999
  294.3'37873—dc21   99-051657

ISBN 0-86171-167-X
06 05 04 03 02
7 6 5 4 3

Project Manager: Amy Morgante
Style editing by Helen Marie Casey and Amy Morgante
Interior layout by Ralph Buglass
Cover design by Gopa & the Bear
Photo research by The McCoy Group
Cover photos © 1999 Photodisc

Printed in the United States of America

Table of Contents

4
.
.
.
.
.

BUDDHIST PEACEWORK

CREATING CULTURES OF PEACE

Preface

These are exciting yet often arduous times for Buddhist peace movements—a fact to which this volume, *Buddhist Peacework*, eloquently attests. From the moving personal accounts by esteemed teachers and activists gathered here, from editor David Chappell's astute and appreciative commentary, and from Joan Halifax's luminous foreword, it's clear that Buddhist communities abound with nonviolent potential. This potential is the planetary resource most threatened by the events of the distressingly violent and troubled century now drawing to a close.

And yet, hope for the future rests squarely on human potential for inner and outer peaceful transformation. As Gandhi once stated about seemingly hopeless causes, "I remain an optimist, not that there is any evidence that I can give that right is going to prosper, but because of my unflinching faith that right *must* prosper in the end."[1] On another occasion he said, "My optimism rests on my belief in the infinite possibilities of the individual to develop non-violence."[2] The leading Buddhists represented here share Gandhi's undaunted faith in humanity.

Buddhist peacework is distinctive, but hardly alone in an empty field. A widespread, yet underreported, current of peace activity is at work in the world as people struggle to put their deeply held peaceable values into practice in the face of massive threats to these same values.

When Buddhist leader Daisaku Ikeda—an essayist included in this book—established the Boston Research Center for the 21st Century in 1993, he charged the Center: Be a force for the evolution of truly universal values—not Western-imposed values—through dialogue that engages scholars and activists on an equal footing crossculturally and interreligiously. *Buddhist Peacework* is the latest in a series of projects the Center has undertaken since its inception to draw attention to global civil society initiatives worthy of public discourse and support. From a people's view of the United Nations to women's views on the Earth Charter and dialogues on abolishing war, we have publicized ethical statements and visions of peace with potential for broad-based grassroots appeal and mobilization. This is the best testimony we can offer to our own version of Gandhi's belief in the people's power to make peace.

With the United Nations' designation of the year 2000 as the International Year for the Culture of Peace and the decade 2001–2010 as the Decade for a Culture of Peace and Nonviolence for the Children of the World, yet another opportunity for dialogue—this time intra-Buddhist dialogue—presented itself. We hope our modest effort to support UNESCO's Barcelona *Declaration on the Role of Religion in the Promotion of a Culture of Peace* serves to deepen public understanding, and particularly religious understanding, of what peace in its fullest sense actually entails. For an informed perspective on the UNESCO declaration, which is included at the back of this volume along with the declaration itself, we are grateful to Janusz Symonides, director of UNESCO's Department of Peace, Human Rights, Democracy, and Tolerance.

Other thank-yous are in order. What lucky star guided us to David Chappell when we had only the vaguest notion of how this project might take shape? For him, it has been a labor of love from the start. A person whose raison d'être is to build trust where it's scarce, he was overjoyed by the prospect of bringing together the views of many revered Buddhist leaders who do not generally have the opportunity to share the same forum. He quickly warmed to the task of shepherding their words to print and then conscientiously pored over each essay to draw out its wider import.

We thank, too, wordsmith and poet Helen Marie Casey for lending, and at the same time restraining, her considerable editing talents. Her light-handed touch preserved the authentic quality of each voice. Amy Morgante, Boston Research Center's publications manager, ably assisted by work-study student Katie Donahue, provided outstanding and enthusiastic leadership to the whole effort throughout, from conception to the final print run.

We are grateful to the representative cross-section of Buddhist leaders who answered our appeal. Their responses share hard-won insights and discoveries gained from the patient, continuous cultivation of both inner and outer landscapes. As the picture on the book cover implies, Buddhist peacework is close to the earth. It is raised by hand and sustained by constant cultivation. Above all,

this book affirms human responsibility, for, as Daisaku Ikeda reminded us in *New Horizons of a Global Civilization,* "The crux of
our challenge is whether to simply be a passenger on the ship of
fate, leaving everything to others, or to take the helm and be responsible for that ship ourselves to search, with the help of all, for
the most desirable course."[3]

—Virginia Straus
Executive Director
Boston Research Center for the 21st Century

1. Mahatma Gandhi, *All Men Are Brothers: Autobiographical Reflections* (New York: The Continuum Publishing Company, 1990), 70-71.

2. Mohandas Gandhi, *Gandhi on Non-Violence: Selected Texts from Non-Violence in Peace and War* (New York: New Directions Publishing Corp., 1965), 26.

3. Daisaku Ikeda, *New Horizons of a Global Civilization,* 1997 peace proposal
(Tokyo: Soka Gakkai, 1997).

Foreword

Many people have observed that where there is the deep shadow of suffering in the life of the world, then there is also penetrating light. Such are the lives, communities, and work of the compassionate people in this important and wise book. This book explores the lives and actions, insights and guidelines of some of the world's most beloved Buddhist practitioners, teachers, and social activists who are currently working to end suffering in the life of the world. These friends from different cultures and schools of Buddhism are all actively engaged in the singular activity of peacemaking. They express their work of compassion in profoundly diverse, wise, and brave ways. And they have used the philosophy, practice, ethics, community building, and beauty of Buddhism to help with this endless work of compassion in action.

Buddhism has since its inception inspired its practitioners to discover the most radical form of inclusivity. This is the realization that all beings in all realms, no matter how miserable, violent, depraved and deluded, have a mind ground that is not only free of suffering and delusion but also not separate from the mind ground of any other being. Our individual suffering also unites us in a community of suffering as well. We may be a suffering buddha, a wounded buddha, a deluded buddha, but our basic nature, our basic mind ground is free from any defilements and not separate from others. Our wounds are commonly shared as well.

It is not necessarily so easy to realize this. Most of us have not allowed ourselves to look deeper than our personality and culture to see and touch who we really are. Yet, Buddhists and contemplatives of many traditions are encouraged to go within in order to discover not only the so-called oneness of all things but also the peace that surpasses understanding, knowing, ideas, and conceptions, the peace that is basic to all beings when they have come home to a deep and abiding state of nonalienation.

This peace, however, is not complacent. Out of this wise peace arises compassionate, nondual action. If we see that we are not separate from others, then we not only share their enlightenment, we also share their suffering. The right hand then naturally takes care of the left hand, with no expectation of thanks or credit. In peacemaking, there is no self, no other; no peacemaker, no victim; no outcome, no gaining idea. Just making and being peace.

Our authors feel that peacemaking is about realizing and living nonalienation from all beings and living this realization as the Bodhisattva does, riding on the waves of change. Making peace is based in the experience of radical intimacy with the world. It is about the most basic realization that enlightenment is not an individual experience, rather it is the liberation of intimacy in our relatedness with all beings. Enlightenment then is ultimately social, and Buddhism, Buddhists, and buddhas serve and awaken with and through relationships that are based in the functional experience of a deeply shared life, a life that is about nonharming and doing good, and a life grounded in kindness, compassion, wisdom, and skillful means.

Thus, we as humans, as spiritual beings, beings who love and feel compassion, cannot hide from the truth of the pervasiveness of the particular suffering and alienation in the world in which we live today. We cannot turn our backs on the tendency to turn the world and its beings into objects which we call "other." We are called more than ever to realize the obvious, that we are not, nor were we ever, living in a world of isolation. We are completely and inescapably interconnected and interdependent.

Like the Buddha 2,500 years ago, Buddhists today work for the liberation of all beings from the illusion of separation. When there is an "other," there is an Auschwitz, a Kosovo, a caste of people we will not touch, a ravaged and raped woman, a clear-cut forest, an abused and abandoned child, a young boy with fear and hate in his eyes and a gun in his hand, a man behind bars medicated or numbed out of his mind and heart, a rundown village of old women whose men have all died in war.

The basic vows that we take as Buddhists remind us that there is no "other." The most basic practices that all of the schools of Buddhism engaged in underscore the fact that there is no "other." The fundamental teachings of the Buddha tell us that there is no "other." Yet we live in a world peopled by those who are subject to the deepest forms of alienation from their own natural wisdom, a world where whole communities see "others" who should be done away with, liquidated, eliminated.

Today, more than any other time in human history, we are living in a kind of intimacy that can destroy or liberate. Our weapons can find their targets within minutes, our diseases can spread like a wildfire in a dry forest, and our delusions can contaminate the minds of millions instantaneously through the media.

At the same time, in the same instant, we can reach through to endless communities and individuals with acts of compassion and sanity, making peace by strengthening values and behaviors based in compassion and wisdom. We can nurture cultures of peace by transforming our own lives through kindness, compassion, and wisdom. We can work actively for economic justice, racial equality, protection of the environment, protection of human rights and the rights of all beings, wise and humane education, the voluntary control of the growth of the world's population, freedom from weapons, domination, exploitation, and colonialism of all forms, and deep and true dialogue with respect for and appreciation of differences and plurality.

We have a responsibility today to work directly with our own suffering and the suffering in our communities, the world, and the environment. We all live under each other's skin, and it is now more than ever functionally intolerable to turn away from injustice, corruption, violence, hatred, greed, and delusion.

The contributors to this volume, and many more individuals and groups around the world, are peacemakers whose lives and work are based in the realization that we are not separate from each other and that we must and can live sane, beneficial, and meaningful lives. Peace, however, is a process not a goal. It unfolds in the very details of our daily lives as well as in the broad brush strokes of the big picture. This marvelous and inspiring book is like the strong timber found in old bridge spans. May each of us, like the friends in this book, be a strong and joyful bridge that helps numberless beings and communities find their way to peace.

—Joan Halifax Roshi
Head Teacher, Upaya Zen Center
Santa Fe, New Mexico

Introduction

David W. Chappell

May all beings be happy.
May all be joyous and live in safety.
Let no one deceive another, nor despise another, as weak as they may be.
Let no one by anger or by hate wish evil for another.
As a mother, in peril of her own life, watches and protects her only child.
Thus with a limitless spirit must one cherish all living beings.
Love the world in its entirety – above, below and all around.
Without limitation.
With an infinite goodness and with benevolence.
While standing, or walking, sitting or lying down, as long as one is awake,
Let one cultivate Loving-Kindness.
This is called the Supreme Way of Living.
– Metta Sutta[1]

This is not a theoretical book. Several of the authors are in political exile, others have endured civil war, and others are struggling to create social equality and justice under the threat of terrorism and arrest. This volume does not offer theories of peace, but is a report on work in progress.

The only person who did not respond to the invitation letters for this volume is Aung San Suu Kyi of Myanmar (Burma). Since she lives under police surveillance, it is likely that she never received our letter. After she was democratically elected as the national leader in 1989, she was placed under house arrest by the ruling military junta. For her bravery and for her refusal to compromise either her political or ethical principles, which are based on nonviolence, she was awarded the Nobel Peace Prize in 1991.

The challenge facing Aung San Suu Kyi is not unlike challenges faced by everyone in this book. Her specific concerns are how could Myanmar, a major Buddhist culture, become a military dictatorship? Twenty years ago it was said that Burma was the most Buddhist country on earth since it had the largest percentage of Buddhists and was not subservient to the capitalist values of the West.

What went wrong? What must be done by Buddhists to build cultures of peace to avoid another Myanmar?

The Buddhists in this volume all share the concern for building a culture of peace. Their responses to the UNESCO *Declaration on the Role of Religions in the Promotion of a Culture of Peace* describe their local efforts to put the goals of the declaration into practice. Buddhism is famous for bringing inner peace, but what about social harmony, human rights, and environmental balance? The challenge for Buddhists today is not just to develop inner peace, but also social justice; not just inner contentment, but social reform and environmental well-being.

Because of her silent presence in this project, and as a voice for her in her struggle, seeing her as a symbol of the Buddhist peacework that is the goal of this volume, and as a testimony to her compassion even toward those who threaten her own well-being, we dedicate this volume to Aung San Suu Kyi.

THE UNESCO PROJECT

Religion touches those intimate levels of the human heart where trust and hurt can lead to either sympathy or hatred. By guiding these responses, religions can inspire either division or reconciliation, war or peace. Recognizing the potential of religion, UNESCO wisely convened a group of religious leaders in 1993 and 1994 to consider how religions could develop a culture of peace instead of war. The resulting declaration offers guidelines and goals for religious peacework in the global community.

The Buddhist voices in this book who are responding to the UNESCO declaration are important because the ideals of UNESCO cannot become reality until local communities and individuals become peacemakers. Many of the practices described by the respondents provide new information for Buddhists and non-Buddhists alike since the authors stand at the cutting edge of new developments in the Buddhist community and reveal new models for Buddhist practice in the modern world.

BUDDHIST VALUES

Buddhists are those who take refuge in the Buddha, his teachings (the Dharma), and the Buddhist community (the Sangha). All

INTRODUCTION

Buddhists are unified in their reverence for these Three Refuges, also called the Three Jewels or the Triple Gem of Buddhism. Unlike Christians who recite the Apostle's Creed, however, Buddhist initiates do not say that they "believe in" the Buddha, the Dharma, and the Sangha, but affirm how they go to these for guidance and refuge.

Buddhists are wary of doctrines and beliefs as potential causes of conflict since they are culturally conditioned, partial, limited, and changing. When doctrines are held too tightly, they can lead to misunderstanding, division, and harm. As a result, Buddhists recognize that there can be many interpretations of the Buddha, his teaching, and the Buddhist community. Instead of emphasizing doctrine, a more central focus for Buddhists has been the goal to lessen suffering by dissolving attachment, hatred, and ignorance, and by recognizing the interdependence and impermanence of existence. As a result, Buddhists have a wide range of practices and ideas, but are notable for developing inner and outer harmony and for avoiding holy wars and conflicts over religious differences.

BUDDHIST COMMUNITIES

There are many kinds of Buddhists based on differences of culture and methods of practice, but a major division exists between monastics and laity because monastics have left family life and made vows of celibacy and poverty. The collection of articles in this volume is almost evenly divided between articles by monastic and by lay Buddhist leaders. Also, Buddhists have always acknowledged different styles and levels of practice, ranging from solitary practice in the forest to practice in groups and in society. Although the Buddha himself began practicing with groups and then as a solitary practitioner, he later became very socially active. Buddhist scholar and social worker Harvey Aronson carefully analyzed early types of Buddhist meditation, but discovered that after enlightenment the Buddha's social activism was motivated not by a special kind of Buddhist compassion, but as an expression of common human sympathy. As an early scripture says:

Monks, there is one individual who arose and came to be for the welfare of the multitudes, for the happiness of the multitudes, out of sympathy for the world; for the benefit, welfare, and happiness

17

of gods and humans. Who is that one individual? The Harmonious
One, the Perfectly Enlightened One.[2]

Early Buddhism forbade monastics to create sectarian divisions,
and this rule was enforced by the Buddhist King Asoka who la-
icized any monastic who was guilty of dividing the Buddhist community (the Sangha). Nevertheless, over time three different streams
of practice arose based on three different scriptural collections, often called the "three turnings of the wheel" of Buddhist teaching.
Early Buddhist scriptures preserved in Chinese and Pali represent
the first turning of the wheel and are the basis for the "Way of the
Elders," or Theravada Buddhism that is found today in Sri Lanka
and Southeast Asia. A few hundred years later, these early scriptures
were supplemented by a large number of other scriptures that contained many new teachings. Most East Asian Buddhists are practitioners of these new scriptures and call themselves the Greater Ve-
hicle, or Mahayana Buddhism. Finally, the third turning of the wheel
is called Esoteric or Vajrayana Buddhism, based on another set of
new scriptures that survive in Tibetan and Chinese. Esoteric Buddhism is practiced in Tibet, Mongolia, and Japan.

Besides these three "turnings of the wheel," each cultural area
has a wide variety of Buddhist organizations, often shaped by political and social factors. Unlike Roman Christianity or the Islamic
Sunnah, Buddhism is very decentralized. There is no central leader
nor organization for either Theravada, Mahayana, or Esoteric Buddhism, and no primary pilgrimage site and no unifying rituals beyond taking refuge in the Three Jewels. The acceptance of diversity
in Buddhism is notable in itself and means that there is a similar
variety in Buddhist peacework.

THE CONTRIBUTORS

The authors in this volume were chosen to reflect the diversity
of Buddhist communities, both culturally and in terms of Buddhist traditions of practice. The Buddhist communities in Sri
Lanka and Southeast Asia, who constitute Theravada (the Way of
the Elders) and share a common set of Buddhist scriptures preserved in the Pali language, are represented by two monks (Ven.
Gunaratana and Ven. Maha Ghosananda) and two laity (Dr. A.K.
Ariyaratne and Acharn Sulak Sivaraksa). These four speak out of a

related geographical area, but also out of Theravada as a stream of Buddhist practice that does not use Mahayana or Esoteric Buddhist scriptures.

Another Buddhist grouping is the Mahayana stream that uses Sanskrit and Chinese Buddhist scriptures in the cultural region of East Asia and is represented by four monastics (Ven. Sheng-yen, Ven. Cheng-yen, Ven. Kosan, and Ven. Jeon) and a layman (Dr. Daisaku Ikeda). One of the largest Japanese Mahayana groups is Jodo Shinshu (the True Denomination of Pure Land), but even though invitations were sent to several leaders, none were able to send a response in time to meet publication requirements. A different cultural region that utilizes Tibetan Buddhist scriptures in the Vajrayana Buddhist stream is represented by two monks (H.H. the Dalai Lama and Bataa Mishigish of Mongolia). The Western authors are leaders who are nurtured by one or another of these Buddhist streams, but who are also practicing in response to Western cultural conditions. Three work out of a Tibetan religious framework (a nun, Ven. Karma Lekshe Tsomo, a former monk, Professor José Cabezón, and a layperson, Professor Judith Simmer-Brown) and two draw on the Japanese Zen tradition (Robert Aitken, Roshi, and Professor Stephanie Kaza).

Perhaps the leader who best embodies this mosaic of diversity and commonality, of the old and the new, is Dhammachari Lokamitra who was born in England but who is a leader in India of the Trailokya Bauddha Mahasangha (TBM) founded in 1978. The Buddha had established an egalitarian community (the Sangha) in contrast to the conventional social divisions of wealth, power, and caste in ancient India, but it disappeared after 1,500 years. Now, almost a millennium later, a new Buddhist community (TBM) has emerged in India among former "Untouchables" who once again use Buddhism to struggle against the old injustices of caste and inequality.

All of these leaders express Buddhist unity and diversity: they share a common reverence for the Buddha, the Dharma, and the Sangha, but understand and practice this reverence in very different ways in their different cultures and regions. As they work creatively in a global context to ease the sufferings of all beings, what is common is their traditional emphasis on the inner cultivation of

19

mindfulness. What is different from the past is that the issues of peace that they address require both private, personal practice and group organization in order to address regional needs and the global framework. An important resource that analyzes these new movements and introduces the work of several of our authors is Christopher Queen and Sallie King, ed., *Engaged Buddhism: Buddhist Liberation Movements in Asia* (Albany: State University of New York Press, 1996).

What is new, and what Buddhists are learning, is to develop an array of new organizational approaches to meet social needs. Unlike the World Bank or the United Nations or the Red Cross, Buddhists insist that peacework cannot be effective to ease the sufferings of all beings without the constant cultivation of mindfulness and inner dialogue. But unlike earlier Buddhists, these leaders insist that morality and mindfulness must lead not only to wisdom and compassion, but also to courageous action that constitutes Buddhist peacework.

ORGANIZATION OF THE BOOK

The 18 essays in the book are divided into three sections, starting with the newest Buddhist social developments in Part One. The principles guiding Buddhist peacework are the focus of Part Two. The book ends by reaffirming the necessity of inner peacework in Part Three. These responses to the UNESCO declaration begin with the new Buddhist social projects and end by reaffirming that inner peace is essential for cultivating a sense of kinship with all people.

Part One highlights new and emerging social programs for building cultures of peace. Dhammachari Lokamitra tells how the so-called Untouchables in India use Buddhism to develop constructive communities and fruitful lives to offset the influence of caste persecution. Based on an integrated view of Buddhism and society, Sulak Sivaraksa has challenged government oppression and founded many new social organizations to promote nonviolent methods to protect the environment, to recover the best of traditional values, and to avoid oppression of people. The International Network of Engaged Buddhists that he cofounded is a symbol of these new Buddhist social movements. Called "one of the heroes of our time" by the Buddhist social activist Joanna Macy, Sulak Sivaraksa has been arrested and risked his life several times in his protest against government and military exploitation and corruption.

Beginning by saving a few pennies a day, Shih Cheng-yen has created the Buddhist Compassion Relief Tzu Chi Foundation, the largest charity organization in Taiwan. It offers assistance in more than 20 other countries. Her leadership has developed collaboration between Buddhism and modern techniques of medicine and social welfare by attracting millions of volunteers. By inspiring so many people with her gentle life dedicated to relieving the suffering of others, Ven. Cheng-yen has been compared to Guanyin (Jp., Kannon), the Bodhisattva of Compassion, who uses a thousand eyes and a thousand hands to see and help those in distress.

Karma Lekshe Tsomo explains the new roles that Buddhist women are creating for greater participation and leadership opportunities in society, and describes the many new organizations and activities that are being produced as resources. Bataa Mishigish shows that traditional Buddhism in Mongolia is resurfacing in the 1990s after communist oppression, but that it needs new educational approaches if Buddhists are to help Mongolians avoid poverty and social deprivation in the new economy.

Part One concludes with a summary by A.T. Ariyaratne of his 41 years of work as leader of the Sarvodaya Movement in Sri Lanka. Based on its volunteer village renewal programs that have transformed more than 10,000 villages, he describes the Buddhist principles that are used for training people to cooperate for collective renewal in the family, village, and nation. All of these Buddhist writers discuss concrete programs—educational, medical, economic, environmental, feminist, and political—that are designed to build social reform, human rights, and cultures of peace.

Part Two reflects concerns similar to Part One, but the authors emphasize the underlying principles that provide the framework, support, and motivation for Buddhist peacework. Practicing Zen Buddhism in the United States, Stephanie Kaza, a biologist, organizes peacework into four phases: repentance, resistance, root cause analysis, and rebuilding moral culture. Because of the scope of environmental deterioration, she emphasizes that recovery work to bring about the necessary systemic changes requires a group effort that is a major challenge for Buddhists. Robert Aitken, cofounder of the Buddhist Peace Fellowship, supports Kaza's point by emphasizing the Buddhist principle that our life evolves only *with* the life of all beings. As a practical device, he advocates the traditional Buddhist practice of making vows to focus energy on tasks that range from comforting the afflicted to afflicting the comfortable, especially new efforts that challenge the social structures that create suffering.

Jeon Chong-yoon tells the story of the revival of the Chontae tradition of Korean Buddhism after a gap of 542 years caused by government suppression. The rapid growth in only 33 years has creatively adapted Chontae Buddhism to the new conditions of modern Korea as stated in three primary principles: Buddhism for society, Buddhism in everyday life, and Buddhism for everyone. Both monastic cultivation and secular activities are emphasized, including Avalokitesvara meditation, tree-planting, adopting rivers and mountains, and education. Judith Simmer-Brown shows how the Shambhala teachings of Chogyam Trungpa (1939-1987) also aimed beyond individual transformation to change systemic social problems. After his death they have taken shape in education programs that embody ethnic, religious, and gender diversity. Balancing inner awareness with social activism, participatory democracy with teacher/leader guidance, Naropa University works to develop an enlightened society. Kosan Sunim lived through Japanese occupation and the Korean civil war, and made a personal vow to do his best for peace in the world. His leadership in various national organizations extends his effectiveness throughout Korean society based on five principles: maintaining the Buddhist monastic rules, teaching the Dharma, cultivating meditation, sponsoring education, and working for interreligious cooperation.

Part Two concludes with Daisaku Ikeda, who recalls facilitating international understanding through person-to-person diplomacy as one way to support world peace. On a local level, he emphasizes the role of small discussion meetings as an arena where the value of each person can emerge in an egalitarian atmosphere that creates social value, which is part of the Lotus tradition that recognizes equality while valuing diversity. Ikeda adds the virtue of courage to the usual Buddhist duo of compassion and wisdom, thereby emphasizing the need for action to challenge militarism, bring relief to refugees, and nurture world citizenship. This book is a concrete example of his peacework. Daisaku Ikeda established the Boston Research Center for the 21st Century in 1993 to foster "dialogue among scholars and activists on common values across cultures and religions, seeking in this way to support an evolving global ethic for a peaceful twenty-first century."[3] His commitment to interreligious cooperation is embodied in the Toda Institute for Global Peace and Policy Research where he appointed an Iranian Muslim, Majid Tehranian, as the first director. His commitment to diversity as a foundation for peace can also be seen in SGI-USA which has grown into the largest Buddhist group in the United States and the only one that is ethnically diverse.[4]

Part Three grounds the social outreach and activism described in the book by emphasizing the foundational principles of the Buddhist life. This foundation is not in the monastery, however, but in the mind, and being in the mind it is portable. Maha Ghosananda writes that "We Buddhists must find the courage to leave our temples and enter the temples of human experience, temples that are filled with suffering." Ghosananda teaches by example by organizing regular peace walks on the suffering soil of Cambodia where 31 percent of the Cambodian people were killed in four brief years (1975-1978) and violent conflict still continues. Hatred can only be overcome by kindness, not by hatred, which keeps the cycle alive. "Reconcilition does not mean that we surrender rights and conditions, but rather that we use love in all our negotiations."

Thich Nhat Hanh and H.H. the Dalai Lama are well-known Buddhist authors in explaining the practice of peace in the midst of life. Thich Nhat Hanh faced constant danger working in Vietnam in the early 1960s, so his words are not theoretical. Even in the midst of war, he was able to avoid dividing the world into "us" and "them" by recognizing the violence within our minds and the common ground that joined him with those who opposed him. His clarity about how to be peaceful in the midst of action interprets our task not as working toward building peace, but as constantly *being peaceful* in our work. Peace cannot be achieved without being peaceful moment by moment. And that means seeing your enemies as your kin.[5]

Constant mindfulness was also emphasized by Ven. Gunaratana as the first step to bringing peace to the world. He resists building a Buddhist identity that stands against other religions by insisting that the virtues of generosity, patience, compassion, appreciative joy, loving friendliness, and equanimity are not owned by Buddhists. Rather, they are shared by all religions and are universal. The key is realizing peaceful attitudes and expressing loving-kindness in our relations with others. Similarly, Ven. Sheng-yen writes that "peace in society begins with peace within oneself," and "To achieve social peace, Buddhism begins with a program of inner peace." While agreeing that changing institutions, laws, and economic structures are helpful to create a peaceful environment, he gives first priority to transforming the minds of individuals. "The world changes according to the state of our mind." Ven. Sheng-yen teaches that everyone must create their own mental space as the foundation for socially engaged Buddhism. "Everywhere is a meditation hall; everywhere is a Buddhist temple."

The understanding of peacemaking as a constant process, rather than peace as a goal, is given further support by José Cabezón who explains the Madhyamaka teaching used by the Dalai Lama. It shifts attention from the goal of peace by deconstructing it—just as it deconstructs all things, whether self, or enemies, or religions—as having no intrinsic self-existence, and focuses instead on developing peaceful conditions. Cabezón balances the Western emphasis on socio-political-economic factors and the Buddhist focus on the inner life, but urges all of us to act. "It is both unrealistic and morally problematic to postpone dealing with issues of social justice until the inner life has been perfected." Trying to end poverty and sickness only by achieving inner peace is both naive and "implicit collusion with the forces of injustice."

The UNESCO declaration was prepared by an interfaith conference involving several Buddhist leaders, including Maha Ghosananda and the Dalai Lama. The importance of interreligious cooperation is supported by many authors. Sheng-yen, Kosan, and Gunaratana especially emphasize interreligious work, and the Dalai Lama also makes a point of affirming religious pluralism and rejecting religious sectarianism. In addition, he specifically outlines five forms of cooperation: intellectual dialogue, mutual practice, five forms of cooperation: intellectual dialogue, mutual practice, interfaith public events to increase motivation, joint pilgrimage, and cooperation in restoring the environment. Primarily, however, he stresses that peacework depends on positive motivation, and religious communities have a special responsibility to disarm hatred, greed, and jealousy while building up tolerance, trust, and compassion. Violence and peace begin and end with the human heart. In his recent book, the Dalai Lama asks that we give kindness a chance and offers a prayer which inspires him in his quest to benefit others:

> *May I become at all times, both now and forever*
> *A protector for those without protection*
> *A guide for those who have lost their way*
> *A ship for those with oceans to cross*
> *A bridge for those with rivers to cross*
> *A sanctuary for those in danger*
> *A lamp for those without light*
> *A place of refuge for those who lack shelter*
> *And a servant to all in need.*[6]

NOTES

1. A rendering of the Metta Sutta, Sutta Nipata I.8, by Christopher Titmuss in Ken Jones, *The Social Face of Buddhism* (Boston: Wisdom Publications, 1989), 384.

2. Gradual Sayings I.14 (cf. T 2.561a.8-16), trans. by Harvey Aronson, *Love and Sympathy in Theravada Buddhism* (Delhi: Motilal Banarsidass, 1980), 3 and 14-16.

3. Boston Research Center for the 21st Century, Newsletter 13 (Spring/Summer 1999), 19.

4. See David Chappell, "Ethnic Diversity in the Soka Gakkai," in Christopher Queen, ed., *Engaged Buddhism in the West* (Boston: Wisdom Publications , 1999).

5. See Thich Nhat Hanh, *Peace in Every Step: The Path of Mindfulness in Everyday Life* (New York: Bantam, 1992 reissue).

6. His Holiness the Dalai Lama, *Ethics for a New Millennium* (New York: Riverhead Books, 1999), 237.

Part I

BUILDING INCLUSIVE COMMUNITIES

Chapter 1

THE DHAMMA REVOLUTION IN INDIA: PEACEMAKING BEGINS WITH THE ERADICATION OF THE CASTE SYSTEM

Dhammachari Lokamitra

B uddhism was dramatically re-established in India when 500,000 so-called Untouchables[1] went for refuge to Buddha, Dhamma, and Sangha in Nagpur in 1956. Little realizing the significance, I arrived in Nagpur on the very day of the twenty-first anniversary of this great event. I had never seen so many people gathered in one place as I saw that day at the Diksha Bhumi, the site of the conversion. The significance of what Dr. B. R. Ambedkar, the leader of the new Buddhists, had done was immediately apparent. Not only could the lives of millions born as so-called Untouchables be transformed radically, but Buddhism would be re-established in the land of its birth. Furthermore, oppressed people throughout the world would have before them an example of social change through the Dhamma.

Encouraged by my teacher, Sangharakshita, in 1978 I returned to work indefinitely in India. I was soon faced with the gravity of the situation I had committed myself to. After my second lecture I was asked how to cultivate skillful states when one's friends and relatives have been abused, raped, and killed. In addition, the state government of Maharashtra had just announced that it was changing the name of Marathwada University to Dr. Babasaheb Ambedkar University. Caste Hindus, not wanting the university named after someone they considered an Untouchable, had reacted in an orgy of violence against the Buddhists in the surrounding towns and villages. Coming from comfortable England, how could I advise those facing hardships so far beyond my limited experience?

DHAMMACHARI LOKAMITRA was born in London in 1947 as Jeremy Goody. He was ordained into the Western Buddhist Order in 1974 by Sangharakshita as a Dhammachari, and given the name Lokamitra. Since 1978 he has been living in India helping to initiate and guide the activities of Trailokya Bauddha Mahasangha, Sahayaka Gana, and Bahujan Hitay, especially amongst the followers of Dr. B. R. Ambedkar. In 1984 he married a local Buddhist, and they have two children.

I soon came to understand the discrimination, harassment, and humiliation that haunt many of the new Indian Buddhists and their *dalit*[2] kin daily and the atrocities that thousands suffer every year. Most have to suffer appalling living conditions and limited employment prospects for no other reason than that they have been born into a group considered by the Hindu religion to be Untouchable. Such conditions lead to a deep resentment, a crippling insecurity, and, perhaps worst of all, a victim mentality which only serves to perpetuate the helplessness and dependency that are part of the heritage of Untouchability. Given what it is like today, what must it have been like 60 or more years ago?

Dr. Ambedkar was born right at the bottom of Indian society. He was a so-called Untouchable. After matriculation—almost unknown for an Untouchable in those days—certain benefactors helped Dr. Ambedkar complete his education in the United States, the United Kingdom, and Germany. Returning to India as one of the most highly educated Indians of his time, Dr. Ambedkar devoted his life to eradicating Untouchability, which affected one-sixth of the Indian population. He soon realized that while politics, education, and other means of social uplift could alleviate some conditions, they could not solve the most fundamental problem. Over hundreds of years the Hindu religion had embedded deep-seated attitudes in the minds not only of the caste Hindus but the Untouchables themselves. Only by getting out of the religion that made them Untouchable, Dr. Ambedkar realized, would the so-called Untouchables have a chance of a better life. Remarkably, Dr. Ambedkar did not turn to communism or violent revolution. He was clear that he wanted a religion that would dissolve the old conditioning and encourage attitudes of dignity and responsibility that had previously been denied the converts as "Untouchables." Buddhism was the religion he discovered.

Buddhism stood for the creation of a Dhammarajya, a society based on the principles of the Dhamma. This society would be based on Dr. Ambedkar's most valued principles of liberty, equality, and fraternity which, he insisted, he learned from the Buddha, not from the French Revolution.[3] The basis of social change was transformation of mind. "The greatest thing that the Buddha has done," he said, "is to tell the world that the world cannot be reformed except by the reformation of the mind of man and the mind of the world."[4]

Dr. Ambedkar saw the Sangha's role as central to a Buddhist society. It would be an ideal model, setting an example for others on how to live. Its members should develop their own minds and strive to help the wider society. The existing *Bhikshu Sangha* fell far short of this ideal, he said, and he called for a new kind of Sangha.[5] Although it is not clear exactly how his ideas on Sangha would have taken shape, he is said to have stated that "In my religion the Upasakas will also be admitted to the Order."[6] He certainly tried to break down the rigid distinction between monk and layman. For instance, after receiving the Refuges and Five Precepts from Ven. Chandramani at Nagpur in 1956, he himself, a layman, led the conversion ceremony of his followers. He emphasized that monks and laity all shared the same commitment to practice the Dhamma. He thought that suitable lay people could be supported to teach the Dhamma.[7]

Tragically, he died just seven weeks after his conversion, leaving the new Buddhist movement leaderless. Imagine the state of his followers at that time: extremely poor, largely illiterate, cut off in a village with little contact with the outside world, and extremely vulnerable to oppression. Most of his leading lieutenants immersed themselves in politics, ignoring the importance he had given to Buddhism. The political squabbles that ensued quickly factionalized the new Buddhists. They badly needed help from their brothers and sisters in the wider Buddhist world but were largely ignored.

Sangharakshita did not forget them. He had lived in India for 20 years and, after Dr. Ambedkar's death, he did what he could to help the new converts understand how to practice the Dhamma. He still kept them in mind after returning to the West in 1964. Under his guidance the Trailokya Bauddha Mahasangha, Sahayaka Gana (TBMSG)[8] was founded in India in 1978. Today, it has more than 20 centers of Dhamma and social activities. From these centers, lecture tours are arranged in an attempt to reach some of the now millions of Buddhists starving for Dhamma nourishment who have not had a chance to understand what it means to be a Buddhist and how to practice. Lecture tours are an aspect of Dhamma work that I have particularly enjoyed. Exhausting though such tours

31

are, it is always inspiring talking to so many people, poor and uneducated though they may be, who delight so much in the Dhamma. In the initial stages of Dhamma practice, retreats are very effective. Most people live in overcrowded homes, with several people to a room, continual noise, and constant family and social pressures. Practicing the Dhamma in the relatively ideal conditions of a retreat works a kind of magic. A balanced program of spiritual practice enables the participants to dwell in more creative and joyful mental states than ever before. This experience of the fruits of the Dhamma confirms and strengthens their faith. They come to understand fully why Dr. Ambedkar said at his conversion to Buddhism, "Now I have taken a new life."[9]

The social activities operate under the name *Bahujan Hitay*, after the Buddha's famous exhortation to go forth for "the welfare and happiness of the many." Bahujan Hitay provides 19 hostels where poor village children can stay while attending local schools. Without such facilities, many would not be able to go to school. It also conducts extensive slum community projects consisting of educational, health, and cultural activities for children, youth, and mothers. All the work is directed and managed by local Buddhists.[10]

The heart of TBMSG is a *Sangha* or spiritual community,[11] the Trailokya Bauddha Mahasangha.[12] This consists of men and women, householders and celibates, who are, in effect, "Going for Refuge" to Buddha, Dhamma, and Sangha. This commitment, Sangharakshita has come to understand, is the central and definitive act of the Buddhist life. He cites the great conversion itself and the contact he had with Dr. Ambedkar's followers after the conversion as factors influencing his understanding of the significance of the act of "Going for Refuge."[13] Sangharakshita's conception of the Sangha comes close to Dr. Ambedkar's: individuals committed to transforming their own minds, to spiritual fellowship with others likewise committed, and to working together to help others benefit from the Dhamma. He speaks of the Sangha as the nucleus of the new society.[14]

I want to look at three practices that we find support "Going for Refuge" to Buddha, Dhamma, and Sangha. The first is taking responsibility. "Going for Refuge" means taking responsibility: not putting responsibility for unskillful thoughts, speech, and actions on to others or on external conditions; accepting responsibility for cultivating skillfulness of body, speech, and mind. We work to reach our goal through practicing ethics, meditation, and study, but more practical measures are also required to extend the sense of responsibility beyond the meditation cushion and Vihara. To make progress we have to become aware of, acknowledge, work upon, and eventually transmute the more gross and unskillful aspects of our characters. Through taking on responsibility by working for the Dhamma and for social transformation, we are extending our "Going for Refuge" into the working situation, testing and strengthening it. This means cultivating and maintaining skillfulness of body, speech, and mind whatever difficulties arise. It means summoning up energy to accomplish what we have committed ourselves to. Most of all it means not being swayed from our commitment, not resting until what we have taken on is accomplished.

This practice is appropriate to people everywhere as a means to transcend their personal limitations. In India, Untouchability has led to attitudes of social, psychological, and material dependence for many. It is common to think that one can do nothing for oneself—any change must come from those in power. Feelings of worthlessness, helplessness, inertia, and passivity inevitably follow this attitude. What you do is of no significance, so why make an effort? Dependence fosters a victim mentality, a state of paranoia in which everything unpleasant that befalls one is part of a conspiracy against one and the social community to which one belongs (from my experience in India there are objective validations for such paranoia, despite it being a subjective state). Helplessness leads to a crippling resentment, which can fossilize mental states or explode in violence. These attitudes are some of the caste system's greatest liabilities, making progress of any kind almost impossible.

Taking active and practical responsibility challenges such attitudes and demands change. We begin to develop self-reliance, confidence, initiative, and creativity. We learn that we can change our mental states, even in the most difficult circumstances. Instead of being a victim of circumstances beyond our control, we see that we can positively affect others and the environment in which we live. Gradually our energies are released from the prison of resentment, becoming increasingly skillful and creative.

33
.
.
.
.

The second practice concerns Sangha, the context in which we are "Going for Refuge." The basic principle of Sangha is *Kalyana Mitrata* or spiritual friendship. Sangharakshita has often quoted the incident in which the Buddha says emphatically to Ananda that Kalyana Mitrata is the whole of the spiritual life.[15] In other words without such friendship, practice of the Dhamma can be very difficult. A Kalyana Mitra regards us through loving kindness and compassion and not through any selfish concern. We can trust and be fully open with such a friend, freely confessing our weaknesses and mistakes. Our faith, inspiration, and energy are stimulated, helping us through dull and difficult periods. Spiritual friends can help us see through the confusions and doubts that divert us from the Path: alone it is so easy to deceive ourselves. Eventually such friendships help us rise above the demands of self-attachment. It is not easy to cultivate such friendships, constant effort being required.

Kalyana Mitrata is one of the basic practices in Trailokya Bauddha Mahasangha throughout the world. In the West, where social isolation and lack of deep friendship are common, the need for this practice is obvious. Indian society has very positive aspects, which include social awareness and a general attitude of friendliness. However, the predominant negative social conditioning in India comes from the caste system, divisive by its very nature. The newly converted Buddhists are affected as much as anyone else. This tendency is not limited to caste but extends to family, region, class, and all areas of social life. The *dalit* and Buddhist communities in India are, as a result, afflicted by a groupism which seems to extend into any positive common endeavor. In the spiritual community our common commitment to Buddha, Dhamma, and Sangha has to exert a stronger pull than the differences and tensions between us. If it does, we can destroy the roots of caste conditioning, individually and collectively. Kalyana Mitrata provides the emotional and spiritual environment necessary for this to happen.

Teamwork, the last practice I want to mention, brings together the practices of taking responsibility and spiritual friendship. Working in a team makes more demands on our sense of responsibility—we are responsible not only to ourselves but to the other team members as well. The success of the team depends on everyone taking responsibility for his or her particular work. There may be a leader or chairman, but only to coordinate, to help members fulfill their individual commitments to the team, and to feel responsible for the common goal, not to take others' responsibility and create dependence. Teamwork, bringing no personal material reward, lessens the possibility of personal intoxication but brings great benefits in helping us to overcome attachment to self.

Teamwork is the principle of Sangha we must apply to the working situation. If we can transform the team with an atmosphere of Kalyana Mitrata, we will have a supportive environment for taking our Dhamma practice out into the world. We work particularly on our communication with each other. Encouraged by each other's commitment, we try to speak openly and honestly, in a friendly manner and politely, helpfully, and harmoniously. This builds up a strong base of trust and enables us to work together harmoniously and thus effectively.

Teamwork has many challenges, and a strong Dhammic base is necessary to help take them on. When we work together, as opposed to come together to practice meditation or study, our level of consciousness can easily drop, resulting in worse communication, not better. Our psychological weaknesses and negative social conditioning will be ready to exploit any cracks in the harmony of the team. If we have established a strong atmosphere of trust through the practice of Kalyana Mitrata, we will be able to reflect upon, take responsibility for, and work on our individual and collective shortcomings. We will be able to use the difficulties and frustrations we encounter creatively. With less personal and collective conflict we, as a team, will be able to do so much more for others.

Taking responsibility, Kalyana Mitrata, and teamwork are practices that enable us to take our "Going for Refuge" to Buddha, Dhamma, and Sangha into the world, effectively working on ourselves and helping others. We are destroying the roots of the old caste conditioning which include dependence, social hierarchy, and divisiveness, and we are creating the nucleus of a new society based on "Going for Refuge" to Buddha, Dhamma, and Sangha. We are doing what we can to fulfill the Dhamma revolution started by Dr. Ambedkar, and bring a strong, renewed Buddhism back to India.

NOTES

1. I use the phrase "so-called Untouchables" because, of course, those so cruelly designated and treated by the Hindu caste system never freely accepted Untouchability. It is therefore not correct to call them Untouchables or ex-Untouchables as that implies giving some validity to the designation. Simply adding "so-called" to the word is not really satisfactory, but it does make it clear that one is not giving any validity to the words.

2. "Dalit" is a word used by many of the so-called Untouchables in their communities to describe themselves. It means "oppressed," and sounds a very different note than "untouchable," although it has its own limitations.

3. Keer, Dananjay, *Dr. Ambedkar: Life and Mission,* third edition (Bombay: Popular Prakashan), 459.

4. Report of the Fourth Conference of the World Fellowship of Buddhists, Kathmandu, Nepal, quoted in Ahir, D. C., *Dr. Ambedkar on Buddhism* (Bombay: Siddharth Publications,1982), 105.

5. Ambedkar, B.R., *The Buddha and the Future of His Religion* (Nagpur: Triratna Grantha Mala, 1992), 14-16.

6. Quoted in Gore, M.S., *The Social Context of an Ideology: Ambedkar's Political and Social Thought* (New Delhi: Sage Publications, 1993), 252.

7. Ambedkar, B.R., *Record of My Talk to the Buddhist Council of Burma. An Enlarged Version,* 1954. Unpublished duplicated copy in the author's possession.

8. In the West, where it was founded in 1967, it is known as the Friends of the Western Buddhist Order.

9. From the Twenty-two Vows Dr. Ambedkar gave to his followers at the time of the conversion.

10. The funding came from the Karuna Trust, set up by disciples of Sangharakshita in the United Kingdom, from Buddhist friends in Taiwan, from grants from government agencies and NGOs in India, and from other donations.

11. I use the word "spiritual" to refer to the cultivation of highly skillful mental states through ethics and meditation.

12. Founded in the West as the Western Buddhist Order in 1968 by Sangharakshita. Members are called Dhammacharis (masc.) or Dhammacharinis (fem.)

13. Sangharakshita, *History of my Going for Refuge* (Birmingham: Windhorse,1988), chapter 10.

14. Sangharakshita, *Buddhism for Today and Tomorrow* (Birmingham: Windhorse, 1996), chapter 3.

15. Samyutta-Nikaya. V,2

SUGGESTED FURTHER READINGS

Ahir, D.C., *Dr. Ambedkar on Buddhism* (Bombay: Siddharth Publications,1982).

Ambedkar, B. R., *The Buddha and His Dhamma* in *Writing and Speeches,* vol. 11 (Bombay: Government of Maharashtra, 1992).

_____, *Annihilation of Caste* (Jalandhar: Bhim Patrika Publications, 1982).

Das, Bhagwan, ed., *Thus Spoke Ambedkar,* Vol.1-4 (Bangalore: Ambedkar Sahithya. Prakashana).

Keer, Dananjay, *Dr. Ambedkar: Life and Mission,* third edition (Bombay: Popular Prakashan).

Sangharakshita, *Ambedkar and Buddhism,* second edition (Birmingham: Windhorse,1989).

_____, *Buddhism for Today – and Tomorrow* (Birmingham: Windhorse,1996).

, *History of my Going for Refuge* (Birmingham: Windhorse, 1988).

Sponberg, Alan, "TBMSG: A Dhamma Revolution in Contemporary India," in Christopher S. Queen and Sallie B. King, eds., *Engaged Buddhism: Liberation Movements in Asia* (Albany: SUNY Press, 1996).

Subhuti, *Sangharakshita: A New Voice in the Buddhist Tradition* (Birmingham: Windhorse, 1994).

These and other books by Dr. Ambedkar and Sangharakshita can be obtained from:

- Windhorse Publications
Dhammachari Dharmashura
11, Park Road
Moseley, Birmingham, B13 8AB
United Kingdom
Tel/Fax: -44-121-449-9191
E-mail: windhorse@compuserve.com
Webpage: http://www.fwbo.org/windhorse

- Jambudvipa
Dhammachari Manidhamma
5, Prashant Apartments
Deccan College Road
Pune 411006
India
Tel/Fax: -91-20-6696812
E-mail: manidhamma@vsnl.com

CONTACT INFORMATION

Information about the activities of TBMSG in India can be had from:

- Jambudvipa (see above)
- The Karuna Trust
Dhammachari Priyananda
St. Marks Studios
Chillingworth Road
London, N7 8QJ
Tel: -44-171-700-3434
Fax: -44-171-700-3535
E-mail: info@karuna.org
Webpage: http://www.fwbo.org/karuna

37

Information about the activities of FWBO in the West can be obtained from:

• FWBO Communications Office
12A,Park Road
Moseley, Birmingham, B13 8AB
United Kingdom
Tel: -44-121-449-8272
E-mail: communications@fwbo.org
Webpage: http://www.fwbo.org

Chapter 2

BUDDHISM AND A CULTURE OF PEACE

Acharn Sulak Sivaraksa

> *"Look how he abused me and beat me,*
> *How he threw me down and robbed me."*
> *Live with such thoughts and you live in hate.*
> *"Look how he abused me and beat me,*
> *How he threw me down and robbed me."*
> *Abandon such thoughts and live in love.*
>
> *In this world hate never yet dispelled hate.*
> *Only love dispels hate. This is the law*
> *ancient and inexhaustible.*
>
> —*Dhammapada:* The Sayings of the Buddha. 1: 3-5

Buddhism has traditionally not been a religion of declarations. The Buddha himself thought long and hard before he decided that his experience of liberation could be taught. It is often said that a teacher can show you the way but cannot make the journey for you. This is perhaps true also of organizations such as UNESCO. They may make many grand declarations. The declarations may be inspirational, informative, crucial even, but in the end someone— some nation, some neighborhood, some society—has to make the journey from wishing for peace to actually causing it to happen.

ACHARN SULAK SIVARAKSA was born in Thailand in 1933 and was educated in England. He returned to his homeland in 1961 to be a lecturer at Thammasat and Chulanlongkorn Universities. In 1963 he founded and for six years edited the *Social Science Review*, which is thought to have played a crucial role in awakening the student awareness which led to the overthrow of the military regime in 1973. Concern for democracy, human rights, and accountable government has been central to Sirvaraksa's life work. He is credited with starting the indigenous NGO movement in Thailand and has been committed in all his endeavors to a rejection of Western consumerist models of development and an emphasis on the importance of the spiritual and religious dimension of human life. Sivaraksa is currently developing an international network on "Alternatives to Consumerism" and a new college in Thailand which will provide an alternative approach to mainstream education.

Perhaps Buddhism has more to say about this on a personal level than an institutional level, but the wisdom to address social issues has been a part of Buddhist teaching from its beginnings. What is required is more a matter of extrapolation than newly inventing a doctrine or policy to apply to social issues. Buddhism ties social concerns together as part of an integrated way of striving for spiritual growth as a person, a member of a community, nation, and planetary society. It is true, to find inner peace, wisdom, and release from suffering is the most obvious purpose of the Buddha's early teachings. However, it was never intended that one would operate either in a vacuum or at the expense of society in general.

THE BUDDHIST *SANGHA* AS A MICROCOSM OF A PEACEFUL SOCIETY

The earliest teachings of the Buddha provided the *Sangha*, or community, with a model for a well-balanced, peaceful society. In the *Vinaya,* a code of conduct for monks, as individuals and as a group, is spelled out. Throughout the entire Pali Canon, the Buddha never describes the spiritual path as being strictly intellectual or moral. Rather, he calls it "Dhamma-Vinaya"—the Doctrine *(Dhamma)* and Discipline *(Vinaya)*—suggesting an integrated body of wisdom, applicable to the personal spiritual journey as well as to living in societies. The Vinaya is thus an indispensable facet and foundation of all the Buddha's teachings, inseparable from the Dhamma. The intention of the Vinaya as a guide for behavior in general and for the everyday lives of monks is to provide an atmosphere in which meditation and personal growth are made possible. In addition, the intention is to allow this to be true for all of the members of the Sangha. The few do not get to meditate and practice the Dhamma at the expense of the others. Another of the intentions of the Vinaya is to allow the monks to exist in harmony with the community from which they receive their material sustenance. At the same time, the monastic community may be a model for the lay community, demonstrating conflict-resolving skills, fairness, and a pragmatic (as opposed to neurotic) approach to materialism. For example, in the *Vinaya-pitaka* of the Pali canon we find examples of procedures for resolving conflicts and disputes which have immense relevance to contemporary situations where the application of democracy, self-determination, transparency, and other characteristics of fair governance would contribute to the peace process.

In the *Ashikarana-Samatha*, several options for ending a conflict without engendering further hostility are discussed. In all cases of conflict, the text states that decisions are made "in the presence of" the Sangha, persons involved, the Dhamma, and the Vinaya. In other cases, acting in accordance with the majority may end a dispute. In a dispute in which the issues have become obfuscated by emotions and insults, both sides may agree that further dispute is not helpful and perform a ceremony to ask forgiveness of each other and reaffirm their solidarity. All of these approaches to creating a harmonious community work together to create a culture of peace within the context of the Sangha, the community that practices the Dhamma together.

THE BUDDHA'S RELATIONSHIP TO HIS CONTEMPORARY SOCIETY: POTENTIAL LESSONS FOR THE NEW ERA

Buddhism has been, from the beginning, an alternative or even revolutionary movement. Walpola Rahula states that "Buddhism arose in India as a spiritual force against social injustices, against degrading superstitious rites, ceremonies and sacrifices; it denounced the tyranny of the caste system and advocated the equality of all men; it emancipated woman and gave her complete spiritual freedom" (Rahula, 1978). The essence of the story of the historical Buddha is that he broke with his born tradition of being a *Kshastriya*, a prince/warrior and future king, and set out on a journey to find a kind of peace which was, in the first place, beyond the illusions and ignorant suppositions about the phenomenal world. Second, he sought a kind of peace which was applicable/attainable to everyone, regardless of caste and wealth. Later he even took tangible steps to ensure that the dhamma was accessible to all by teaching the same ultimate message in various forms, establishing an inclusive religion. Although there is some debate as to the nature and potential for the attainment of ultimate enlightenment, the process of enlightenment is open to all. The spirit of cooperation is a product of the quest for enlightenment and also a prerequisite.

When the Buddha came to see his materially rich life at the royal court as hollow and essentially meaningless in the face of the seemingly inevitable cycle of birth, old age, sickness, and death, he left his comfortable surroundings and went to seek the advice of those who were the leading spiritual teachers of the day. There are for me two important lessons in this story that relate to peacebuilding in our world today. Number one is renunciation. Without a clear sense of revulsion for violence, ignorance, and oppression, it is impossible to break free. Revulsion is a strong word, but it implies an almost physical force, like the poles of two magnets. It pushes you away, away from even very comfortable surroundings into unknown, possibly frightening, territory. But this is the only way. Renunciation doesn't literally mean a physical move from where you are. Most commonly it is a mental process, a deep dissatisfaction with the status quo and a strong desire to seek alternatives. This is often amplified in the Theravada tradition by meditation on the repellent aspects of material life, including the stench of a corpse and the reality that the corpse is us one day. The capricious nature of aesthetic appeal is also emphasized wherein the flower is beautiful but quickly turns yellow and dies. It was the same flower all along but our mind-created ideas can elicit awe or revulsion based on what, under examination, turn out to be the most trivial of factors.

The second point is that dissatisfaction with the status quo must inspire action. Breaking old habits is hard to do, and the idea of renouncing violence is a long way from doing something about it. Pontificating about the grand scheme of things is useless until one looks inside, makes a personal choice, and then acts on it.

The Buddha left the palace, which under ordinary circumstances wouldn't be an easy thing to do. For peacemakers in the world today, the openness to interpretation of this lesson is large. Given that we are mired in the workings of an interconnected world, perhaps the ultimate reality of renunciation is not so much at question as the symbolic nature of it and the kind of frame of mind one must cultivate. A two-step outline for building peace consists of (1) looking at the roots of violence carefully and honestly, not sugarcoating anything about the realities of life, consciousness, or culture and (2) taking action based on an honest appraisal of causes and conditions, looking at the root causes, and attempting to remedy the problem through cultivating a proper frame of mind and letting action follow in a more spontaneous than rational fashion.

THE MIDDLE WAY: REDISCOVERING REAL FREE WILL

The Buddha devised an integrated system that addresses both intellectual and pragmatic concerns simultaneously. That is the Middle Way. The intellectual component of the Middle Way is freedom from extremes. In the metaphysical or philosophical sense, freedom from extremes is neither to be attached to the idea that things are eternal (whether material or mental is irrelevant) nor that they are unreal, nonexistant in the ultimate way. The more practical side of the Middle Way is advice on how to live in the world as we must, to accept the provisional reality of what our senses tell us, but without attachment and with a minimal of elaboration based on the emotions, desires, and general wildness of the mind.

It is very interesting to note how, in the declaration, several of the points made are essentially Westernized statements of applying the Middle Way to particular issues. In fact it is the Middle Way which will ultimately allow us to create a culture of peace. As one can see, the tendency toward extremism is fueling most of the conflicts around the world. A political Middle Way will be a proximate cause of peace when the underlying conditions are in place. One of the first conditions, as mentioned, is the balancing of the economic and social systems to be fair, fair within individual countries and fair on a global level, fair in protecting basic human rights and fair in utilizing the earth's resources. The Middle Way recognizes the usefulness of institutions and technology but not at the expense of local control over how they are implemented in a given community.

WORKING FOR A PEACEFUL AND FAIR SIAM

In my native land of Siam, we have been through these struggles for human rights, for fairness of economic policy, and we have seen much suffering during these struggles. In line with the Buddhist model of establishing peace, both inner and outer peace, the first step in our nonviolent struggle has been education. We look at the root cause of injustice and violence on a personal level, and this may help us understand how it operates at a societal level. The most important application of a personal examination of the roots of nonviolence is not to become a saint but to develop the discipline and personal courage, strength of will, to undertake nonviolent struggle. Resorting to violence often seems like the only way to get what we want; at the least, it seems faster and more certain. But if we resort to violence we are locked in a violent spiral which will surely end in our defeat. Even if we win our rights, if it is by violence we will just as surely lose them through violence. A lack of moral legitimacy promotes conflict. Seeking a personal understanding of violence in ourselves and meditating, praying, contemplating—in order to lessen the violence inside us—obviously cannot by itself be a singular force for social change. What it can do is give us clear vision, not clouded by hatred. It can give us a firm ground to stand on and faith in our convictions. It can help us to link our head and our heart and also to draw strength from Mother Earth, as did the Buddha. When we identify the seeds of violence, perhaps we may not uproot them, but we plant seeds of peace in their place. All of this is necessary in order to cultivate the inner strength to persist in nonviolent struggle.

So the first step, the real beginning of our struggle in Siam, is to go back to our roots and to use the Buddhist tradition of cultivating personal peace to engage the violence in the world around us effectively. I have many organizations at work trying to teach Siamese people to relearn and honor their Buddhist heritage so that they may be more peaceful—this applies to the common people as well as the top officials. If they learn to be more peaceful and fair in a significant way, perhaps our struggle would be assisted and shortened.

The second step application of the Middle Way, in my case, is beginning from the ground up. The Middle Way is applying the wisdom gleaned from great teachers and illustrious doctrines to real situations. After people are educated about the roots of violence and the necessity for a firm commitment to nonviolent struggle, we begin to train them in organizational skills. In order to effect nonviolent change in the social structure, they must be able to address issues in an informed manner. They must learn how to use the existing government channels.

Much has been made of the fact that peace is not the absence of war. Peace is neither a negative concept nor the flip side of an inverse partnership. Peace is a proactive, comprehensive process of finding common ground through open communication and putting into practice a philosophy of nonharm and sharing resources.

The concrete steps toward a culture of peace which we have been working on here in Siam deal directly with the issues of communication and understanding between peoples and moving from that understanding to action which is aimed at making society more fair. The spiritual component plays an important role in these projects, but it is not the domain of a single spiritual path. It is rather the establishment of conditions which allow for the freedom to discover within oneself the characteristics of the spiritual life. This is real peace. Perhaps disputes and conflict will always be. But within the context of a diverse society that has many religious traditions, there is a plethora of ways in which conflicts may be understood and dealt with nonviolently.

PEACE AS A NONVIOLENT STRUGGLE FOR JUSTICE

In order to create a culture of peace, first we must make society more just, more fair, and give equal rights to all people. The imposition of so-called peace has, in fact, at times been a tool of suppression. Look at the many programs for pacification undertaken throughout history and the world. In many cases, the institutionalized definition of peace is tantamount to the suppression of righteous struggles for equal rights and justice. In other cases, the institutionalization of peace is really propaganda for maintaining the status quo of an unjust government or system. Thus, the development of a culture of peace really begins at ground level. There is never a reason for violent struggle, in the Buddhist way. Still, realistically speaking, you cannot expect the hungry and the oppressed whose basic human rights are violated to sit still while intellectuals and technocrats debate the vagaries of peace. Peace to these people means being free to attain their potential in life, to raise a family, find a place in their community, and to be able to have control of at least the most crucial aspects of their destiny. This point is absolutely important if a culture of peace is ever to be.

CONCLUSION

The Declaration on the Role of Religion in the Promotion of a Culture of Peace is a good starting place from which we may go forward into the next millennium with the aspiration of improving society. By recognizing the importance of input from the world's wisdom

45

traditions, it taps into the deepest well of insight for directions and actions we must undertake. No longer is it satisfactory to limit us to the view that human progress is measured solely by material invention and expansion. A society that does not enable and support all of its members to pursue their personal vision for spiritual growth is hollow and doomed to endless squabbling over material goods and political power. Whereas the last renaissance eventually led to a diminution of the role of spirit in society, a new renaissance is reawakening the sense that there is a deeper purpose to life than ego-driven pursuits. A spirit of brotherhood and sisterhood may be awakened by the dawning realization that we are linked by a common purpose to improve ourselves, our community, and our society, and that this goal is immeasurably furthered by dedicating our life to finding common ground.

SUGGESTED FURTHER READINGS

Various books by Sulak Sivaraksa, such as *Global Healing* (1999), *Loyalty Demands Dissent* (1998), *Socially Engaged Buddhism* (1988), and *Seeds of Peace* (1992) can be obtained from:

Parallax Press
P.O. Box 7355
Berkeley, CA 94707
Tel. 510-525-0101.

The journal *Seeds of Peace* is a thrice annual publication of the International Network of Engaged Buddhists (INEB) that can be ordered at:

P.O. Box 19, Mahadthai Post Office
Bangkok 10206, Thailand
Tel./Fax: 66-1-433-7169;
E-mail: ineb@ipied.tu.ac.th

Swearer, Donald K., "Sulak Sivaraksa's Buddhist Vision for Renewing Society," in Chistopher S. Queen and Sallie B. King, eds., *Engaged Buddhism: Buddhist Liberation Movements in Asia* (Albany: SUNY Press, 1996).

CONTACT INFORMATION

- Sulak Sivaraksa
  Santi Pracha Dhamma Institute
  117, Fuangnakhon Road
   Opposite Wat Rajabopit
  Bangkok 10200
  Thailand
  Tel: 662-223-4915
  Fax: 66-2-222-5188; 225-9540

Chapter 3

A NEW MILLENNIUM OF GOODNESS, BEAUTY, AND TRUTH

Venerable Shih Cheng-yen

As the new millennium approaches, a review of the twentieth century compels us to face the obvious fact that the more material gains we have, the further lost we become. We have not improved our minds or spirits. Even though we have been privileged with unprecedented technological advancements, we are still drawn into a whirlpool of greed, belligerence, and ignorance.

Racial discrimination, disagreement over political ideologies, confrontations between economic interests, and hunger for power have brought on two world wars and numberless national conflicts. In Kosovo, for example, many have been forced to leave their homes or have even lost their lives because of ethnic discord. People cannot live peacefully together and, as a result, many suffer.

PURIFY YOURSELF, RESPECT ALL BEINGS

Many natural disasters are also caused by human beings. The Buddha said, "All creatures share a common karma because we all receive the results of our actions." When people have less and less respect for Mother Nature, she will surely respond with endless calamities. Just see how many fatal disasters have happened in the world: great floods have inundated many tracts of fertile land in China; an earthquake instantly leveled Armenia, a city in

DHARMA MASTER CHENG-YEN was born in 1937. When she was 23 years old, she left home to become a Buddhist nun and, in 1963, she became a disciple of the highly revered Dharma Master Yin Shun. Living a simple life with only the basic necessities, the Master has actively pursued her work of helping the poor and educating the rich. In 1966, she established the Compassion Relief Tzu Chi Foundation, now the largest charitable organization in Taiwan, with offices in more than 20 countries. In 1991, Master Cheng-yen received the Philippine Magsaysay Award, the "Asian Nobel Prize." Her publications include: *Still Thoughts, People Have Twenty Difficulties, Returning to the Home of the Soul,* and *The Thirty-seven Principles of Enlightenment.*

Columbia; there have been enormous tsunamis in Papua, New Guinea, and devastating floods, droughts, and tidal waves in North Korea; Hurricanes Mitch and Georges swept across several Central American countries. All of this has left any number of people suffering from the pain of hunger and cold.

Why have people become too disrespectful toward each other to remember what gratitude, contentment, good will, and understanding are? The reason is that there is not enough love, that there is no awakening of our innate universal love. If we remember that all creatures in the universe are one, we will know how to let go of our egotism, eliminate our mutual misunderstanding, and put aside our selfishness. We will then return to the true, clear essence of our human nature, and from the depths of our hearts will arise a reverent love for all beings.

We hope that the world will be a Pure Land of peace and joy. However, only by purifying human hearts, eliminating avarice and hostility, and activating the innate compassion in every person can we give of ourselves selflessly. Only by activating our conscience, revealing the intrinsic love hidden in our hearts, and planting the seeds of goodness can we change evil to good, calamity to good fortune.

Of course, we must start with ourselves. We must purify ourselves and promote happiness and harmony in our families. We can then extend our care and concern to our community and society. When every society can live in harmony, then the whole world will be peaceful and free of disasters. This is what I pray for every day: "May human minds be purified, may people live in peace, and may there be no disasters in the world."

EVERYONE HAS GREAT LOVE

The Buddha's teachings are not so difficult or profound. They are directions for our daily lives. Therefore, grounded on the spirit of the Buddha and endeavoring to put what he taught into practice in daily life, the Tzu Chi Foundation began by doing charitable work, and then gradually expanded its activities into the eight fields of charity, medicine, education, culture, international relief, bone marrow donation, environmental protection, and community volunteerism. "We learn from what we do and we do what we have learned." In this way, we experience the meaning of the admonition, "Let the Buddha be in your heart, the Dharma in your words, and love in your deeds."

Every step of the way has been in accordance with the teachings of the Buddha. For more than 30 years, millions of people have enthusiastically responded and joined in the good work, without complaint or regret. I deeply believe that in every heart there exists priceless great love.

In our charity work, we provide material necessities, medical care, and spiritual consolation for the sick and elderly. We not only help the poor, but also educate the rich by showing them that giving and service are more meaningful than pursuing wealth, power, and prestige. We are grateful to both our long-term care recipients and to disaster victims when we give them food, clothing, care, and companionship, for without their misfortune we would find no opportunity to serve. The poor and wretched receive help, the rich and fortunate activate their love, and thus both can be grateful to each other.

In order to show respect for all life, we have worked tirelessly to establish a medical care network that includes two hospitals in Taiwan and a system of mobile free clinics in many countries around the world. What is special about our medical service is the attitude of the personnel. Our doctors and nurses are taught to treat patients as they would their own relatives, and to heal them in both body and mind. They not only treat the symptoms of a disease, but they also consider how a patient's illness affects his life and family. Our hospital volunteers—the unique "software" of the Tzu Chi Hospital—gently console patients' hearts and care for their bodies. Patients facing the end of their lives are taught how to maintain tranquility and peace of mind.

In order to purify human minds, the importance of education must not be overlooked. Tzu Chi teachers "treat all children with the hearts of parents and treat their own children with the hearts of bodhisattvas." In this way, the love that they teach will truly sprout, grow, and blossom. The teachings of my book, *Still Thoughts*, are presented in order to plant the seeds of compassion and great love in every student. We have seen the results of many years' efforts in these lively, well-mannered youngsters. We are now working to set

49

up a complete system of education, from kindergarten to graduate institutes.

Social education is no less important than academic education. Our cultural mission is thus an essential task for the new century. Technological advancements have brought us from two-dimensional printed words to three-dimensional images. In addition to our Tzu Chi magazines, newspapers, and other publications, we now have our own cable television channel. Through these media, Tzu Chi broadcasts true stories of people acting out of great love so that the spirit of compassion and love can enter every home to purify people's minds and stimulate the love in their own hearts. In addition, our Still Thoughts Hall in Hualien, eastern Taiwan, is a major center for the propagation of the dharma. Through meetings, lectures, photo exhibitions of Tzu Chi members at work, and other activities at the hall, we hope to plant the Buddha's teachings firmly in human hearts and lead them onto the right path.

GREAT LOVE TRANSCENDS ALL BORDERS

Whenever disaster strikes, Tzu Chi people, like living bodhisattvas, are the first to respond to calls for help. Our international relief work shows the truth of the Buddha's teaching that "All beings are equal." When you see with your own eyes a family huddled on a small, tottering roof in the middle of a flood, waiting to be rescued, do you care what their nationality is? At that moment, you only think of how to save them from their suffering. This is the meaning of "Great mercy even to strangers and great compassion for all." Tzu Chi relief team members pay their own way to disaster areas to help distribute relief supplies, grateful for the opportunity to help the suffering. Overcoming obstacles of time, space, and politics, the foundation has provided material and medical relief to victims of war, flood, and drought in such countries as mainland China, Cambodia, Thailand, Rwanda, Ethiopia, South Africa, Papua New Guinea, Afghanistan, and Kosovo.

Tzu Chi has established the world's third largest marrow donor registry, which has handled more than 100 marrow transplants both in Taiwan and abroad. This realizes the Buddhist teaching, "Give your head, eyes, marrow, and brain to others." Transplants are carried out in an atmosphere of gratitude: recipients are grateful for new life, while donors are grateful for the opportunity to personally experience the joy of saving a life.

Give whenever you can, whether a little or a lot. Strive persistently with equanimity and patience. You will soon reach the level at which "There is no giver, there is no receiver, there is no gift." Giving and receiving will be nothing more than part of the natural order of things. This may seem like an impossible ideal, but in fact anyone who really wants to can become a bodhisattva in this world.

It is everyone's responsibility to protect our earthly resources, and it is everyone's duty to be grateful for our blessings and to create new blessings. When Tzu Chi environmental protection volunteers work so hard to collect, sort, and recycle garbage, they not only keep the environment clean—but more important—they learn to humble themselves. When they can humble themselves and eradicate their pride and egotism, they will get along well with others and show their concern for the people and things around them.

In addition, we especially promote community volunteering in order to show our concern for all the problems of our communities, advocate respect for our parents, look after senior citizens, and encourage everyone in our communities to walk on the Path of the Bodhisattvas. We hope to make it possible for everyone in our communities to be as compassionate as Kuan Yin Bodhisattva and as loving as Amitabha Buddha. We believe that if each and every local community can reach this ideal, then all communities together can build an ideal world in which the elderly are cared for, friends are trusted, and the young are nurtured.

JUST DO IT

Tzu Chi is constantly working to broaden the road of love and the Path of the Bodhisattvas. Through constant development of our missions, we aim to encourage more people to participate in our work so that they may comprehend the meaning of religion, put human values into practice, and open their hearts. When everyone plants the seeds of good karma together, they are sure to receive good fortune.

Tzu Chi people have walked on the path of love for more than thirty years. We have experienced success and disappointment, but we have always fearlessly upheld the attitude of "Just do it!" Having

51

grown from the original 30 members to the millions of members of different nationalities, races, and languages throughout the world today, we have walked with one heart and one mind on one path to accomplish our mission. If everyone can give love without asking for anything in return, we can certainly look forward to a world of peace. I pray that many more people will join us to lovingly create a new millennium of goodness, beauty, and truth.

SUGGESTED FURTHER READINGS

Master Cheng-yen, *Still Thoughts* (Vol. One, 1996; Vol. Two, 1998). (Taiwan: Still Thought Cultural Mission Company).

_____, *The Sutra of the Bodhisattvas' Eight Realizations* (Taiwan: Tzu Chi Cultural Publishing Company, 1999).

_____, *The Thirty-seven Principles of Englightenment* (Taiwan: Tzu Chi Cultural Publishing Company, 1999).

Lotus Flower of the Heart – Thirty Years of Tzu Chi Photography (Taiwan: Still Thought Cultural Mission Company, 1997).

Tzu Chi Quarterly (Taiwan: Buddhist Compassion Relief Tzu Chi Foundation, since 1977).

CONTACT INFORMATION

- Tzu Chi Compassion Relief Foundation
21 Kanglo Village
Shinchen Hsian
Hualien County
Taiwan, Republic of China
Tel: (886) 03-8266779
Fax: (886) 03-8267776
Website: http://www.tzuchi.org.tw/

The Tzu Chi four major missions—charity, medicine, education, and culture—are being carried out by Foundation members worldwide. Visit the Tzu Chi web site for information on the nearest Tzu Chi branch office.

Chapter 4

BUDDHIST WOMEN IN THE GLOBAL COMMUNITY: WOMEN AS PEACEMAKERS

Venerable Karma Lekshe Tsomo

Historically, apart from a few minor scrapes, Buddhists have had a fairly good record on tolerance and nonviolence. After all, Buddhist practice is designed to create wise, ethical, compassionate beings. The Buddha taught that "Hatred ceases not by hatred, but by love alone," and his golden rule was, "Do not do to others what you would not wish done to you." Recently, however, Buddhist countries have become notorious arenas of genocide and brutality. Burma, Cambodia, China, Sri Lanka, Tibet. What went wrong?

Today, with people throughout the world linked through closer communications, technology, and economic ties, individuals in the world community and their well-being have become increasingly interconnected. These closer connections can be tremendously beneficial, but they can also be a source of problems. Greed and consumerism in one part of the world can lead to hunger, social injustices, and political instability in even the most remote corners of the world. Creating a harmonious human family requires greater understanding, respect, and compassion than ever before. Without genuine dialogue and concern for the happiness of others, tensions will mount, erupting in violence that threatens us all.

VENERABLE KARMA LEKSHE TSOMO is an instructor at Chaminade University and an affiliate at East-West Center in Honolulu. She holds M.A. degrees in Asian Studies and Asian Religion from University of Hawaii at Manoa, where she is a doctoral candidate in Comparative Philosophy. She is secretary of Sakyadhita: International Association of Buddhist Women and the director of Jamyang Choling, a network of seven Buddhist education programs for women in the Indian Himalayas. Her publications include: *Sakyadhita: Daughters of the Buddha, Buddhist Through American Women's Eyes, Sisters in Solitude: Two Traditions of Monastic Ethics for Women, Buddhist Women Across Cultures: Realizations, Swimming against the Streams: Innovative Buddhist Women,* and (with David W. Chappell) *Living and Dying in Buddhist Cultures.*

53

BUDDHISM'S CONTRIBUTION TO PEACE

What can Buddhism contribute toward creating a more peaceful future? Because a peaceful world consists of peaceful individuals, Buddhism's most useful contribution is the practical techniques the Buddha taught for developing patience, contentment, generosity, and inner peace. For creating a culture of peace, some system of mental cultivation which trains the mind to respond constructively in difficult circumstances is essential. Buddhist meditation techniques for cultivating mindfulness, wisdom, and compassion are invaluable resources for dealing with stressful situations and emotional conflicts. These practical tools can help us calm our anger, curb our desires, and develop wisdom for dealing constructively with the challenges of living in an often stressful, violent, corrupt, and competitive world.

His Holiness the Dalai Lama reminds us that happiness comes from replacing our self-centered attitudes with the wish to help others—generating loving kindness and compassion even toward those who harm us. The surest way to achieve world peace, he says, is to reduce our inner arsenal of greed, anger, ignorance, and self-cherishing. "For some, climbing mountains is the greatest achievement, but for Tibetans, it is overcoming ego." The Dalai Lama continues to generate thoughts of loving kindness even toward those who intentionally harm him and his people, refusing to participate in the destructive spiral of violence. For his powerful, consistently nonviolent example, His Holiness was awarded the Nobel Peace Prize in 1989.

Human beings today live in a very different environment than when the Buddha lived. More than ever, wise and ethical Buddhist leaders have a responsibility to convey the Buddha's peaceful teachings authentically in new cultural environments. Buddhism offers meaningful alternatives that are more useful than ever to the current glamorization of wealth, power, and violence. These include not only meditation, but also guidelines for sustainable living, harmonious interpersonal relationships, and ethical decision making. Buddhists work to provide effective spiritual and social leadership by embodying the Buddhist ideals of moral integrity, fairness, compassion, and harmony.

Buddhists have always been active in the community as teachers, counselors, and healers, but today Buddhist insights are also needed on such issues as racism, sexism, environmental destruction, bioethics, economic injustices, hatred, and rage. With 10 percent of the world's population on the verge of starvation, Buddhists are challenged to combine spiritual transformation with social transformation. In addition to meditation and prayer, they must demonstrate their commitment to peace and human happiness in tangible ways.

GENDER IMBALANCE WITHIN BUDDHISM

More than 2,500 years ago, the Buddha articulated the radical idea that all human beings have equal spiritual potential, including women, and put the idea into practice by establishing an order of nuns. The early Buddhist communities of India were probably the world's first examples of democratic institutions, but over the years power and resources have become concentrated in the hands of a few, mostly men. Often women are bypassed in decision-making and lack opportunities for education and religious training. To correct the gender imbalance that has developed within Buddhism and to bring Buddhist institutions more in line with the tradition's own egalitarian ideals, an international conference on Buddhist women was convened in 1987 in Bodhgaya, India, and Sakyadhita, the International Association of Buddhist Women, was born. As idealistic as it may sound, the fledgling association's very first objective was the promotion of world peace.

Since then, an alliance of Buddhist women leaders and practitioners has worked steadily to bring down barriers and help women achieve equal opportunities. We have concentrated our efforts especially on benefiting women in developing countries and helping in areas of greatest need. Subsequent conferences in Thailand, Sri Lanka, Ladakh, Cambodia, and the United States have acted as catalysts to create a new vision of what is possible for Buddhist women. These grassroots efforts have galvanized energies and resources for badly needed education projects, peace efforts, healthcare training, women's shelters, literacy programs, leadership training, monastic training, meditation retreats, and economic development projects for women. Sakyadhita's international, nonsectarian

55

gatherings have provided opportunities for women to engage in dialogue with our counterparts from other countries about their aspirations and concerns. As a result of these gatherings, Buddhist women are developing leadership skills and the confidence to work for the advancement of ourselves and our communities.

THE SOCIAL AND SPIRITUAL MISSION OF SAKYADHITA

From the beginning, Sakyadhita's aim has been to create bonds of friendship and understanding among nuns and laywomen from a variety of countries and practice traditions. Working in harmony with monks, laymen, and followers of other religious traditions, Sakyadhita has become the world's most active international Buddhist women's organization, reaching out to more than 280 million Buddhist women through conferences, publications, a website, and community-based education and training programs. Much of the strife in the world today is attributed to differences of religion and ideology, so Sakyadhita has taken the initiative in promoting ecumenical understanding through panel discussions, small group discussions, research, and publications. Sakyadhita's diversity is evident in the variety of ethnic, religious, educational, and economic backgrounds of our members and staff. We have found that uniting representatives of various backgrounds on working committees is an excellent way to clear away doubts and misconceptions of other faiths, and develop a genuine appreciation for one another's beliefs. Interdenominational services and pilgrimage tours are also great opportunities to learn more about the ideals, interpretations, meditation methods, chanting styles, and symbolism of one another's traditions.

Sakyadhita's special focus is working to achieve equal opportunities for women in Buddhism. A significant aspect of the effort to achieve gender equity within Buddhism has been the struggle to gain equal access to ordination. Monasticism has been central in Buddhism's development from the start and the order of fully ordained nuns established by the Buddha himself continues today in China, Korea, Taiwan, and Vietnam. Reclaiming women's right to wear the robe as full-fledged members of the Buddhist monastic community is crucial for ensuring women's rights and opportunities within Buddhist institutions. Sakyadhita has therefore encour-

56

aged research on Buddhist women's history and the Buddhist monastic codes (*Vinaya*) to promote women's equal status and access to ordination. As a result of Sakyadhita's advocacy, ordination ceremonies and monastic training programs for nuns are gaining greater acceptance and support in India, Nepal, Sri Lanka, and the West. These efforts are critical not only for nuns, but also for achieving full participation for all women in the various Buddhist traditions.

BECOMING AGENTS OF PEACE

To become effective agents of peace, we are experimenting with new participatory styles of leadership, exploring new models of community, and developing truly democratic organizational skills. For centuries, women have been excluded from or on the margins of religious institutions—serving as workers and supporters without any voice in the organizations' aims or methods. Learning from these experiences, Sakyadhita members have forged new directions in inclusive, participatory leadership. Women's grassroots organizations often lack sufficient funding to pay staff members, so it becomes all the more crucial to fully acknowledge and value volunteer efforts. Committee members and coordinators on both the international and local levels are empowered to organize conferences, publications, research, and other activities. It may take five months to produce a brochure, but everyone who wishes is welcome to offer her ideas at every stage of its production. In addition to engendering a greater sense of involvement and commitment, this inclusive, responsive style of organization gives women a chance to develop friendships, respect, wisdom, and confidence in their own and each other's abilities.

In a matter of just a few years, many worthwhile projects have developed from Sakyadhita members' commitment to benefiting others. In Thailand, shelters for victims of violence and for women living with AIDS as well as a "Home of Peace and Love" for single mothers have been built. In India, numerous education projects, healthcare initiatives, monastic training programs, and a handicraft center for women in remote Himalayan regions have been developed. In Sri Lanka, a nuns' training center, counseling programs, hospice training, and education programs for women in the villages have been created. In Nepal, several education centers for nuns

57

and laywomen have been founded and an orphanage is planned. In 1994, Sakyadhita members sponsored a visit of His Holiness the Dalai Lama to Hawaii, titled "Compassion for World Peace," with events attended by more than 15,000 people. CDs, audiocassettes, and videotapes of these events were created to bring the Dalai Lama's message of peace and compassion to an even wider audience. Sakyadhita has joined with women around the world to protest population transfers, torture of prisoners, forced sterilizations, cultural genocide, and other human rights abuses in Tibet and around the world.

Sakyadhita's Sixth International Conference on Buddhist Women in February 2000 in Lumbini, Nepal, honors Mahamaya, the Buddha's mother. Focused on the theme "Women as Peace Makers: Self, Family, Community, World," the conference will give Buddhist women opportunities to share their knowledge and experiences. Women from developed and developing countries will acquire practical skills in workshops on meditation, leadership, reproductive ethics, conflict resolution, environmental health, and peacebuilding skills. The workshops on "Women for a Peaceful Millennium—Learning Peace Building Skills" will feature role play, skits, poster sessions, performances, panel discussions, and small group discussions. Through these hands-on activities, participants will gain skills that they can immediately implement and share with members of their own communities. The Sakyadhita conferences have been many women's first experience speaking at a public gathering. This experience of speaking in a safe environment has helped many women develop the confidence and public relations skills they need to effectively engage with the media and to publicly express their ideas and the needs of their communities.

CORRECTING GENDER INEQUALITIES

An important aspect of Sakyadhita's mission has been awakening women to their own potentialities and imparting the confidence and training needed to maximize those potentialities. Among people in more affluent countries, this has involved educating people about the conditions of women in developing countries and alerting them to the fact that the gender problem has not yet been solved. Among people in developing countries, it has meant educating people about the attainments of nuns and laywomen in other Buddhist countries and throughout Buddhist history. Sakyadhita members have published numerous books documenting their research on women in Buddhist cultures: *Sakyadhita: Daughters of the Buddha; Thai Women in Buddhism; Buddhist Women across Cultures; Women under the Bo Tree; Buddhism through American Women's Eyes; Buddhism after Patriarchy; Sisters in Solitude; Buddhism with Open Eyes; Buddhist Women across Cultures; Women Living Zen; Swimming against the Stream: Innovative Women in Buddhism;* and so on. As a result of Sakyadhita members' efforts, women are now being included more often in Buddhist forums and women's concerns are more frequently being discussed.

Sakyadhita's aim is not simply to benefit women. Our work stems from the realization that inequalities lead to injustices and injustices inevitably lead to strife. For example, gender inequalities are the cause of violence against women and children perpetrated daily in homes around the world—homes where young people learn the values and habits that affect the rest of their lives. Strengthening women is a way of correcting inequalities, preventing violence and injustice, and building more peaceful societies at the most fundamental level—the family.

Women have played little, if any, role in the decisions that consign their sons and daughters to wars, brothels, gangland killings, and drug-infested streets. Now it is time for women to demonstrate that peace is possible, using every means at their disposal—including prayer, meditation, peace education, the arts, and the political process. Women are creating alliances committed to actualizing peace on all levels: in our hearts, families, communities, and world. Buddhist women are helping each other learn meditation skills to nurture inner peace, communication skills to foster family peace, organizational skills to build community peace and to work for world peace. This global alliance of women is helping change the earth's climate from storm to calm.

The enlightened attitude that Buddhism teaches—the wish to free all living beings from suffering—is timely. Buddhist compassion teaches us to place others' needs before our own and to work ceaselessly for the well being of all. Each individual has a responsibility to help alleviate the sufferings of the world. Buddhist women are now taking Buddhism's message of peace and compassion and translating it into action. Each time a person sits and observes the stillness of her own heart, each time she resolves a misunderstanding, each time she speaks out against injustice, she takes responsibility for a small portion of humanity's problems and the world becomes a more peaceful place. The movement for gender equity in Buddhism not only encourages women to develop their own spiritual resources, but helps them become leaders in community development, ecumenical dialogue, and international peace efforts.

SUGGESTED READINGS

Dresser, Marianne, ed., *Buddhist Women on the Edge: Contemporary Perspectives from the Western Frontier* (Berkeley: North Atlantic Books, 1996).

Friedman, Lenore, *Meetings with Remarkable Women: Buddhist Teachers in America* (Boston: Shambhala, 1987).

Klein, Anne Carolyn, *Meeting the Great Bliss Queen: Buddhist, Feminists, and the Art of the Self* (Boston: Beacon Press, 1995).

Murcott, Susan, *The First Buddhist Women: Translations and Commentaries on the Therigatha* (Berkeley: Parallax Press, 1991).

Tsomo, Karma Lekshe, ed., *Buddhism Through American Women's Eyes* (Ithaca: Snow Lion Publications, 1995).

_____, *Buddhist Women Across Cultures* (Albany: State University of New York Press, 1999).

_____, *Sakyadhita: Daughters of the Buddha* (Ithaca: Snow Lion Publications, 1988).

PERIODICALS

Sakyadhita: International Association of Buddhist Women. Sakyadhita, 1143 Piikoi Place, Honolulu, HI 96822, Ph: 808-524-9588, Email: tsomo@hawaii.edu, Website: www2.hawaii.edu/~tsomo.

Yasodhara: Newsletter on International Buddhist Women's Activities. Dr. Chatsumarn Kabilsingh, Faculty of Liberal Arts, Thammasat University, Bangkok 10200, Thailand, Fax: 66-2-613-3140.

CONTACT INFORMATION

• Sakyadhita: International Association of Buddhist Women
  1143 Piikoi Place
  Honolulu, Hawaii 96822

Chapter 5

THE OPPRESSION OF BUDDHISTS IN MONGOLIA

Venerable Lama Bataa Mishigish

INTRODUCTION

In Mongolia, the roles of monks and nuns have undergone enormous change in this century. In order to appreciate the challenges for Buddhists in Mongolia today, I will describe Buddhism during the Communist period and contrast this with Buddhism in today's democratic system.

MY EARLY EXPERIENCE OF BUDDHISM

I was born in Ulaanbaatar, Mongolia, in 1972, and in the summer of 1990 I became a monk. I have seen how Buddhists lived when they lacked religious freedom. When I was in high school, teachers were not allowed to talk or teach about religion. There were no textbooks that provided true secular studies of religion at any educational level. In my childhood, I found out about Buddhism from my grandma, who is a Buddhist. When my grandma thought it was the time, she took me with her to the monastery, which I enjoyed. She took me to the only active monastery, Gandan, where peaceful-looking, quiet, older monks gave away delicious rice with butter and raisins, especially to the children. I could see older people in the prayer hall prostrating to the big ancient statues of Buddhas, reciting something, and burning incense.

At the time, everything was very new and interesting. Because of movies I saw and books I read containing antireligious propaganda, I and other children had thought about monks as "yellow feudal," as greedy and hungry for money, as ready to swallow everything in order to gain wealth. At the monastery, however, I never noticed

VENERABLE LAMA BATAA MISHIGISH was born in Ulaanbaatar, Mongolia, in 1972. In 1990, he became a monk and studied Buddhism at Tashichoeling Monastery until 1996. In 1996, he went to Hawaii to study English. Presently, he is pursuing a master's degree in religious studies at the University of Hawaii.

any threat to my grandma and me. My grandmother looked pleased that her ten-year old grandson was respectful to the monks and ceremonies, and she asked me to recite a short prayer to Green Tara. She warned me that I should not let anyone know I knew the prayer. If someone knew, I would have been considered a young supporter of religious dogma, which could have caused bad rumors about my family members. The confusing thing was that everything I saw on television or read from the textbooks about monks was really contradicting what my grandma told me and what I experienced.

In the 1970s, it was common for monks walking in the street, dressed as monks, to be attacked by small kids who threw rocks and yelled at them. The children expressed their hatred as best they could. This was only one of the many ways that young people abused the monks who were seen as the most dangerous and inhuman beings of that time. Elders could do almost nothing to tell the truth. They were afraid of getting caught and being charged with participating in pro-religious propaganda. In almost every movie or book, monks were described as "counterrevolutionaries" and "class enemies" who tried to destroy all the good things. The party propaganda's major target was the teenagers of school age whose minds were like blank pages for absorbing anything against Buddhism and monks. They were taught that Buddhism was an opiate of the people and an obstacle to individual development.

Every individual was forced to be either antireligious or nonreligious at that time. Therefore, whoever went to temple or was involved in religious activity was considered uneducated, or nationalist, or anti-Communist. They were pressured by the Communist party and were condemned and criticized publicly. They had no place to freely exercise their religious practice in society. The only way they could practice was secretly getting together in an isolated safe place and burning a few butter lamps to have a religious service. They even had to wrap up their bells and other religious instruments with a piece of cotton to make less sound and not to attract strangers' attention. The monks at the monastery were strictly forbidden to instruct and practice any religious teaching outside of the monastery. Looking back, I realize what religious oppression was and how it negatively affected people's lives.

OLD BLACK DAYS IN THE 1930S

Many of the following stories of events I have heard from the old monks whose teachers were killed, brothers arrested, and whose home monasteries were completely destroyed. As they remembered the "old black days," their eyes filled with tears and they wept out of pain and grief, not for what they themselves experienced, but because they remembered their teachers, fellow monks, and brothers, all of whom were executed. During the 1991 visit of His Holiness the Dalai Lama, I could see not only monks, but also old men and women, bitterly crying for the loss of people close to them and the loss of their faith. Buddhism was more than some superficial religion to them; it was the most meaningful aspect of their lives. This religious persecution that had occurred was a great tragedy for the whole of Mongolia. It continued for almost 70 years.

The 1921 national revolution had brought many positive results, such as political independence and Western secularization. However, in religious life, it had challenged Buddhism not only as a religion, but also as a cultural heritage, and a valuable core of traditions, arts, and unique social and political integration. The major obstacle to the authority of the Communist party-guided government and its implementation of the new policy of indoctrination was Buddhism and its teaching. Therefore, the most crucial part of this new anti-religious campaign was to eliminate Buddhist activities and gradually make Buddhism disappear from social life. In the past, Buddhism had played a strong role in the unification of the nation as a powerful social institution. During the Communist regime, if Buddhism had remained as strong as it had been, the national interest of the Mongols would strongly have been against the interest of Communist expansion in the territory.

In the name of modernization, the Mongolian People's Revolutionary Party (MPRP) with its Comintern advisors began implementing reformation programs that strongly challenged the religious freedom of the people. The reformation was to eliminate all the monks who were in higher political positions and get rid of them by charging them with political errors. It aimed at depriving all the monks of their political, economic, and social rights. Later, with the new campaign of collectivization, cattle and other fixed wealth of temples and monasteries were confiscated in order to

63

economically weaken the Buddhist organizations and stop their activities. The next program was the imposition of heavy taxes both on individual monks and on temples. Between 1930 and 1932, 30,000 monks were forced to leave monastic life.

In retaliation for several antireligious campaigns, the people, including armed monks, rebelled against the government and the whole country exploded in open rebellions. The monks and civilians had no other way to regain their religious freedom because they no longer had basic rights and were considered "enemies." Many of them were arrested and shot because of false political charges. The only hope for them was to rebel. They had nothing to lose.

Unfortunately, all the rebellions were smashed and the leaders were arrested, brutally tortured, and shot. Following those rebellions, the government strictly forbade the construction of religious buildings and religious teachings. In 1927, religious organizations had held approximately 3.6 million cattle and the number decreased to 80,000 in 1937. In 1932, there were about 800 major religious centers throughout the country. But in 1938, 760 of the remaining centers were closed and many of them were destroyed. By 1940, only several hundred monks remained of some 120,000 in the 1920s. They lived in the 11 remaining religious centers.

The older monks were forced to live in the country and the younger monks became workers in the new factories and some of them joined the military. By joining the military service, young monks were no longer considered as "yellow feudal" or as a "social parasite;" rather they were welcomed as intelligent supporters of the Communist propaganda. In 1937, under the name of the antireligious propaganda and antinationalism movement, massive religious persecution took place in a silent way, which caused Buddhism to completely disappear, after more than four centuries, from the everyday life of the Mongols. The number of people, including monks and civilians, that were killed during the persecution is not clear yet. It was a black period of Mongolian history in which brothers killed each other, friends persecuted one another, and students became enemies of their teachers.

The government finally released some monks and permitted a few monasteries to open, but these later decreased to only one with a total of 100 monks. Most of the monasteries were torn down and some remaining monasteries were used as museums. Today in the country, there are ruins of many old monasteries. The ruins serve as a lesson about what happened and a warning that such repression should never be repeated.

BUDDHISM IN MODERN MONGOLIA

The party kept a careful eye on every religious activity during the Communist period. By 1970, there was only one functioning religious center, Gandan Monastery in Ulaanbaatar, which had a limit of 100 monks. The head of Mongolian Buddhism at that time was Khambo Lama Gombojav, who prepared the stage for the future revival of Buddhism. The Khambo Lama was the founder of the first Mongolian Buddhist College and the Asian Buddhist Conference for Peace (ABCP). Even though it was founded with the direct support of the Communist political organizations and held their ideologies, the ABCP was very active in involving other religious organizations in Asia in peace-oriented friendly cooperation. The ABCP has 16 national centers in Asian countries, and it also has an NGO status with the UN. Domestically, it supported religious and cultural preservation and provided some limited religious service to the public.

To develop support for its political ideology, the government financed new projects to reconstruct some temple buildings for preserving cultural values and to organize international activities to increase international goodwill for their Communist states. During the Communist regime, there was a Council for Religious Affairs that regulated and controlled religious activities according to party policy. However, the monks took advantage of this political support to preserve the faith of the majority and to keep alive the valuable traditional customs of their cultural heritage. Even though most of the monks had lost hope for a revival, the older generation was very responsible in passing on their religious and cultural traditions to the next generations.

At the end of 1989, a democratic movement brought a peaceful victory over the old political system and its Communist ideologies. The Communist party and its political committee, which had controlled the country for about 70 years, wisely resigned and put an

65

end to the totalitarian government system. The new democratic movement officially aimed at establishing a democratic foundation both for legitimizing human rights, political democracy, and a liberal economy. The people welcomed the human rights movements and were pleased with the opportunity to have their religious faith and practice revived after a long religious persecution.

Even today, if you ask young Mongolians if they have any faith, most of them would say that they consider themselves Buddhists. Because their grandparents and parents are Buddhists, they themselves were born and raised in Buddhist families and within Buddhist culture. Due to its long existence in society, Buddhism itself has become an inseparable part of daily life, especially for older generations. It is hard to understand why people clung to their faith in Buddhism so strongly after the brutal and almost complete institutional destruction. In reality, Buddhism in Mongolia has planted deep roots in every field of social life.

According to today's statistics, there are more than 140 monasteries and temples, including four convents, throughout the country, with two Buddhist colleges and two Buddhist intermediate and high schools. The number of monastic organizations has increased rapidly.

Many young people of the 1990s were interested in following the religious tradition and became monks. Some old monks, who spent their early lives at monasteries, provided the religious education. Some of the first monk-students of the 1970s were responsible for the religious education of young and novice monks. There is a big gap between the old monks of above 80 years of age and young monks below 30 years. This gap negatively affects the education of young monks.

Between 1990 and 1993, most of the current monasteries and temples were independently reopened by a group of old and young local monks. The first challenge they faced was building new monastery or temple buildings. In rural areas, they used *gers*, traditional tents, until they built their own small buildings for religious purposes. Due to financial constraints, even today many of them are still in the *gers*. The second problem was educating young monks who had no religious educational background. Gandan Monastery had the single college that provided religious education. However, the capacity of the college to educate young novice monks was very limited. In addition to its college education, the college began a two-year training program for young monks. This program serves hundreds from rural areas and teaches them the basics of religious practice and service. Afterward, many young monks were eager to get a higher religious education, but few of them had the opportunity to improve their education. With the support of the Indian government and Tibetan religious organizations, many monks have been sent to India to continue their religious education. They are specializing in philosophy, medicine, and art.

Most of the 140 monasteries, especially temples in rural areas, have fewer than ten resident monks today. Some young monks went to central areas, where bigger monasteries exist, because they want more education and better support for it. In the last four years, the number of new novice monks has rapidly decreased. In addition, because of its declining social status, many young people are no longer interested in becoming monks. Religious education is considered outdated and too traditional amongst the youth. They prefer to be educated in a more Western way, rather than the traditional religious way. Monastic organizations cannot support improvements in their educational system. Only a few monasteries even have a computer. There are outdated books and source materials and a limited faculty.

There is no central religious organization that manages and organizes monasteries and their activities. Bigger monasteries have a strong desire to be independent but middle-sized and small temples prefer to cooperate with and receive assistance from bigger ones. A standardized educational system is needed to prepare educated monks and nuns. Monastic organizations need generally accepted monastic regulations and rules to jointly cooperate not only with one another, but also with other social institutions. Most monastic organizations barely guarantee their monks' and nuns' living standards. Such organizational and economic weakness causes individual monks to lack education and social status.

Young monks between 18 and 27 years of age, according to the law, now have to join the military service. The only possibility not to serve is by paying a large amount of money as compensation. However, monks usually can't afford to pay so that most young monks must serve in the military. Religious institutions and individual monks should jointly oppose this kind of law which contradicts monks' religious convictions.

Religious organizations are struggling to overcome their economic, educational, and social constraints. Monks and nuns need modern education to deal with today's challenging social issues and maintain Buddhist traditions and cultures.

SUGGESTED FURTHER READINGS

Moses, Larry W., *The Political Role of Mongol Buddhism* (Bloomington, Indiana: Asia Studies Research Institute, 1977).

Pozdneyev, Aleksei, M., *Religion and Ritual in Society: Lamaist Buddhism in Late 19th Century Mongolia* (Bloomington, Indiana: The Mongolian Society, Inc., 1978)

CONTACT INFORMATION

• Lama Bataa Mishigish
P.O. Box 514
Ulaanbaatar 46
Mongolia
Tel: (808) 944-6131
E-mail: bataa@hawaii.edu
Lamabataa@hotmail.com

Chapter 6

SARVODAYA SHRAMADANA'S APPROACH TO PEACEBUILDING

A. T. Ariyaratne

In traditional Buddhist families of Sri Lanka, from their early childhood children are made to learn and recite certain Pali stanzas. At their young age they may not understand the meaning and significance of these but as they mature they do. The meaning of some of these stanzas is as follows:

- *I venerate and follow the Buddha, His Teachings, and the Community of Monks.*
- *I shall abstain from: taking away sentient lives, stealing, sexual misconduct, untruth, and consuming intoxicants.*
- *I offer these colorful, fragrant, and good quality flowers to the Buddha knowing that like these flowers, as time passes by, I will gradually fade and wither away. So is my body impermanent.*
- *I understand that the essence of the Teaching of the Buddha is: Refraining from doing all evil, cultivating the good, and purifying my mind from all defilements.*
- *I shall always strive to help all living beings to overcome physical suffering, fear, and mental suffering.*

All the mental and emotional ingredients necessary for the building up of a culture of peace are found in the above words.

There were times in our history when there was total peace and harmony in our country. In modern times, why do children take to violence as they grow to adulthood? Why do we have a society today which is far from peaceful? Why do governments invest more and more in weapons and war preparations? Why are we on a path to the destruction of our life support systems in the environment?

A.T. ARIYARATNE is a community educator who founded the Sarvodaya Shramadana Movement of Sri Lanka and is its current president. For 41 years he devoted his life to build this movement, which is active today in over 11,600 villages in Sri Lanka. Dr. Ariyaratne's writings and speeches have been edited and published by Professor Nandasena Ratnapala as seven volumes of *Collected Works*.

One of the unique teachings of the Buddha is the theory of dependent arising. Everything is related to every other thing. If there is no peace in a society, there should be a variety of interdependent and interrelated causes that bring about such a situation. All these causes have to be attacked simultaneously and removed to make a reversal of the processes that have brought about a loss of peace in our society so that we can rebuild a culture of peace.

The Sarvodaya Shramadana Movement of Sri Lanka has evolved during the last 41 years an integrated self-development approach to counteract the causes that bring about conflicts, crimes, and war. The vision on which this approach is based has been developed from the Buddha's teachings. Some of those in popular religious practices were stated above. In this article I am presenting some practical examples of peacebuilding activities from Sarvodaya Shramadana experience. *Sarvodaya* is a word coined by Mahatma Gandhi which we have adopted to mean the well-being of all or the awakening of all. *Shramadana* means the gifting or the voluntary sharing of one's labor and resources for the awakening of oneself and others. This movement, therefore, is striving to build up a society where the well-being of all is ensured. In other words, the goal of Sarvodaya is a no poverty/no affluence society where there is sustained peace and justice for all.

If religious teachings are to have an influence on the lives of people, these teachings have to be applied to the day-to-day living of human beings. There should be no discrepancy between the teachings and the practice. All human beings—both as individuals and as families, groups and communities—have their basic, secondary, and tertiary needs. Basic needs pertaining to a healthy environment, clean water, adequate clothing, optimum food requirements, sanitation and health, energy needs, communication, education, and cultural as well as spiritual needs have to be satisfied first. Without looking to governments or other external agencies, the Sarvodaya Movement assists people to organize themselves with their own self-reliance and community participation to satisfy as many of these needs as possible.

One methodology adopted is to pool all the resources the people are voluntarily prepared to share in a psychological, social, and physical environment that is created for a few days to satisfy one or more of these needs. Such an arrangement is called a Shramadana camp. Here men, women, and children in a village, sometimes along with the neighboring villagers, prepare all the logistical requirements. They decide on the kind of work they should do and prepare the tools and equipment necessary for that task. They arrange for the food, water, medical care needed in case of injury, and temporary accommodation for lodging the volunteers. All the participants work in a Shramadana camp.

The camp begins with a community meditation and recitation of the five precepts pertaining to moral conduct. Inspirational songs outlining the above-mentioned Buddhist thoughts are sung before people take their tools and get to physical work in organized groups. Some may work building the required access road to the village; others will be digging a series of wells to provide for clean drinking water to the village community, while yet others may be planting trees to enrich the village environment. It can be anything that falls within the category of basic needs for which they will be donating their labor, skills, knowledge, and even land and other resources. Before the work begins, during the lunch break, and in the evening, the participants sit together in a circle on the ground and conduct what is known as "family gatherings." The idea behind the term "family gathering" is that the whole world is one family, and all of them represent humanity in microcosm. All religious, caste, race, linguistic, class, national, or political differences are of no importance in these family gatherings. Instead, meditations on loving kindness for all beings, songs, dances, and other cultural items that promote the concept of "one world, one people" occur. Discussions related to the constructive work at hand, learning a variety of useful subjects such as health and sanitation, and the practice of nonviolence in everyday life also form part of the agenda of family gatherings.

Shramadana camps have been taking place for the last 41 years. They continue as the first Sarvodaya step for building inner and outer peace in human personalities and groups. In hundreds of places where the Ten Thousand Villages Sarvodaya Development Program is going on, these camps are conducted during weekends and holidays with the participation of hundreds of people in each village. From a physical and material development aspect, the contribution made by Shramadana to village reconstruction work is very large. But what is more important for us is the psychological and spiritual transformation brought about in individuals and communities by participating in this work. We believe that by raising the level of spiritual consciousness of people in a physical and social environment where needs are satisfied as a result of self-reliance, we are laying a strong psychosocial foundation for lasting peace within human minds and among human communities. But this is only the beginning. This initial process is supplemented and consolidated with other Sarvodaya programs.

Generally, a Shramadana camp is followed up with the organization of six formations of different age groups in the community. The first is the children below five years of age—the preschool group. The second is the children of compulsory school age—6 to 16 years. The third is the youth group composed of those above 16 years up to about 28 years. The fourth is the mothers' or women's group. The fifth is the farmers' and artisans' group and the sixth is the general elders' group, which is composed of village elders such as the religious leaders, government servants, native physicians, and so on. A full-time Sarvodaya volunteer is in charge of assisting the village communities to organize these groups and guide them in relating themselves to continue with activities pertaining to their need satisfaction. At this stage, in addition to their own labor, skills, and resources, whatever help from the governmental and other agencies is available is utilized. Instead of a confrontational attitude, a harmonious relationship is established with these agencies.

As the above groups are established and function, the communities graduate from a process of spiritual, psychological, and social infrastructure building that they participated in during the initial Shramadana camps to a nonviolent institutional building stage. The next level of evolution of a Sarvodaya development process is obtaining legal recognition or incorporating their village-level Sarvodaya Shramadana Society. This is not like a national constitution because in the village society's rules and regulations many practical principles and guidelines embodying spiritual, moral, and ethical values are included.

For example, Buddha's advice to the people of Vajjin Village Republic of his time, which we call the Seven Factors of Non-degeneration, is incorporated in the rules of the Sarvodaya Village Society. These rules are very simple and intelligible even to a child, but they are very profound from a culture of peace point of view. In the 25 member elected executive committee of the Sarvodaya Shramadana Society of a village, according to their rules, it is obligatory to elect at least three children between seven and 15 years, three youths, and three women. In this way, vested interests and domination of the society by self-centered adults are eliminated and the pursuit of the highest codes of ethics is encouraged. This is the Sarvodaya path to justice and peace through a participatory democracy that evolves from the bottom up. This kind of unorthodox total approach to peacebuilding demands lots of sacrifice and patience, and it is time-consuming. However, when we look at the unique position Sarvodaya holds today in the peacebuilding task of our society, after 41 years of continuous work carried out in over 10,000 villages, we can conclude that there is no shorter path to transform our society from a psychology of killing and threats to kill to one that is life-enhancing and spiritually fulfilling.

Having achieved a collective psychological drive, social organization, and legal recognition, the village society has to acquire appropriate technological and managerial know-how to improve their livelihood. Having taken to a path of cooperation based on an ethical code rather than giving in to the prevailing competitive, unethical, and violent market forces promoted by the broader society, the critical choice now before the village community is in the sphere of technology, finance, and economy.

The community has to contend with much stronger political, economic, technological forces backed by both national and multinational vested interests. The latter not only possess the financial and political clout but also have at their disposal a very powerful communication technology that can take their message to the remotest communities in the country. These forces, along with their allies both from the governmental and certain nongovernmental sectors, try to perpetuate poverty and powerlessness of the majority of people and promote the status quo by palliative means. What is needed, however, is a fundamental transformation of the consciousness of all in a spirit of compassion, understanding, and nonviolence to change the existing economy of violence to one of a culture of peace.

The initiative to build a culture of peace through people's self-development at the grassroots has reached horizontally to every part of the country. Networking these villages in clusters of ten (a pioneering village, four intermediary villages, and five peripheral villages) and then getting these clusters to network at divisional and district levels with a national headquarters has been accomplished. This network is active today trying to tackle people's secondary needs like those pertaining to education, health, economy, and a livable environment. Sarvodaya is also anxious to do whatever it can to turn around the economy and technologies to promote a nonviolent society and finally to take up the issue of crimes in the country including the unnecessary war that is going on in the northern and eastern provinces. With this in view, Sarvodaya villages which have completed pre-economic stages of their development are now taking action to start savings, credit, and micro-enterprises programs and establish Sarvodaya development banks in their villages. Already over 300 such banks have been established and are functioning; 3,000 more are ready to establish their own banks after going through legal procedures. Other villages will follow suit. The main objective of the Sarvodaya development banking system is to relieve the village community from the debt burden and help them to have their own monetary resources to start their own agricultural, agro-industrial, and other income-generating projects and enterprises and also create service opportunities for the village youth.

Though these programs appear to be mainly economic, they promote a very important peace process, i.e., building trust among different racial, religious, or ethnic groups. For example, when a member of the society has to take a loan from the Village Development Bank, five or six others in their group have to be the guarantors. There is no collateral required for the poor to take loans from the Sarvodaya bank. In the group there may be Buddhists, Hindus, Christians, and Muslims, or Sinhalese and Tamils. By this process an immense trust and personal bond is created among different communities. Instead of having conflicts between them, together they can now confront other basic issues like poverty, exploitation, environmental degradation, crimes, alcoholism and drug problems, and other social ills. This becomes a cooperative effort cutting across race and religious divides.

So far I have described the processes Sarvodaya has implemented to transform individuals and groups and how these influence the Sri Lankan society as a whole. These are generally not seen and not so much considered as serious peacebuilding processes or even as activities that are in reality putting Lord Buddha's teachings into action. Of course, in the numerous activities that Sarvodaya initiates, not only Buddhist, but also the harmless customs and traditions of non-Buddhist religions are given equal place; for example, in a "family gathering," the first opportunity to observe their religious practices is given to the minority religious groups before the majority performs their recitations or rituals. Then together they participate in a common meditation.

People expect quick solutions to the culture of violence that prevails today. They forget that this culture has been caused over a long period of time by multifarious factors, including a lack of a social vision, violent technologies that eat up our ecological wealth and destroy our environmental health, and highly centralized political and economic institutions that do not suit our value systems. On the one hand, Sarvodaya is patiently and silently rebuilding the foundations of the required new social order. On the other hand, Sarvodaya has been organizing quite a number of visible people's participatory peace programs with the participation of thousands of people during the last two decades. There are peace seminars, peace conferences, peace camps, and peace meditational walks. In the meditation walks and mass meditation campaigns, numbers ranging from 5,000 to 120,000 have participated. The longest meditational walk was 81 miles from the sacred city of Kandy to the ancient sacred capital of Anuradhapura. This kind of program occurs at least once a month in different places in the country, including the troubled areas.

Sarvodaya has 12 independent national organizations which support the movement as a whole. Among them we have the Sarvodaya Women's Movement, Sarvodaya Legal Services Movement, and Sarvodaya Shantisena (Peace Brigade) Movement. The Shantisena Movement alone has more than 100,000 young people, organized

75

in groups of 11, dedicated to working for peace. They play a pioneering role in peace walks while they conduct regular Shantisena Peace Camps with the participation of all ethnic communities in different parts of the country.

The latest and newest innovative venture of Sarvodaya is Vishwa Niketan, a peace center for all nationalities to come together for developing both inner and outer peace. It is established in the belief that world peace can only be attained through the cessation of conflicts within ourselves. Buddha has taught us that we should not violate the Five Cosmic Laws that affect humans, other living beings, the plant kingdom, and even our physical environment. These are universally effective laws pertaining to the genetic systems (*Bija Niyama*), seasons (*Utu Niyama*), causality (*Kamma Niyama*), all phenomena (Dhamma *Niyama*), and consciousness (*Citta Niyama*). Vishwa Niketan functions by obeying these laws.

Vishwa Niketan provides a serene and tranquil internal and external environment conducive to the development of peace, harmony, and spiritual growth. To contribute to the spiritual revival of humankind in Sri Lanka and throughout the world, it promotes the learning, teaching, and practicing of the universal teachings of the Buddha in a spirit of loving kindness to all living beings. Vishwa Niketan asserts human rights and human duties as the basis of peace and justice in every community of the world. It promotes interfaith, interracial, interpolitical, and interstate understanding. It sponsors actions that promote cooperation between communities and religious denominations, providing a neutral ground for the dissolution of disputes arising within communities as well as those on a larger scale between countries.

The heart of the peace center consists of a series of indoor and outdoor meeting places where people can gather to discuss ways of achieving peace and resolving conflicts, receive training in the form of seminars and workshops, or engage in group or individual meditation. There are platforms beneath shady trees, informal seats on rock outcroppings, as well as covered verandas, and a large meeting hall, *Samadhi*, for more formal gatherings.

The peace center has 14 *kutis* (accommodation retreats with attached toilets) in four buildings known as *Metta* (Loving Kindness), *Karuna* (Compassion), *Muditha* (Altruistic Joy), and *Upekkha*

(Equanimity). Between them, these can accommodate up to 24 people at a time. The kitchen and pantry facilities are common. The layout and realization of the center have been carefully designed to be conducive to the purification of the mind, with great attention paid to all the details, both aesthetic and practical.

In conclusion, I must reiterate that the Sarvodaya philosophy is principally motivated by the teachings of the Buddha. It is supplemented by the lessons learned by the nonviolent struggles of Mahatma Gandhi, Martin Luther King, and others in the field. Yet Sarvodaya is not a movement of Buddhists exclusively. It is a movement for all religious groups and also for those who have no particular religion. We in Sarvodaya believe that religions should assist human beings and human groups to overcome internal defilements such as greed, ill will, and egotism, and promote internal spirituality so that beneficence, sharing, morality, and enlightenment will evolve within them. The ultimate objective of Buddhists and other religious individuals should be building a critical mass of spiritual consciousness on this planet—which is the surest way to live in a culture of peace.

SUGGESTED FURTHER READINGS

Ariyaratne, A.T., *Collected Works*, Volumes 1-7.
Vishva Lekha Publications
No. 41, Lumbini Avenue
Ratmalana, Sri Lanka

Bond, George D., "A.T. Ariyaratne and the Sarvodaya Shramadana Movement in Sri Lanka," in Christopher S. Queen and Sallie B. King, eds., *Engaged Buddhism: Liberation Movements in Asia* (Albany: SUNY Press, 1996).

CONTACT INFORMATION

• Sarvodaya Shramadana Headquarters
No. 98, Rawatawatte Road
Moratuwa, Sri Lanka
Tel: 94-1-647159; 94-1-645255
Fax: 94-1-647084; 94-1-646512
E-mail: arisar@sri.lanka.net

Part II

REBUILDING MORAL CULTURES

Chapter 7

KEEPING PEACE WITH NATURE

Stephanie Kaza

"Peace" is a term often riddled with romantic idealization, projection, and doublespeak. Political agendas and moral values of peacekeeping are not necessarily aligned in situations of conflict. Contemporary Buddhist leaders describe peace as something you do as spiritual practice. For Thich Nhat Hanh, each calm, mindful breath or step can be a step generating peace and awareness. For His Holiness the Dalai Lama, peace comes from the practice of kindness and compassion. Buddhists who take up the bodhisattva way are encouraged to practice equanimity or patience to sustain peacekeeping in everyday life. One way to define peace, then, is the cultivation, through practice, of a state of mind which can envision and manifest peaceful relations with others. Internal and external peace are seen as mutually regenerating and co-creative. Here in particular, I will look at cultivating peaceful relations with the natural world.

Peace can also be seen as the absence or at least minimization of suffering. Though Buddhists recognize that suffering is inevitable in human life, one can make an effort to reduce or eliminate some forms of suffering. Buddhist philosophy and practice emphasize the principle of nonharming or *ahimsa*. "Nonviolence," as this is sometimes translated, means more than the absence of violent acts or thoughts. It means acting positively toward constructing peace. The opening stanzas of the *Dhammapada* state, "For hate is not conquered by hate: hate is conquered by love. This is a law eter-

STEPHANIE KAZA is Associate Professor of Environmental Studies at the University of Vermont where she teaches religion and ecology, international environmental studies, radical environmentalism, ecofeminism, and nature writing. Professor Kaza is the author of *The Attentive Heart: Conversations with Trees*, a collection of meditative essays on deep ecological relations with trees, and numerous articles on Buddhism and ecology. Her new book *Dharma Rain: Sources of Buddhist Environmentalism* (forthcoming January, 2000), which she co-edited with Kenneth Kraft, is an anthology of classical and modern texts that lays a foundation for a Buddhist approach to environmental activism.

nal."[1] Thai teacher Buddhadhasa suggests that peace means being true friends to all beings and to one's self. Thus peacekeeping, from a Buddhist perspective, includes ending not only violence in human society, so widespread across the planet, but also violence towards plants and animals, rivers and oceans.

Clearly there are ample opportunities for peacemaking in the end-of-the-century escalation of the war against nature, what some have called "World War Three." A first step in keeping peace with nature calls for contact with ecological suffering in the world today. One must meet directly the ravaged land of industrial clearcuts, the chemical soup of polluted waters, the sprawling megacities filled with traffic and smog. In these places of life-threatening deterioration, peacemaking as a practice has real consequences for both human and nonhuman beings.

Reducing suffering can be a moral, political, spiritual, and practical peacemaking goal. One can begin by recognizing the suffering caused by the Three Poisons—greed, hate, and ignorance—in all their many forms. Acknowledging cruelty in treatment of trees and animals, for example, can awaken compassion and generate motivation for policy changes and public education. Resisting consumerist lures can help manage the suffering of greed through simplifying personal possessions. Combating the ignorance of stereotyping can open up avenues for understanding, not only between social groups but in relations with plants and animals. In most peacemaking dialogues, the primary parties are human beings. If we want to reduce environmental suffering, those dialogues will need to recognize the nonhumans who have been harmed and propose appropriate peacemaking measures to redress this harm.

One way to begin this work is to look for examples in some of the common realms of peacemaking action. I will organize my ideas around a model that includes four phases of emotional and spiritual work: 1) repentance, 2) resistance, 3) root cause analysis, and 4) rebuilding moral culture. This framework presents opportunities which can be taken up in pieces or as a whole, in whatever order is appropriate for the situation at hand. Most examples will reflect my familiarity with socially-engaged Buddhism, particularly in the area of environmental work. Perhaps they can inspire similar actions elsewhere or provide springboards for creativity in moving toward a peaceful and healthy environment, as well as society.

Repentance acts provide opportunities to recognize wrongdoing in the past and present, with the hope of preventing similar misdeeds in the future. With regard to the natural world, this may mean expressing grief, remorse, or regret that people have done such extensive and unthinking damage to other living beings. Repentance also acknowledges human fallibility and the limits of human wisdom and understanding. Accepting these elements of the human endeavor, one might choose to be more cautious regarding the ecological impacts of human projects.

As part of her Deep Ecology work, scholar-activist Joanna Macy has developed a number of workshop activities that allow participants to express their difficult feelings regarding human impact on other beings.[2] In the "Truth Mandala," people come forth to speak in witness to their concerns for the earth. A central circle is divided into four quadrants representing fear, sorrow, anger, and deprivation. The ritual or ceremony is a series of testimonies, made powerful by the cumulative weight of feelings in the group. In "The Council of All Beings," created with Australian rainforest activist John Seed, people allow themselves to be called by another life form to speak on its behalf at the Council. Using masks to indicate the other voice, the plant and animal representatives share their current ecological troubles with each other. They then invite several humans into the center of the circle to call humans to account for their actions. In the last round, the life forms offer their unique powers to the humans to help them see how to heal the damage they have caused to the planet.

Rochester Zen Center and affiliates hold regular repentance ceremonies as part of the yearly ritual cycle. In 1992, the Vermont Zen Center hosted the annual Buddhist Peace Fellowship (BPF) meeting over the Columbus Day holiday in October. That year marked the 500th anniversary of the "discovery" of America, an event seen as misnamed and culturally destructive from the perspective of indigenous peoples. BPF members participated in a Zen repentance ceremony adapted for the occasion to address the tensions of colonizer and colonized. Sitting in *zazen*, they passed the incense bowl around and spoke their regrets and remorse quietly, honoring "all our ancient twisted karma/ from beginningless greed, hate, and delusion." The simple but formal ceremony allowed people to be present with the power of this complex karma and its far-reaching effects.

Resistance, or holding actions, call attention to suffering, often with a forceful message of "STOP," "no more," "this is not okay." They aim to stop or reduce destructive activity, buying time for more effective long-term strategies. Protests of various scales help to define the dimensions of what is morally acceptable to the concerned public. Such actions open up dialogue and bring issues to the community for reflection. As people stand together to express concern, they act in solidarity, finding a common base for correcting injustice and improving ecological relations.

In Thailand, Buddhist monks have gained international recognition for galvanizing local people to address environmental violence in their villages. Two of the most effective methods have been tree ordination ceremonies and peace witness walks.[3] The tree ceremonies grew out of the frustration of village monks with the national plundering of local forests. Villagers were suffering loss of food, firewood, and homes. In response, forest monks took traditional orange monks' robes and wrapped them around senior trees in the forest in a formal ordination ceremony. This designated the largest local trees as "priests" and protectors of the forest, sending a strong moral message to those who would cut them down. Others known as "development monks" have led environmental pilgrimages around polluted lakes, inviting local people to walk with them in solidarity as witnesses to unsafe water and unplanned urban growth. A group of peacemaking monks who call themselves "Dhammayatria" are continuing to organize more such walks across Thailand as important rounds of moral resistance to excessive suffering.

In the United States, Buddhist activists have joined resistance efforts for forest protection and nuclear arms reduction. A small group who call themselves "ecosattvas" were impelled to protest the logging of old growth redwood groves in northern California. Drawing on local support from the Humboldt County eco-sangha and national support from the Buddhist Peace Fellowship, they led people in creating a large prayer flag covered with human hand-prints of mud. This served as visual testimony of solidarity for all who participated in Headwaters forest actions. The next year, several ecosattvas made a pilgrimage into the heart of the Headwaters, carrying a Tibetan treasure vase. Activists had taken the vase to San Francisco Area sangha meetings and invited people to offer gifts and prayers on behalf of the redwoods. The vase was ceremonially buried beneath one of the giants to strengthen spiritual protection for the trees.[4]

American Buddhists have also joined in resistance efforts against nuclear weapons and below-ground nuclear waste storage. At the Nevada Test Site near Las Vegas, Buddhists from the Buddhist Peace Fellowship offered an adaptation of a Buddha's birthday ceremony as support for those planning to commit civil disobedience and step across federal lines. Under Joanna Macy's leadership, a study group met for several years, taking the position that nuclear waste was safer above ground where it could be monitored. Using imagination combined with careful investigation, they developed an alternate vision of nuclear guardianship based in Buddhist spiritual practices.[5] Around the same time, Japan had arranged for several shipments of plutonium to be reprocessed in France and then shipped back to Japan. Zen student and artist Mayumi Oda helped to organize resistance to stop these shipments of deadly nuclear material. One ship was temporarily stopped, and although shipments resumed, the actions raised awareness in Japan and the United States, affecting Japanese government policies.

Root cause analysis applies peacekeeping methods to the structural origins of suffering. In-depth examination is necessary to address the entrenched patterns of systemic violence. Much suffering results from business policies or cultural customs that rationalize environmental destruction. A subgroup of the International Network of Engaged Buddhists and the Buddhist Peace Fellowship who call themselves the "Think Sangha" is engaged in just such structural analysis of global consumerism. Collaborating between the United States and Southeast Asia, they have held on-line and on-site conferences targeting "Alternatives to Consumerism." Through global trade analysis and review of economic policies, they show

how Western-style consumerism is taking its toll on local culture.[6] Thai activist Sulak Sivaraksa points out the moral problems of neocolonialist expansionism in "Think Big" development approaches.[7] Santikaro Bhikkhu shows how greed, hate, and ignorance take on structural form in leading social institutions. For example, rationalized hate or aggression is central to the military; rapacious greed for natural resources is standard in many economic structures.[8]

American scholars have also prepared structural analyses using Buddhist principles to shed light on environmental violence and press for better human-nature relations. Rita Gross, Buddhist feminist scholar, has laid out a Buddhist framework considering the impact of pronatalist values and policies on global population issues.[9] Process theologian and meditator Jay McDaniel has developed spiritual arguments for compassionate treatment of animals as a fundamental human responsibility.[10] Buddhist scholar Kenneth Kraft discusses the eco-karma and eco-koans of nuclear waste and the challenges activists face in undertaking socially engaged practice.[11] Sociologist Bill Devall has integrated Buddhist principles with Arne Naess's Deep Ecology philosophy, urging simplification of needs and wants.[12]

Reclaiming moral culture is the social transformational work critical to accomplishing systemic change from the ground up. This work lies in the arenas of family, home, school, and community, where moral values have traditionally been cultivated. With escalating fragmentation of landscapes and attention spans, moral reflection has taken a backseat to consumerism. Long-term peacekeeping depends on reversing such decline by cultivating moral responsiveness to other beings and to the life of Earth itself.

The practice of *ahimsa* or nonharming lies at the foundation of peacekeeping practice aimed at reducing environmental suffering. All the Buddhist precepts are based fundamentally on nonharming of self and others. Practicing the first precept, "not killing," raises moral dilemmas around food, land use, pesticides, pollution, and cultural economic invasion. The second precept, "not stealing," raises questions about global trade and corporate exploitation of resources. "Not lying" brings up issues in advertising and consumerism that promote exploitive cultural values. "Not engaging in abusive relations" points to a broad realm of cruelty and disrespect for nonhuman others. "Not using drugs and alcohol" can be interpreted broadly to include the toxic applications of insecticides and herbicides.[13] Practicing restraint and nonharming directly reduce suffering in the context of rapidly deteriorating global ecosystems, loading the odds for more peaceful relations with nature.

For many students, environmental awareness and personal lifestyle change flow naturally from a Buddhist practice commitment. Many people are turning to vegetarianism and veganism as compassionate food choices for animals and ecosystems. Others are committed to eating only organically grown food in order to support pesticide-free soil and healthy farming. Thich Nhat Hanh has strongly encouraged students to examine consumption habits, not only around food and alcohol, but also television, music, books, and magazines.[14] Buddhist values of restraint and simplicity are celebrated in "International Buy Nothing Day," a moral protest event targeted for the busiest shopping day right after Thanksgiving.

Practicing moral relations in community is perhaps the most demanding challenge of the Three Refuges. In a speedy, product-driven society, most students are drawn to the calming effects of meditation practice and the personal depth of student-teacher relationships. From a green Buddhist perspective, sangha work means not only the challenges of personal and institutional relations, but also creating sustainable ecological relations. Because of the scope of environmental deterioration, reparations work can only be effective done in collaboration or community. Working together for mutual support can not only prevent activist burnout but offer the opportunity to develop *kalyana mitta,* or spiritual friendship.

Retreat centers act as focal points for transmitting Buddhist values to committed Buddhist practitioners and the visiting public. To the extent that practice places reinforce ecological caretaking with spiritual principles, they provide a cultural model for moral commitment to the environment. For example, Green Gulch Zen Center in northern California demonstrates institutional responsibility for the environment through its food practices, waste recycling, and water use. By cooking vegetarian, it withdraws support from the inhumane institutional practices associated with factory animal farming and animal slaughter. It also avoids contributing to the accelerated clearing of global rainforests for cattle pasture and beef imports. Food served at Green Gulch includes as much in-season produce as possible from the organic farm. Food waste goes into large compost piles adjacent to the farm and garden. Water for human use and farming is drawn from local sources and managed according to the year's rainfall. Printed materials such as the introductory booklet on Green Gulch environmental practices help educate visitors about these institutional commitments.

Zen poet and ecophilosopher Gary Snyder brings his sangha work home through the framework of bioregional thinking and organizing. His basis for this is more than moral and ecological; it is aesthetic, economic, and practice-based. From his perspective, the bioregional community "does not end at the human boundaries; we are in a community with certain trees, plants, birds, animals."[15] He encourages others to take up the practice of "reinhabitation," learning to live on the land with the same respect and understanding as the original indigenous people. Snyder has been a leader in establishing the Yuba River Institute, a bioregional watershed organization working in cooperation with the Bureau of Land Management. They have done ground survey work, controlled burns, and creek restoration projects engaging the local community in the process. "To restore the land one must live and work in a place. To work in a place is to work with others. People who work together in a place become a community, and a community, in time, grows a culture."[16] Snyder models the level of commitment necessary to reinhabit a place and build community culture that might eventually span generations.

These four arenas of peacemaking—repentance, resistance, root cause analysis, and rebuilding moral culture—offer strong potential for rebuilding damaged relations with the natural world. The list of environmental war zones has been well documented; the litanies of loss are well known to people of many regions. A peacemaking commitment for a healthy world now must include restoration of moral relations with nonhuman beings. Working together, Buddhists and non-Buddhists can find ways to help each other in undertaking this important and life-sustaining work. May this work help reduce the suffering of plant and animal beings caught in the web of human activity and may it bring awakening to those who follow the peacemaking path.

NOTES

1. *The Dhammapada*, trans. Juan Mascaro (London: Penguin Books, 1973).

2. Joanna Macy and Molly Young Brown, *Coming Back to Life: Practices to Reconnect Our Lives, Our World* (Gabriola, British Columbia: New Society Books, 1998).

3. These and other environmental activist examples are described in Stephanie Kaza and Kenneth Kraft, eds., *Dharma Rain: Sources of Buddhist Environmentalism* (Boston: Shambhala, 2000 forthcoming).

4. Wendy Johnson, "A Prayer for the Forest," *Tricycle* 8:1 (Fall 1998), 84-85.

5. Joanna Macy, "Guarding the Earth," *Inquiring Mind* 7(2):1,4-5,12, Spring 1991.

6. See 1998-1999 issues of *Seeds of Peace* for reports and announcements of these events.

7. Sulak Sivaraksa, *Seeds of Peace* (Berkeley: Parallax Press, 1990).

8. Santikaro Bhikkhu, "The Four Noble Truths of Dhammic Socialism" in *Entering the Realm of Reality: Towards Dhammic Societies*, ed. Jonathan Watts, Alan Senauke, and Santikaro Bhikkhu (Bankok: Suksit Siam, 1997), 89-161.

9. Rita Gross, "Buddhist Resources for Issues of Population, Consumption, and the Environment" in Mary Evelyn Tucker and Duncan Ryuken Williams, eds., *Buddhism and Ecology: The Interconnectedness of Dharma and Deeds* (Cambridge: Harvard University Press, 1997), 291-312.

10. Jay B. McDaniel, *Earth, Sky, Gods, and Mortals: Developing an Ecological Spirituality* (Mystic, Connecticut: Twenty-third Publications, 1990).

11. Kenneth Kraft, "Nuclear Ecology and Engaged Buddhism" in Mary Evelyn Tucker and Duncan Ryuken Williams, eds., *Buddhism and Ecology: The Interconnectedness of Dharma and Deeds* (Cambridge: Harvard University Press, 1997), 269-290.

12. Bill Devall, *Simple in Means, Rich in Ends: Practicing Deep Ecology*, (Salt Lake City: Peregrine Smith Books, 1988).

13. Green Gulch Zen Center Ecological Precepts, *Buddhist Peace Fellowship Journal*, Summer 1990, 33.

14. Thich Nhat Hanh, *For a Future to Be Possible* (Berkeley: Parallax Press, 1993).

15. David Barnhill, "Great Earth Sangha: Gary Snyder's View of Nature as Community," in Mary Evelyn Tucker and Duncan Ryuken Williams, *Buddhism and Ecology: The Interconnectedness of Dharma and Deeds* (Cambridge: Harvard University Press, 1997), 192.

16. Gary Snyder, *A Place in Space* (Washington, D.C.: Counterpoint Press, 1995), 250.

SUGGESTED FURTHER READING ON BUDDHISM AND ECOLOGY

Batchelor, Martine and Brown, Kerry, eds., *Buddhism and Ecology* (London: Cassell Publishers, 1992). One of five introductory volumes on the five major world religions and the environment, this set of essays addresses Buddhist teachings and practice and how they apply to ecological issues.

Chapple, Christopher Key, *Nonviolence to Animals, Earth, and Self in Asian Traditions* (Albany: State University of New York Press, 1993). Origins of the practice of nonviolence in early India with applications to contemporary issues such as vegetarianism, animal protection, death by choice.

Gottlieb, Roger, ed., *This Sacred Earth* (New York: Routledge, 1996). The most complete anthology on a wide range of religious traditions and their teachings for the environment.

Kapleau, Philip, *To Cherish All Life: A Buddhist Case for Becoming Vegetarian* (San Francisco: Harper and Row, 1982). A compelling argument for vegetarianism based on Buddhist thought and practice.

Kaza, Stephanie, *The Attentive Heart: Conversations with Trees* (New York: Ballantine, 1993). Meditative nature writing essays from a Zen deep ecological perspective, with a particular interest in meeting individual trees as sentient beings.

Kaza, Stephanie and Kraft, Kenneth, eds., *Dharma Rain: Sources for a Buddhist Environmentalism* (Boston: Shambhala, out in January, 2000). Anthology of classical and modern texts, including advice and reflection from Buddhist environmental activists.

Macy, Joanna, and Brown, Molly Young, *Coming Back to Life: Practices to Reconnect Our Lives, Our World* (Gabriola Island, B.C.: New Society Publishers, 1998). Practical experiential exercises to introduce deep ecology and Buddhist principles into environmental perception and organizing.

Nhat Hanh, Thich, "The Sun My Heart" in *Love in Action* (Berkeley: Parallax Press, 1993). Mindfulness teachings as they relate to interdependence from an ecological and spiritual view. Guidelines for practicing with the Jewel Net of Indra and the ten penetrations.

Seed, John, Joanna Macy, Pat Fleming, and Arne Naess, *Thinking Like a Mountain: Towards a Council of All Beings* (Philadelphia, PA: New Society Publishers, 1988). Practices for weaving together deep ecology with Buddhist reverence for life, including guidelines for leading a Council of All Beings workshop/ceremony.

Sivaraksa, Sulak, *Seeds of Peace* (Berkeley: Parallax Press, 1992). Essays on economic development in Thailand and its relationship to Buddhist principles and Western consumerism.

Snyder, Gary, *The Practice of the Wild* (San Francisco: North Point Press, 1990). Penetrating essays from Buddhist revolutionary bioregionalist poet-philosopher Snyder on the natural world and Zen Buddhist teachings and practice.

Tucker, Mary Evelyn, and Duncan Ryuken Williams, eds., *Buddhism and Ecology: The Interconnectedness of Dharma and Deeds* (Cambridge: Harvard University Press, 1997).

CONTACT INFORMATION

- Buddhist Peace Fellowship
  P.O. Box 4650, Berkeley, CA 94704
  Tel: (510) 655-6169
  Fax: (510) 655-1369
  E-mail: bpf@bpf.org
- International Network of Engaged Buddhists
  (contact through the Buddhist Peace Fellowship)

Chapter 8

THE NET OF VOWS

Robert Aitken, Roshi

The UNESCO *Declaration on the Role of Religion in the Promotion of a Culture of Peace* is a document that stands on the shoulders of human rights declarations that stretch back to the Magna Carta in 1215. There is, however, a shift in this present document from a bold assertion of rights to an emphasis on the responsibility we share in realizing those rights with and for others. This is a shift toward *swaraj*, "self-government," by which Gandhi meant resisting acquisitive powers that would destroy cultures of communal self-reliance, and pursuing the requisites of a sustainable society.[1]

In this paper, I will seek to show how Buddhism and Buddhists contribute to a culture of peace in two ways: First, by enhancing and clarifying the spirit of *swaraj* and offering a common rationale for work toward peace, social justice, and the protection of all beings; and second, by practical organizing in the Buddhist spirit to ameliorate suffering and to challenge covetous and exploitative systems.

BUDDHIST VOWS

The vow lies at the root of the Buddha Way. Very early Buddhist vows were reformulated in a verse by Chih-i, sixth-century founder of the T'ien-t'ai school, and are recited as "Bodhisattva Vows" in

ROBERT AITKEN, ROSHI, is one of the founders of the Buddhist Peace Fellowship and the long-time roshi of the Diamond Sangha in Honolulu, Hawaii. He first began to study Buddhism while a prisoner of the Japanese during World War II. After the war, he continued his studies at the University of Hawaii, where he received a master's degree in Japanese studies. He traveled frequently to Japan during the 1950s and 1960s, and in 1974 was appointed *sensei* (teacher) by Kamakura-based Zen master Yamada Koun Roshi. In 1985, Yamada Roshi gave Aitken transmission as an independent roshi. Robert Aitken is well known for his writing and socially-engaged Zen teaching; his peace and social justice activism; and for his support of Native Hawaiian, same-sex, and women's rights issues in the islands. He has also been a long-time advocate of Buddhist-Christian dialogue.

very similar forms throughout Mahayana Buddhism to this day. One translation reads:

> The many beings are numberless, I vow to save them;
> Greed, hatred, and ignorance rise endlessly, I vow to abandon them;
> Dharma gates are countless, I vow to wake to them;
> Buddha's way is unsurpassed, I vow to embody it fully.[2]

The first line expresses the Bodhisattva imperative to enable others to cross over (to the other shore of liberation) and, while the next lines are apparently vows for personal transformation, they bear altruistic implications as well. Then a century or so after Chih-i, we find a subtle shift in the tenor of vows that were set forth as a kind of manual of Buddhist practice in the *Flower Ornament Sutra (Huayanjing)*. Here is an example:

> When I see flowing water
> I vow with all beings
> to develop a wholesome will
> and wash away the stains of delusion.[3]

Like the Bodhisattva Vows, there is no hint of socioeconomic concern in the vows of the *Flower Ornament Sutra*, but the latter vows express an aspiration to live an ideal life *with* all beings, and thus encourage change, rather than to assume the role of an agent with salvific power. Gandhi, who stressed the importance of living *with*, would approve.[4]

The Vietnamese Buddhist teacher Thich Nhat Hanh encourages the formulation of modern vows. I was inspired at one of his early workshops to put together a book of my own. An example:

> With tropical forests in danger
> I vow with all beings
> to raise hell with the people responsible
> and slash my consumption of trees.[5]

Though they may be formulated to meet contemporary conditions, modern Buddhist vows are still rooted in the central thesis of the *Flower Ornament Sutra:* the containment of all in the one.[6] This dream of inclusion in which "I am large; I contain multitudes," this hologram of all beings as myself, is the hidden reality of our world. "All beings by nature are Buddha," wrote Hakuin Ekaku in his "Song of Zazen," concluding "This very body is the Buddha."[7]

But it is the *Flower Ornament Sutra* that uncovers the inclusive nature of this very body, and sets forth our intimate task of evolving *as* our countless members. This is the perennial foundation of *swaraj*, with its political and economic implications.

With this experience, the revolution the world awaits can be moistened. Even without such an experience, the Bodhisattva who is sustained by the net of her vows can stand fast in the face of benighted authority and network from her niche.

HUMAN RESPONSIBLITITY

But I must not oversimplify. Buddhist teaching places responsibility upon human beings for maintaining harmony and enhancing maturity, but rulers who have professed the Buddha's Way have governed oppressively down through the ages, and Buddhist teachers have neglected their vows and played political games. Governments in South and Southeast Asia to this day can include the five main Buddhist precepts in their respective constitutions, yet violate them outrageously. The late Zen master Haku'un Yasutani is currently under fire for his nationalist pronouncements during World War II. Yet we can turn to that same Yasutani Roshi for cogent criticism of nationalism and group-centered views. In 1967 he wrote:

> Unenlightened people have this karmic illness of considering whatever they attach themselves to to have a self. If they make a group, they consider the group to have a self. If they attach themselves to the nation, they consider the nation to have a self.[8]

With this critique, resting on a clear understanding of the transitory nature of life—that all things, including self and soul are fundamentally without substance—the dangerous fallacy of egocentrism in the individual and group is set forth. Here rises nationalism; here rises corporate arrogance and exploitation; here rises structural and systemic violence, racism, sexism, and caste systems; here rises the ruthless despoliation of oceans, forests, wetlands, and family farms; here rises acute danger to the Earth itself.

Yasutani Roshi's apparent shift in views from subservience to governmental dominion to a social and political application of perennial truths is a small prototype of the extended axial shift that

Buddhism and Buddhists have been undergoing gradually since the rise of the Mahayana 2,000 years ago. In the course of this prolonged history of laicization from the monastery to the world, we find only the rare monk who might be involved, say, in a peasant revolt, for until modern times Buddhist clerics have been either aloof from, or part and parcel of, their political system. Today, however, the old vows must mean what they say. Now or never, *swaraj* must be our watchword.

CAUTIONARY TALES

In his recent essay, "A New Economy for a New Century," Lester R. Brown sets forth the cautionary analogy of Easter Island history as a worst case scenario for the world. In a few short decades during the sixteenth century, the agrarian society on this isolated island fell completely apart. The population expanded, more and more land was cleared for crops, and remaining trees were used as fuel and as rollers to move giant obsidian images into place. There was no wood for houses; people began to live in caves; soil erosion ruined farmland; food became scarce; conflicts arose; and there were even cases of cannibalism.

Professor Brown comments:

> As an isolated territory that could not turn elsewhere for sustenance once its own resources ran out, Easter Island presents a particularly stark picture of what can happen when a human economy expands in the face of limited resources. With the final closing of the remaining frontiers and the creation of a fully interconnected global economy, the human race as a whole has reached the kind of turning point that the Easter Islanders reached in the sixteenth century.[9]

Easter Island couldn't sustain itself following its despoliation, and we see the same fascist spirit of Lebensraum on Turtle Island, the powerful turning upon the weak, with decency the loser for Hund and Maus alike. The dynamics of the system are clearly set forth in corporate brochures and national propaganda: *we* first and foremost. Globally the upshot is the hologram consuming its members. The Blue Planet dies from self-absorption. It is a mad imperative that drives this deliberate acceleration of entropy, an imperative that all human beings share, as the Easter Island model shows. It explodes out of control, however, with the technology that Europeans and Euro-Americans have developed and continue to develop, and now the world is in mortal jeopardy.

Yet this expansionism is only a touch away from the compassionate. The schizophrenic and the bodhisattva have the same world view. *Everything is interconnected.* This interconnection is the Net of Indra, in which everything contains everything else. It is "dependent co-arising," in which everything acts in conjunction with everything else. The bodhisattva embodies and enables this cosmic dynamic. The schizophrenic is equally large, containing all beings, but the dynamic is corrupted, for it is only this particular "I" that includes others, and all the individual others must be made to serve *me.* All the arrows of the sociogram point to *me:* the individual *me,* the family *me,* the corporate *me,* the ethnic *me,* the national *me.* The dynamics spin quickly out of control with ruin so devastating that it must be covered up and even denied.

Arthur Miller writes in connection with the sanctions against Iraq:

> Few of us can easily surrender our belief that society must somehow make sense. The thought that the state has lost its mind and is punishing so many innocent people is intolerable. And the evidence has to be internally denied.[10]

SIGNS OF HOPE

The acquisitive and exploitative system is firmly entrenched, and its vigor cannot be overestimated, yet across the world people are reclaiming the power that is more generally yielded to the institutions of money. An array of cooperative programs in wholesale and retail sales, agriculture, forestry, credit and savings, energy, industry, insurance, housing, and so on, flourish virtually everywhere, together with alternative movements for the advancement of disadvantaged, endangered, and displaced people, animals, and plants. Implicit in such compassionate programs and movements is an appeal to conscience, the sense we have in common, the sense that we are in common, which flares forth in organized confrontation and even disobedience under especially benighted dominion.

Buddhists motivated and empowered by their vows are in place as propagandists, organizers, leaders, and members in some of these programs and movements, and there are many such undertakings that are wholly Buddhist.

In the United States, the Buddhists Gary Snyder and Joanna Macy have for many years been in the forefront of writers and speakers for the protection of the Earth and its waters, forests, and animals. The Dharma Gaia Trust raises money for Buddhist-inspired ecological restorative projects in Asia and the developing world. The Los Alamos Study Group, founded and led by a Buddhist, confronts and publicizes the ongoing American nuclear weapons program. The Karuna Center organizes workshops for reconciliation in war-troubled parts of the world, and does practical social work among refugee women. The Buddhist Peace Fellowship (BPF), with 4,000 members, conducts a variety of socially engaged Buddhism activities in the United States, Australasia, and Asia, including a Buddhist Alliance for Social Engagement (BASE) program for apprentice activists in ecology, social justice, and simple living programs.

The BPF journal, *Turning Wheel,* is an important voice for Dharma activists. The BPF is also active in prison visitation and reform, including opposition to the death penalty, as are the Engaged Zen Foundation, Zen Mountain Monastery, the Prison Dharma Network, and others. Homelessness and hunger are addressed by the Dorothy Day House in Seattle, led by Buddhists. Hospices are run by the Zen Hospice Project and the Maitri Hospice for People Living with AIDS, and Buddhist communities are organized around racial and women's concerns, and issues of the elderly, of gays and lesbians, and of teens at risk. The PeaceMaker Order is made up of people ordained as activists. Such enterprises as the farm of Green Gulch Zen Center serve as models for sustainable gardens while providing healthy food.

Similar programs and movements can be listed for Europe, notably the Leeds Network of Engaged Buddhists and the Italian Engaged Buddhist Network. In Asia, the International Network of Engaged Buddhists, headquartered in Bangkok, concerns itself with consumerism, the protection of forests, and peace and social justice issues, particularly those relating to women. Sarvodaya in Sri Lanka is a long-established village self-reliance movement. The AIDS Project of Thailand, the Karuna Trust of India, the peacemaking Dhammayietra in Cambodia, and such educational programs as the Universal Education School in India, and the Tamang Girls' School in Nepal, are also worthy of mention.

A few of these programs are simply ameliorative; most have a spirit that challenges the conventional; and a few are forthright in their confrontation. Some, like the Green Gulch Farm, are organized in the spirit of the IWW,[11] to create the new within the shell of the old. Cooperatives and private enterprise organized in the spirit of the Buddhist-inspired text *Honest Business* provide various examples of Buddhist peacework.[12] Other examples would be individual Buddhist participation in radical movements which use civil disobedience to oppose nuclear weaponry and war and to fulfill ecological, social justice, and peacemaking ideals.

The International Network of Engaged Buddhists has sponsored conferences and seminars over the past 15 years that have been devoted to cultural and economic evaluation and future studies. Inspired by Buddhadasa Bhikkhu and his successors Sulak Sivaraksa and Santikaro Bhikkhu, the INEB movement is linked with the Buddhist Peace Fellowship and its own social analysis and visualization. David Loy and other Buddhist thinkers identify problems in their essential configurations and enable their readers to name them in their vows and to visualize practical ways to resolve them.

This task of visualization and resolution is both individual and social. How do we, through the lens of our vows, view the dismantling of the public school system? The oppressive role of the market and government in universities? The decline in the quality of life in middle classes and below? The ever-widening gap between rich and poor, the white and the people of color? Discrimination by gender? Above all, how shall we deal with the monstrous juggernaut that bombs in the name of diplomacy, coopts and destroys small farms and home industry and forests and the very ocean in the names of free market economy and national interest? The system stinks to high heaven of greed, hatred, and ignorance, but standing aside and complaining cannot bring any sort of transformation. Engaged Buddhists who pull together with common understanding and dedication can bring fulfillment to the implicit vow of Hakuin Ekaku: "This very place is the Lotus Land."[13] This is not magical thinking, but the Way—step by step—the Tao itself.

NOTES

Nelson Foster, Greg Mello, Alan Senauke, and Diana Winston helped in the preparation of this paper.

1. Galtung, Johan, *The Way Is the Goal: Gandhi Today* (Ahmedabad: Gujarat Vidyapith, 1992) 189; Jack, Homer A., *The Gandhi Reader: A Sourcebook of His Life and Writings* (New York: Grove Press, 1994), 221, 229, 237-238.

2. Aitken, Robert, trans., *Encouraging Words: Zen Buddhist Teachings for Western Students* (San Francisco: Pantheon, 1993), 172. The translation should be considered tentative.

3. Cf. Cleary, Thomas, *The Flower Ornament Scripture*, 3 vols. (Boulder: Shambhala, 1984-87), I: 321.

4. Erickson, Erik H., *Gandhi's Truth: On the Origins of Militant Non-Violence* (New York: Norton, 1969), 251.

5. Aitken, Robert, *The Dragon Who Never Sleeps: Verses for Zen Buddhist Practice* (Berkeley, CA: Parallax, 1992), 61.

6. Cleary, *The Flower Ornament Scripture*. III: 347.

7. Aitken, trans., *Encouraging Words*. 179-180.

8. Yasutani, Haku'un, *Flowers Fall: A Commentary on Zen Master Dogen's Genjokoan*, translated by Paul Jaffe (Boston: Shambhala, 1996), 49.

9. Brown, Lester R., et al., *State of the World 1999: A Worldwatch Institute Report of Progress Toward a Sustainable Society* (New York: Norton, 1999), 11.

10. Quoted from *The Nation*, December 14, 1998, by Carmen Trotta, "Sanctions and Their Victims," in *The Catholic Worker*, Vol. LXVI. No. 2, March-April, 1999.

11. IWW stands for Industrial Workers of the World, the anarchist union that was crushed by the Wilson and Harding administrations, though its spirit continues to inspire the anti-capitalist, non-Communist left.

12. Phillips, Michael, and Rasberry, Salli, *Honest Business: A Superior Strategy for Starting and Managing Your Own Business* (Boston: Shambhala, 1996).

13. Aitken, trans., "Hakuin Zenji's 'Song of Zazen'," in *Encouraging Words*.

SUGGESTED FURTHER READINGS

Buber, Martin, *Paths in Utopia* (Syracuse: Syracuse University Press, 1996).

Callicott, J. Baird, and Ames, Roger T., eds., *Nature in Asian Traditions of Thought: Essays in Environmental Philosophy* (Albany: State University of New York Press, 1989).

Galtung, Johan, *The Way Is the Goal: Gandhi Today* (Ahmedabad: Vinod Revashankar, 1992).

Henderson, Hazel, *Building a Win-Win World: Life beyond Global Economic Warfare* (San Francisco: Berrett-Koehler Publishers, 1996).

Loy, David, *Lack and Transcendence: The Problem of Death and Life in Psychotherapy, Existentialism, and Buddhism* (Atlantic Highlands, N.J.: Humanities Press, 1996).

Macy, Joanna, *World as Lover, World as Self* (Berkeley: Parallax Press, 1993).

CONTACT INFORMATION

The best website for engaged Buddhist practice is the Buddhist Peace Fellowship at: www.bpf.org which will guide you to many other sites. For the farm at Green Gulch Zen Center, begin at the San Francisco Zen Center: www.sfzc.com, and go to "Our Three Center." The website for the Karuna Center for Peacemaking is: www.karunacenter.org. The website for the Maitri Hospice for People Living with AIDS is: www.wenet.net/~maitri/.

Chapter 9

THE ACTIVITIES OF THE KOREAN BUDDHIST CHONTAE ORDER TOWARD WORLD PEACE

Venerable Jeon Chong-yoon

At the dawn of a new century and millennium, science and technology continue to advance by leaps and bounds to make our lives more convenient, prosperous, and comfortable. On the other hand, we are facing serious global problems that human beings have never experienced before. These include: ecological crises; the collapse of moral and spiritual values; and nuclear abuses. These problems are threatening the well-being and survival of all human beings. Therefore, all of us should join together in solving them.

The UNESCO 1994 *Declaration on the Role of Religion in the Promotion of a Culture of Peace* is of great importance. Our Order, the Korean Buddhist Chontae Order, has, in fact, already been engaged in various activities that are in line with the recommendations of the declaration and which are based on our three major practice guidelines: Buddhism for Society, Buddhism in Everyday Life, and Buddhism for Everyone. All of these activities promote peace in the world.

The first two parts of this paper provide an overview of our Order's history and activities in line with the guidelines. The last part attempts to present specifically our activities in education, social welfare, and cultivation of the *Avalokitesvara* meditation, all of which are essential in promoting world peace.

VENERABLE JEON CHONG-YOON (Buddhist name: Un-deok) was born in Uljin, Korea, in 1938. In 1961 he became a Buddhist monk as a disciple of the Most Venerable Sangwol-won-gak, and in 1963 he graduated from Dongguk University with a degree in economics. Recognizing his contributions to society, the Korean government decorated Jeon with the Order of Civil Merit, Sokryu Medal in 1991. Jeon Chong-yoon currently holds several positions: President, the Executive Council of the Korean Buddhist Chontae Order (1980-); Vice President, the Council of Korean Buddhist Orders (1983-); President, Chungbuk Taekwondo Association (1981-); and Vice President, the Council for International Cooperation of the Buddhist Communities in Korea, China, Japan (1994-).

I. A BRIEF HISTORY OF THE KOREAN BUDDHIST CHONTAE ORDER

The Chontae Order was founded in the Sui Dynasty, China, by Master Chih-i (538-597), one of the greatest Chinese Buddhist philosophers. The Chontae Order was established based on the *Lotus Sutra*, the doctrinal classification system known as "The Five Periods and the Eight Teachings," and the religious practice called "the simultaneous contemplation of the threefold truths in one thought."

The doctrine of the Chinese Chontae Order was introduced to the Korean Peninsula during the Paekche Dynasty (B.C.E.18-C.E. 663) by Master Hyon-gwang. The Chontae Order in Korea was founded in 1097 by Master Uich'on during the Koryo Dynasty (918-1392), during which time it prospered greatly.

During the Choson Dynasty (1393-1910) the Chontae Order was severely persecuted. One of the Choson government's policies was to favor Confucianism and to suppress Buddhism. In 1424, the Chontae Order in Korea, along with other Buddhist orders, was dissolved.

In 1966, 542 years after the dissolution, the Chontae Order was reestablished in Korea by the Most Venerable Sangwol-won-gak. This newly founded Order is now called the Korean Buddhist Chontae Order (hereafter, KBCO).

The Most Venerable Sangwol (1911-1974) ranks equally with Master Uich'on as the great founder of the Korean Chontae Order. He was born in the city of Samch'ok, Korea, in 1911. His secular name was Park, Jun-dong. Sangwol is his Buddhist name and Won-gak is his posthumous Buddhist name. He was born a generous, compassionate, and sagacious person. He was praised and trusted by many people.

When he was nine years old, his beloved grandfather passed away. The death of his grandfather came as a great shock to him and led him to seriously contemplate life and death. At the age of 13, he left home in search of the truth which would answer for him questions about living and dying.

In 1945, at the age of 35, the Most Venerable Sangwol moved to the *Lotus* site beneath Sobaek Mountain and built a small cottage.

This was how Kuinsa Temple, the headquarters of today's KBCO, was built.

He made two vows at the cottage: one to attain the Great Enlightenment, and the other to save sentient beings from suffering. He soon began rigorous practices of calmness and insight (*samathavipasyana*) based on the Chontae doctrine. One day at dawn, through his intensive practices, he finally achieved the Great Enlightenment. It is said that the room brightened with mysterious rays of light that lasted for three days. He was 41 years old.

After the Great Enlightenment, the Most Venerable Sangwol made up his mind to fulfill his vow to save sentient beings from suffering. Shortly after he began to teach the ordinary people at Kuinsa Temple, his name spread widely. Many people throughout the country came to see, hear, and follow his teachings.

With his great wisdom and compassion, he did, in fact, save many people from their sufferings. His teaching of the correct Buddhist practice and doctrine led his followers close to enlightenment. Finally, Chontae Buddhism flourished again at the Kuinsa Temple.

Today our Order is recognized as an example of remarkable growth and progress among Korean religious communities. The foundation of our Order's growth and progress was laid by the Most Venerable Sangwol. Our Order was greatly expanded during the tenure of our second Supreme Patriarch, Venerable T'aech'ung (1974-1993). Growth and progress are continuing under the leadership of our third Supreme Patriarch, Venerable Toyong.

Our Order's organization consists of 351 temples, 457 Buddhist monks and nuns, and more than 1.7 million lay followers. We are especially proud to have Kwanmunsa Temple, one of the largest temples in Asia, and Samgwangsa Temple, one of the biggest urban temples in Korea.

We are also proud to be a major contributor to international cooperation among the Buddhist communities in East Asian countries. For example, our Order played a leading role in organizing a regular interchange program among the Chontae orders of Korea, China, and Japan. In addition, we hold the International Academic Conference on Chontae Buddhism every year.

II. THE THREE MAJOR PRACTICE GUIDELINES OF THE KOREAN BUDDHIST CHONTAE ORDER

The Most Venerable Sangwol taught the people to seek beyond their material good fortune. He greatly emphasized Mahayanic bodhisattva practice through Buddhist education. He also asserted the importance of true faith, and cultivated support for this practice. His thoughts led to the idea of the New Buddhist Movement.

The main ideas of the New Buddhist Movement can be summarized as follows: "invigorating the society through the well-established Buddhist teachings" and "practicing the Buddhist teachings in daily life." These are the founding spirits of KBCO.

The first idea is based on the doctrines of "the union of the Three Vehicles in One" and "perfect interfusion of Threefold Truth." The second idea is based on "nonduality of the Buddhist way and secular affairs" and "immutable pureness amid defilement."

The Most Venerable Sangwol was well aware of the problems caused by "Hermit Buddhism." With an emphasis on practicing the founding spirit, he tried to revive the true Buddhist teachings that would embrace everyone without any form of discrimination. The remarkable growth of our Order has been made by the observance of the founding spirit.

All of our religious activities are firmly based on the founding spirit of our Order. There are three major specific guidelines to practice the founding spirit: Buddhism for Society, Buddhism in Everyday Life, and Buddhism for Everyone.

To practice the ideas of Buddhism for the Society, our Order has been seeking to lead followers to perform community service for society and to be generous to others. The Most Venerable Sangwol exhorted his disciples to live up to the ideal of Buddhism for Society, saying, "One who destroys others' happiness for his or her own sake will never be happy. It is our followers' supreme duty to build the society where everyone can lead a happy life. We can do it by reconstructing morality and purifying social evils with wisdom and compassion."

Our Buddhist educational activities have been very helpful in leading followers to practice this guideline. Education has been affecting our followers' way of thinking and living, making them more willing to undertake magnanimous and altruistic actions.

106

Buddhists should practice the Buddhist teachings, while diligently performing their own everyday duties. Doing so, they will fulfill the second guideline: Buddhism in Everyday Life. Most of our monks, nuns, and lay devotees show a good example of practicing the second guideline by working hard during the day and constantly cultivating the *Avalokitesvara* meditation at night.

The farms owned and worked by our Order provide another example of this teaching. Our monks and nuns grow grain, fruit, and vegetables without using chemical fertilizers. The farms provide our Order with almost all of the crops needed to be self-sufficient. Our farming without using chemical fertilizers also helps to protect the environment.

Buddhism for Everyone aims to make harmonious solidarity in all religious activities between the monks, nuns, and lay people. This guideline strongly shows that our Order doesn't aim to be the preexisting "Hermit Buddhism" or "Mountain Buddhism." Instead, we have been establishing our temples in cities, not on mountains.

Buddhism for Everyone establishes the participation of our lay followers in all financial affairs of our temples. Owing to our observance of the third guideline, our Order is well known for our accountability and sincere activities.

III. THE ACTIVITIES OF THE KOREAN BUDDHIST CHONTAE ORDER FOR PROMOTING PEACEFUL CULTURES

Activities in education, social welfare, and cultivation of the *Avalokitesvara* meditation are essential to a harmonious and peaceful society. Our Order has been making every effort to engage in these three activities, described as follows.

Education

We established Kumkang Buddhist College to provide Buddhist education in 1983. Knowledgeable professors teach Buddhist doctrines to our monks, nuns, and lay followers on two campuses without tuition fees. The students are expected to be future leaders who may play an important role in developing peace in our society.

To expand Buddhist education further, a four-year college for lay students is under construction. It will open in 2003. We also have the Chontae Buddhist Research Institute as our Order's research facility to develop various ways to contribute to society effectively on the basis of Chontae Buddhist doctrine.

In addition to the education mentioned above, our lay followers have been also educated at temples. The focus of temple education has been on the two major Buddhist doctrines: the doctrine of *pratityasamutpada* and the doctrine of *karma*.

Through this education, our lay followers understand well why they should live in harmony with other people, cultures, and societies. They are deeply aware that one's virtuous actions towards others and nature lead to a truly happy life.

The core of Buddhist doctrines, *pratityasamutpada*, says that one's existence depends on other beings. According to the doctrine, each of us is not a separate individual. We can survive only when depending on others. Therefore, we should live in harmony with diverse people, cultures, and societies. We should care for the wellbeing of others.

According to the doctrine of *karma*, one will experience the direct results of his or her own actions. In other words, one's good fortune arises from his or her good actions and one's misfortune from his or her bad actions. These actions include physical and verbal behaviors, and even thoughts. Therefore, one's virtuous actions towards others and nature lead to his or her own happy life; harmful actions to others and nature lead to his or her own suffering.

Our Order is certain that these educational activities have affected our followers' ways of thinking and living. The effects of this education have been shown in many areas. For example, the lay followers help each other in more effective ways and voluntarily offer financial aid to needy people through their charity organizations at temples. They are also willing to participate in our social welfare projects and our movements to protect the environment.

Social Welfare and Environmental Protection Activities

Our Order is recognized as one of the leading organizations for social welfare in Korea. We have been making efforts to promote social welfare in many ways, including continuous financial aid to helpless children and elderly people, educational activities for criminals, and programs for rehabilitating handicapped people.

Since the 1990s, our Order has initiated some of our own social welfare systems. For example, we operate nursery schools in our temples where experts and volunteers look after the children of Buddhists and neighboring non-Buddhists at no charge. We also operate libraries in our temples, which provide comfortable and emotionally stable spaces for the younger generation who are vulnerable to social violence. Our schools for Korean and Chinese language are open to anyone,

Environmental protection is also very important for social welfare. As mentioned before, our education of *pratityasamutpada* and *karma* doctrines has changed people's ways of living so that they are environmentally harmonious and nature-friendly.

Our Order has been campaigning for the improvement of the entire nation's environment. For instance, between 1970 and 1975 we raised more than two million trees and planted them on the mountains. This project was so successful that it became a good model of how a religious organization could protect the environment in a practical way.

Each and every temple of our Order is responsible for cleaning up a mountain and a river. The Young Buddhists' Association for Environmental Protection was organized nationwide, and its members are devoting themselves to the related activities.

Cultivation of the *Avalokitesvara* Meditation

The Buddhist teachings for establishing peaceful cultures must be implemented as a continuous practice. For our Order, the strength of practicing the teachings comes from our cultivation of the *Avalokitesvara* meditation. We guide followers to cultivate the meditation constantly and sincerely in everyday life.

Most of our lay followers individually cultivate the *Avalokitesvara* meditation every night. There are also intensive meditation programs in which they participate in groups at temples. At every temple twice a year, month long intensive meditation programs are held. In addition, we frequently have three-day or one-week long meditation programs.

The *Avalokitesvara* meditation is mental absorption by reciting the name of the *Avalokitesvara* bodhisattva. This practice is in accordance with the *Avalokitesvara Bodhisattva* chapter of the *Lotus Sutra.* The chapter says: "If living beings with pain and torment call single-mindedly upon the name of the *Avalokitesvara* bodhisattva, the bodhisattva will soon listen to their voices and make all of them relieved from their sufferings."

Almost everyone's mind is filled with greed. However, Buddhism emphasizes the state of mind that has nothing to do with greed at all. This doesn't mean that we should seek refuge outside of this world where we live. Rather, it means that we should seek self-purity amid this contaminated world. Becoming a pure mind, not tainted by greed, is the purpose of the *Avalokitesvara* meditation.

During *Avalokitesvara* meditation, we chant constantly the name of the *Avalokitesvara* bodhisattva with a unified mind. As long as there is an egoistic element in one's mind, the subject will remain separated from the object. In that state of mind, it is not possible to repeat constantly the name *with a unified mind.* Thus the *Avalokitesvara* meditation can only be perfectly cultivated when one abandons such egoistic elements and oneself completely.

We can enter into the perfect *Avalokitesvara* meditation with rigorous and great efforts. Consequently, our greed, anger, and stupidity will vanish and in turn we will become compassionate, calm, and wise.

By practicing pure *Avalokitesvara* meditation, we believe, you will realize that the *Avalokitesvara* bodhisattva is *you,* and *you* are the *Avalokitesvara* bodhisattva. Your pure mind is the *Avalokitesvara* bodhisattva.

SUGGESTED FURTHER READINGS

Chappell, David W. ed., *T'ien-T'ai Buddhism: An Outline of the Fourfold Teachings* (Tokyo: Daiichi Shobo, 1983).

Hurvitz, Leon. tr., *Scripture of the Lotus Blossom of the Fine Dharma* (New York: Columbia University Press, 1976).

Swanson, Paul, *Foundations of T'ien-T'ai Philosophy: The Flowering of the Two Truths Theory in Chinese Buddhism* (Berkeley: Asian Humanities Press, 1989).

The Journal of the Research Institute for Chontae Buddhist Culture Vol.1 (Seoul: The Research Institute for Chontae Buddhist Culture, The Korean Buddhist Chontae Order, 1998).

CONTACT INFORMATION

- Kuinsa Temple (the headquarters of the Chontae Order)
  Kuinsa Temple, 132-1 Baekja-ri, Youngchoon-myun, Danyang-gun, Choongchung-buk-do 395-830, Korea
  Tel: (444)423-7100
  Fax: (444)420-7399
  E-mail: kuintem@chollian.net
- Kumkang Buddhist College
  Kwanmunsa Temple, 56 Umyon-dong, Socho-gu, Seoul 137-140, Korea
  Tel: (2) 576-6401
  Fax: (2) 574-1541
  E-mail: kuintem@chollian.net

111
.
.
.
.

Chapter 10

SHAMBHALA: "ENLIGHTENED WARRIORSHIP" FOR PEACE

Judith Simmer-Brown

UNESCO has provided a tangible challenge to religious communities to seriously examine how they might assiduously pursue peace, not only as a one-time project or demonstration but as a comprehensive culture which reorients the values of the complex times in which we live. In these responses, Buddhists like myself must address how our individual communities are participating in this important endeavor for the future peace and happiness of the world.

My tradition of Tibetan Buddhism has for centuries spoken with conviction about the "dark age" in which the awakening of beings is increasingly hampered by the promulgation of greed and aggression, making it seemingly impossible to live in peace and happiness. Many Tibetan texts speak of this age as one dominated by family feuds, civil wars, lawsuits, incurable diseases, cataclysmic weapons, and other recurrent calamities. When such phenomena arise, it is incumbent upon spiritual beings to employ whatever means may be necessary to reverse the pattern of excruciating suffering and degradation.

Tibetan Buddhism has always promoted powerful methods of personal transformation focused on transmuting the energy of aggression, attachment, and bewilderment into compassion and wisdom. These methods begin with individual commitment to unmask the egocentric preoccupation which has, from beginningless time, caused such harm to others as well as oneself. When we realize that

JUDITH SIMMER-BROWN is professor and chair of Religious Studies at Naropa University in Boulder, Colorado. She has practiced Vajrayana Buddhism since the early 1970s, and is a member of the board of directors of Shambhala International, a network of Buddhist meditation centers in North America, Europe, and Asia. She is also on the board of the Society of Buddhist-Christian Studies. Her forthcoming book is entitled *Dakini's Warm Breath: Feminine Principle in Tibetan Buddhism* (Shambhala Publications).

all beings, like ourselves, have the simple yearning to be happy and to avoid suffering, it is difficult to ignore the cries of the world. In the tradition of the *bodhisattva*, meditation upon exchanging oneself with others has served as the core of personal and societal transformation. In Tibet, this meditation employs certain loving-kindness contemplations which serve as reminders that we can individually place the needs of others before our own needs, sparking the "turning of the tide" of egocentric concerns. This is an essential beginning to the nurture of a culture of peace.

However, in contemporary society the factors which contribute to a degradation of dignity of human life are systemic, environmental, and complex, rendering merely individual efforts insufficient to the task. For this reason, the Tibetan Buddhist teacher Ven. Chogyam Trungpa Rinpoche (1939-1987) brought the transmissions of another important Tibetan tradition to his communities in the United States, Canada, and Europe. This is the tradition of Shambhala, a secular lineage of teachings traced back to pre-Buddhist Tibet. Ironically, this lineage is associated with the favorite warrior-hero of Tibet, Gesar, who vanquished enemies and paved the way to a utopian society, known popularly in the West as "Shangri-la."

Through centuries of interaction with Buddhism, this tradition became an esoteric transmission regarding the cultivation of "enlightened society," universal in scope, compassionate in intention, and peaceful in methods. These teachings were transmitted, like Vajrayana Buddhism, in two ways: through spontaneous discovery by rare and qualified teachers as *terma* ("hidden treasures") and through transmission from guru to disciple. Chogyam Trungpa, Rinpoche, received these transmissions in both manners and through his "hidden treasure" discoveries applied the ancient vision of enlightened society to the contemporary complexities of militarism, consumerism, and environmental degradation.

While Trungpa Rinpoche presented completely traditional Tibetan Buddhist teachings and practices to his Western students, he had a particular passion and urgency about the transmission of the Shambhala vision and practices he had received. Having fled a medieval and isolated Tibetan society overrun by militant Communist China, he was deeply affected by the forces of materialism

114

which drive contemporary international values, and he devoted his final decade of teaching to ways to ameliorate the violence and greed he observed. Central to his Shambhala teachings was the importance of "enlightened warriorship" based on gentleness and courage.

Shambhala warriors battle only their own fear—the cause of violence and of the loss of heart which has so plagued the world. When we quietly plumb the depths of our fear, we discover profound humanity, a kind of openhearted tenderness and authenticity which is known in the Shambhala as "basic goodness." This is experienced by every human as a "genuine heart of sadness and joy" in which all struggle, aggression, and alienation actually stops and real care for others arises. According to Shambhala, this experience already lies at the heart of every religion, people, and culture. Only when the various practices, institutions, and cultural supports to this experience are cultivated can authentic enlightened society dawn.

In Shambhala communities, enlightened warriorship is cultivated on three fronts simultaneously. First, it takes place in individual practice of meditation and the gentle warrior's arts of Asia: calligraphy, *ikebana* (flower arranging), martial arts such as *kyudo* (Zen archery), *haiku* or spontaneous poetry, and *bugaku/gagaku* (Japanese court dance and music). These highly formal disciplines are ways for the warrior to express the "genuine heart of sadness and joy," the experience of open heart and inherent dignity shared by all human beings. When one executes a brush stroke of black ink on white paper, one can see one's own core confidence and care in a very literal way. However, these same insights may dawn in the practices of many religious traditions, whether it be contemplative prayer in Christianity, the five-time *salat* prayer of Islam, Hindu yogic practice, the Jewish *shabbat*, or the Native American sundance. The experience of basic goodness is obviously not the property of any particular religious tradition.

The Shambhala teachings have also focused on the practice of daily life in whatever form it may take. Rinpoche suggested that his students create Shambhala households in which the dignity of each person could be expressed in sane and artistic surroundings and routines, balancing the demands of family, children, livelihood, and practice. No matter how embattled or pressured daily life may be, domestic details can manifest contemplative qualities of simplicity

115

and gentleness. Rinpoche also encouraged respect and veneration for the power of place. Every environment has inherent self-existing power which has been honored in many different traditions. Wherever we find ourselves, these unique energies of the physical world influence our lives. If we are able to harmonize and magnetize those energies into our homes and lifestyles, natural dignity will arise for ourselves and our neighbors and communities. Shambhala warriors are encouraged to create living situations which invoke the sacredness of the everyday in this way.

At the same time, Shambhala must be realized in participation in forms of the larger society, for individual efforts are never sufficient to fully actualize the gentleness and courage of enlightened warriorship. It is essential to identify the humanizing tendencies of whatever society in which one lives, and to fully participate in encouraging and enhancing them for the benefit of all members, no matter what religious practice, ethnic or racial origin, gender, or economic level they may represent. Shambhala has a vested interest in promoting religious and cultural pluralism, racial and ethnic diversity, and peace. As I read it, the UNESCO declaration is an excellent statement of many of the principles of Shambhala texts.

Within these mandates, the international Shambhala communities have pioneered the development of a variety of cultural forms to address community issues. In the first generation of Buddhism in the West, which has focused so heavily on individual practice, these forms are unusual in their scope and strength. Of course, Shambhala has created structures for religious practice and education, but it is also developing contemplative approaches to child-raising, elder care, hospice, psychological counseling, and community building.

One particular area of focus has been the creation of schools which inculcate a sense of enlightened warriorship, employing a variety of world wisdom traditions in a kind of secular spirituality. Shambhala has developed a preschool; elementary, middle, and high schools in Colorado and Nova Scotia; and Naropa University in Colorado. The curricula of these schools are not religious or dogmatic. Instead, they promote age-appropriate skills necessary for creating enlightened society. For example, on the early childhood level, children at Alaya Preschool are taught the customary subjects like fundamentals of word and sound, motor skills, artistic creation, and imaginative play. But what sets the Alaya curriculum apart from other preschools is the emphasis on social and communication skills and conflict resolution. Public school teachers note that Alaya graduates who enter area kindergartens are extraordinarily gifted in interactive and problem-solving skills. These youngsters are placed in classrooms to seed these skills for others.

In the Buddhist- and Shambhala-inspired college, Naropa University, the curriculum encourages the development of five qualities so crucial for the development of enlightened society: awareness of the present moment, communication, critical intellect, resourcefulness, and effective action. Studies in the humanities, social sciences, and arts are designed to integrate intellect and intuition and to prepare the student for service in tangible ways. The curriculum is designed to more intimately acquaint the student with her or his personal journey and to extend that journey to the benefit of others. Graduates are trained in psychotherapy and body therapies, gerontology, early childhood education, hospital chaplaincy, environmental activism, religious studies, and in the arts, whether literary, fine, or performing.

The leading edge of Naropa University's discourse currently lies in the areas of religious pluralism and racial and ethnic diversity. The convert Buddhist communities in North America experience *de facto* segregation—most Western Buddhists are white, and people of color are present in large numbers only among the Nichiren Buddhist members of the Soka Gakkai International. In addition, convert generations are notoriously exclusivist religiously, and North American Buddhism is no exception. The impetus to discuss these issues generally comes not from concern about political correctness. The simple matter of setting quotas, writing policies, and recruiting diverse student, faculty, and staff populations could be done by a few administrators with generous budgets. Within the University, discussions which began between a few over coffee or in private conversation have now generalized to a University-wide personal and group contemplation of "difference." The Diversity Awareness Working Group (DAWG) has set the tone for nonideological, personal communication on these issues, which is rapidly affecting the entire campus.

JUDITH SIMMER-BROWN

These discussions are taking place in an environment which has
turned its attention more generally to issues of social engagement
spurred by contemplative practice. North American religion has
generally been characterized by a polarization between social activism on the one hand and contemplative spirituality on the other. In
the current generation of Western Buddhism, however, contemplative practice and social engagement are co-emerging as mutual supports. Profound meditation leads naturally to genuine engagement,
and vice versa. In the Shambhala communities, and especially at
Naropa University, these two intimately interact with each other.

This is especially found in the Engaged Buddhism master's degree program, which couples contemplative practice with training
in social engagement, a combination designed to tame fanaticism
in the activist even while it arouses engagement in the potentially
complacent contemplative. Engaged Buddhism chaplain interns are
working with the sick and dying in hospital settings, with the homeless, with the mentally ill, with men and women in prison, and
with troubled youth. Yet, in most of Naropa's graduate programs,
students are trained in contemplative engagement with the suffering heart of the world, and Naropa's alumni are working in a variety of engaged settings in a variety of professions.

In the large Shambhala community settings, the central issues
are a bit different. Most compelling are the questions of how organizations and institutions may function in a way which appropri-
ately engages the members and yet which can also allow the institution to act decisively. The Shambhala view suggests that a pure grassroots democratic model is limited in effectiveness while an exces-
sively hierarchical model divorced from its constituency may become despotic. Effective communities (and enlightened societies,
for that matter) must combine these models in order to manifest
awakening. Rinpoche spoke of "natural hierarchy," based upon the
enlightened leadership of awakened mind. But if the leadership of
a society becomes divorced from the dignity and sanity of its constituency, disaster can ensue; if leaders and community members
lose touch with basic goodness and the genuine heart of sadness
and joy, they can forget to place the needs of others before their own.

Within these considerations, Shambhala is exploring ways in which
a community may grow and develop while preserving respect for

its heritage. This is especially difficult in a large international community initially founded by a charismatic teacher. After Trungpa Rinpoche died in 1987, a period of chaos followed which threatened the survival of the community. This caused an extended period of retrenchment, conservatism, and contraction. Eventually, however, the question of succession and leadership was settled with the empowerment of Ven. Sakyong Mipham Rinpoche, the eldest son of Trungpa Rinpoche. Mipham Rinpoche has refused to assume ongoing management of the community and has empowered a diverse group of leaders to teach, govern, and manage community activities. In the meantime, he has taken a keen personal interest in grassroots organization, cultivation of youth and children, engagement outside the Tibetan Buddhist world, and education. The Shambhala community has recently paid special attention to the support of its international practice and retreat centers, its international Buddhist and Shambhala training programs, and its many affiliated groups and organizations. Plans for the future are now broader in scope and more universal in vision.

During the period of retrenchment, many individuals from the Shambhala community branched out to engage in a variety of secular vocations in areas of social services, education, and business ventures. In fact, Shambhala members have pioneered several nationally recognized innovative programs in the areas of elder care, environmental initiatives, and socially conscious business ventures. For example, the leadership of New York's Greystone Foundation, founded by Tetsugen Glassman, Roshi, has come from senior members of Shambhala, as has the Prison Dharma Network and National Prison Hospice Association.

The structures of the reconfigured Shambhala are still young, but the community appears to be moving out of a merely exclusivist phase focused primarily on itself and its own survival. The challenge which lies ahead is whether Shambhala as a community can actualize the original vision of enlightened society so cherished by its Tibetan forefather and his lineage of teachers. In particular, can Shambhala dare to take leadership in nurturing a culture of peace in the way many of its individual members so inspiringly already have?

119

SUGGESTED FURTHER READINGS

Bernbaum, Edwin, *The Way to Shambhala: A Search for the Mythical Kingdom beyond the Himalayas* (Garden City, N.Y.: Anchor Books, 1980).

Hayward, Jeremy and Karen, *Sacred World: The Shambhala Way to Gentleness, Bravery, and Power* (Boston: Shambhala Publications, 1998).

Chogyam Trungpa [Rinpoche], *Shambhala, The Sacred Path of the Warrior* (Boston: Shambhala Publications, 1988).

CONTACT INFORMATION

- Naropa University
  2130 Arapahoe Avenue
  Boulder, Colorado 80302
  Telephone: (303) 444-0202

- Shambhala International
  1084 Tower Road
  Halifax, Nova Scotia Canada B3H-2Y5
  Telephone: (902) 425-4275

Chapter 11

MY WAY OF PILGRIMAGE TO PEACE

Venerable Kosan Sunim

INTRODUCTION

In the closing year of the twentieth century and in the face of mounting threats to the sustainability of human well-being and the Earth's environment, we are seeing a new rallying of religious communities to recover and update the teaching and practice of peace. In this context, the United Nations has declared the year 2000 the International Year for the Culture of Peace. Here I understand the word "peace" in a broad sense and use it to include the pursuit of nonviolence, socioeconomic justice, human rights, and ecological balance. To live in peace should be understood as pertaining to both personal fulfillment and social well being, the subjective quality of life, and objective living conditions. This broadened notion of peace suggests that a diversity of sectors within a society and a diversity of relationships between societies are important to deal with the complexity of peacebuilding in the world. Although governmental leaders as well as nongovernmental institutions and leaders have played important roles in peacebuilding, they cannot attain lasting peace without participation and support from the people of the world.

Religion is a core element in culture. Obviously, religious and spiritual leadership is one of the most influential factors in managing peace activities. Accordingly, there have been many meetings of religious leaders to discuss peace around the world. One example is

VENERABLE KOSAN SUNIM was born ManGun Oh at Ulju-gun, South Korea, in 1933. He left home for Pomosa Temple and became a disciple of the Venerable Tongsan in 1945. He was given the name Kosan when he became a novice monk in 1948 and was fully ordained in 1956. In 1961 he was transmitted Lectureship from the Venerable Kobong and in 1972 was transmitted Preceptorial Mastership from the Venerable Sokam. Kosan assumed Abbotship of Ssanggye-sa Temple in 1975. He was elected Chief of Court of Chogye Order in 1994 and became President of Chogye Order and President of the Korean Conference on Religion and Peace in 1999.

a significant meeting, organized by UNESCO in Barcelona in 1994, "The Contribution by Religions to the Culture of Peace." As a result of the meeting, the *Declaration on the Role of Religion in the Promotion of a Culture of Peace* was issued. Although the declaration was made five years ago, the world situation is no better now than at that time. In a sense it is worse. The content of the declaration still appeals to me because it pays attention to religion's commitment and responsibility. It is worthwhile to review the declaration to check our progress and to more effectively plan for the future.

PERSONAL REMARKS ON UNESCO'S DECLARATION

First, I can say that I am in full sympathy with the concerns of the participants at the Barcelona meeting that the "situation of the world, such as increasing armed conflicts and violence, poverty, social injustice, and structures of oppression" has been getting worse. In addition, I recognize that religion is important in human life, especially in regions of conflict around the world such as the Middle East, Northern Ireland, and Kosovo. The situation is also serious for people in Korea.

Regarding the section entitled "Our World," I am in full accord. In part, this is because I am confirmed in the reality of dependent origination, a basic teaching of Buddha, that "we are all interdependent and share an inescapable responsibility for the well-being of the entire world."

The statement entitled "We face a crisis" recognizes the pervasiveness of suffering. We should awaken and bring it to an end. With respect to the diversity statement, "Unless we recognize pluralism and respect diversity, no peace is possible. We strive for the harmony which is at the very core of peace," Korea seems to be an exemplary country of religious diversity and harmony. History, in fact, shows that the spirits of harmony and reconciliation have been the most important characteristics of the Korean Buddhist tradition.

Regarding the sixth statement, "Religious people have too often betrayed the high ideals they themselves have preached. We feel obliged to call for sincere acts of repentance and mutual forgiveness, both personally, and collectively, to one another," I myself have repented of the violent occurrence at a temple in Seoul last year. (The incident occurred between two groups of political monks with different interpretations of denominational laws who competed for an administrative post in their order. Although I was in a mountain retreat at the time and had no connection to the monks, I was shamed and deeply saddened by the worldwide news reports of the incident. These monks did not follow the Buddhist path of nonviolence and our tradition of reconciliation, but rather upset other Buddhists and people around the world.) Events in the world should be seen as they are, no matter how good or bad. However, I also believe that "peace is possible."

Regarding the section on peace which states that peace "implies that love, compassion, human dignity, and justice are fully preserved," this meaning of peace does not contradict Buddhist understanding, but is in congruence. I myself have experienced that "peace is a journey," as is life. Therefore, I have worked for peace as though taking a pilgrimage, which is "a never-ending process." Relating to the section on commitment, through my meditative practices, I also made a vow to "be at peace with" myself and to lead other people to the same goal. When I work for temples and the Order, I commit myself "to support and strengthen" my community "as the nursery of peace." During my period of teaching and educational service, I have emphasized "education for peace, freedom, and human rights, and religious education to promote openness and tolerance, environmental and social justice."

With respect to the section on religious responsibility, I have personally recognized this responsibility and tried to do my best "to encourage conduct imbued with wisdom, compassion, sharing, charity, solidarity, and love." I have also been promoting "dialogue and harmony between and within religions…sincere fellowship on our earthly pilgrimage." As for the final section, "Appeal," I have prayed to Buddha and the gods for peace. In short, I have fully adopted the message of the declaration in my private life and in my work.

Responding further to the declaration, I would like to share my thoughts and my experiences working for peace in Korea with colleagues around the world. I will first describe my Buddhist studies and practices as guidelines for peacebuilding, my peace activities, and finally my vision of peace for the world.

MY RELIGIOUS STUDIES AND PRACTICE RELATING TO PEACE

I was born in 1933 to a peaceful Buddhist-Confucian family in a farming village in Ulju County in the southeast part of Korea. It was a hard time because the Japanese occupied the Korean peninsula, and most people in the countryside suffered from starvation and maltreatment under the colonial rule. My parents had five sons and two daughters. I was the fourth son and grew up with good care in a loving family. My father was a Buddhist as well as a Confucian scholar. Therefore, in my childhood, I was educated not only in the normal curriculum at a public elementary school but also in the traditional Confucian classics under my father, who was always concerned for others. When I was 13 years old and studying in a junior high school, my mother suddenly passed away. I was deeply shocked and could not accept the fact of her death, but continued to mourn. I lost peace of mind. All I wanted was to recover peace of mind by meeting my mother, and I asked my father where I could see her again. My father told me that I could see her at a Buddhist temple. Therefore, I went to Pomo-sa temple in Pusan where I met the Venerable Tongsan, a famous *Son* (Ch'an/Zen) Master in Korea. When I asked the Venerable how I could meet my mother, he said that I could see her through a hundred days of prayer to Avalokiteshvara Bodhisattva with intensive contemplation. I decided to stay at the temple and started to practice the prayer and contemplation. At the end of the prayer period, I saw my mother in meditation and recovered peace of mind. I realized the certain reality of life and understood some teachings of Buddha. I was fortunate to have such a thoughtful father and to meet the Venerable Tongsan and be accepted by him as his disciple. After three years' training, I became a monk and was fully ordained in 1956.

From the time I received the precepts of a novice monk until now, I have practiced traditional Buddhist meditation. In 1961, I graduated from Chigji-sa Kangwon, a Buddhist seminary at Chigji Monastery. In the same year, I was transmitted a lectureship from the Venerable Kobong, a well-known lecturer of scriptural studies as well as a *Son* Master. In 1972, I was also transmitted Vinaya mastership from the Venerable Sokam, an eminent preceptor. In

1974, I graduated from the Graduate School of Administration at Dongguk University in Seoul. During my period of study, I obtained Buddhist knowledge and wisdom about peace from both scriptures and masters. Some major texts of my scriptural studies were *Avatamsaka Sutra, Saddharma-pundarika Sutra, Perfect Enlightenment Sutra, Vajracchedika-prajnaparamita Sutra, Brahmajala Sutra, The Awakening of Faith,* and *Record of Sayings* of Ch'an Master Kaofeng and Ta-hui. Regarding my own research on textual studies, during my time teaching at various seminaries I compiled a Buddhist dictionary and wrote several commentaries for scriptural students, such as *Lecture on the Heart Sutra, Lecture on the Awakening of Faith,* and *Lecture on the Lotus Sutra.* For meditation practitioners, I wrote *Son, the Way of Enlightenment.* I can say now that my life of study and practice was a way to seek the reality of life and peace of mind for others and for myself through Buddhist wisdom and meditation.

MY ACTIVITIES PROMOTING PEACE IN OUR SOCIETY

Because I experienced Japanese colonial rule and the Korean War, 1950-53, I made a vow to work hard for peace in the world. Regarding my peace activities, they can be classified in five different fields: (1) precepts, (2) Dharma preaching, (3) *Son* meditation, (4) education, and (5) interreligious cooperation. Regarding precepts, I give Buddhist precepts as ethical and moral guidelines of how to live for oneself and one's community for both the clergy and lay Buddhists. There are various precepts based on the situation of the Buddhist community in Korea. There are five precepts for lay Buddhists; ten precepts for both male and female novices of the Order; 250 precepts and 348 precepts for fully ordained monks and nuns respectively; and bodhisattva precepts, ten major and 48 minor ones, for all monks, nuns, and lay people. During the 30 years I have taught precepts and exercised my Vinaya mastership, I have held about 300 ceremonies at which I have given precepts to about 100,000 people including monks, nuns and lay Buddhists. For instance, at the annual precept ceremony of Nunginsonwon in Seoul this year, I gave boddhisattva precepts to about 4,000 lay people, and I have held a similar ceremony there for a decade. I have never hesitated to go to hold the ceremony, no matter the place, time, or number of people. I have been invited to hold the ceremony by many temples around Korea, scores of times in a year. On every occasion of the precept ceremony, I have always taught people that the principal spirit of the precepts is to manage a healthy and peaceful life for the individual as well as for the community. I have emphasized the fundamental precepts: to abstain from (1) harming living beings, (2) taking what is not given, (3) sexual misconduct, and (4) false speech. These would be the basic guidelines for a way of living in peace for everyone, with deeds of loving-kindness, generosity, contentment, and truthful communication.

As a Dharma lecturer, I have taught people Dharma not only for Buddhist wisdom but also for peace in the world. On every occasion I have always advised and encouraged people to live the Bodhisattva's life, which is good for both oneself and others. I have also pointed out the ultimate goals of Mahayana Buddhists: that one should attain Enlightenment and build a Pure Land in this world both for the individual and for a society of peace and justice. As a professional and academic lecturer, I have taught the traditional Buddhist scriptures to monks and nuns at seminaries through commenting on and interpreting the Buddhist messages as they apply to the present situation and to Buddhist leadership toward the Dharmic society, an ideal world. As an ordinary Dharma preacher, I used to present the social teachings of Buddha, such as interdependence, compassion, harmony, and right way of life. I believe that an appropriate Dharma mission is one of the most effective ways to bring peace to both the personal and social spheres.

Regarding *Son* meditation, I have confidence that this is the best way to attain a peaceful mind in general and Enlightenment in particular. When I exercised the *Son* mastership for about ten years at Ssanggye-sa monastery, I taught practitioners that through practicing concentration and contemplation in meditation they could purify and calm their minds, and then they would obtain wisdom and compassion from that state of mind. Because one's action and speech are derived from one's mind, one should control one's mind in order to act and speak for peace and righteousness in the world. Whenever I have occasion to talk to people about practices, I always emphasize meditation practice to make the fundamental change in personality, for transforming the mind is the root of the

126

tree. I think that to make peace for an individual and the world, we should make peace in our minds first.

To promote peace in the world, education seems one of the most important ways. Based on my experience, to influence the personality through education, the earlier we start, the better it is. Therefore, in 1983 I established a kindergarten, named Lumbini, at Sokwang-sa temple, a temple I founded in Puchon City near Seoul. It has usually accommodated about 350 children and teaches them to develop peaceful and compassionate personalities. Since I was elected a trustee of the Dongguk University in 1995, I have emphasized its direction to develop a person not only as an intellectual but also as a leader of harmony and peace in society. The curriculum of Dongguk includes meditation practice as a required class for all students. The educational complex has about 20,000 graduate and undergraduate students and includes a senior high school, a junior high school, and an elementary school, which has several thousand boys and girls. In 1996, I founded a scholarship to support needy students and asked them to return their fruits to society.

Because I think that interreligious cooperation is essential for peace in society, I took the presidency of the Korean Conference on Religion and Peace (KCRP) in 1999. KCRP consists of six major religions in Korea, including Christianity, Confucianism, and an indigenous religion. As an adviser I also support the United Religions Initiative of Korea, which was established in 1999. Since the Vatican has invited me to an assembly of religious leaders from around the world in October 1999, to further cooperation between different religions, I will join them and then visit the World Council of Churches in Geneva to talk about world peace.

MY VISION OF PEACE IN THE WORLD

In the new century, interreligious cooperation for world peace will be seriously needed. I envision that cooperation among religions for peace will increase locally and globally. As president of the Korean Buddhist Chogye Order, of the Association of Korean Buddhist Orders, and of the KCRP, I will work for peace not only among Buddhist communities but also among various other religions. Moreover, as an advisor and an executive member of some governmental and nongovernmental organizations—for example, the 2002

127

World Cup Organization and the Sanctuary of Arts—I will use all my positions to work for peace and betterment in the world. I believe that if all religious people are united and do their best to work for peace, our dream of peace will be realized on Earth.

SUGGESTED FURTHER READINGS

The Korean Buddhist Research Institute, ed., *The History and Culture of Buddhism in Korea* (Seoul: Dongguk University Press, 1993).

The Korean Buddhist Research Institute, ed., *Buddhist Thought in Korea* (Seoul: Dongguk University Press, 1994).

CONTACT INFORMATION

* Korean Buddhist Chogye Order
  45 Kyonji-dong, Chongno-gu
  Seoul 110-170 KOREA
  Tel: 82-2-2264-8260; Fax: 82-2-2264-8261
  Contact person: Venerable Jinwol
  E-mail: jinwol@cakra.dongguk.ac.kr

  Current projects of the Korean Buddhist Chogye Order include: *Chabi ui Sahoihwa Undong* (A Movement for Socialization of Compassion) and *72 Hours Peace Project.*

Chapter 12

THE SGI'S PEACE MOVEMENT

Daisaku Ikeda

It was just a quarter of a century ago, in 1974, that I paid my first visit to China. A little girl asked me. "Why have you come here?" I told her: "I came here to meet you."

Some three months later, during my first visit to the Soviet Union, Premier Alexei N. Kosygin asked me what my basic ideology is. I replied: "We are committed to the values of peace and culture—the underlying basis of which is humanism."

BUILDING A CULTURE OF PEACE

I have, in all, visited 54 countries. I have come to realize that, regardless of differences in outlook or ideology, so long as people share the common aim of working for the happiness and lasting peace of all humanity we can invariably reach an understanding of one another as human beings and open the door to solidarity based on friendship and trust.

At the time when I proposed the normalization of Japan's diplomatic relations with China in September of 1968, the Cultural Revolution was raging and Sino-Soviet conflict was escalating. Within Japan, meanwhile, there was growing fear of a "Chinese menace." All in all, it was not an atmosphere in which one could easily start talking about friendship with China. Even so, I made my call for friendship with China in the spirit of remorse for the historical fact that, even though Japan owes much of its culture to

DAISAKU IKEDA was born in 1928 in Tokyo, Japan, and joined the Soka Gakkai ("Society for the Creation of Value") at age 19. As a disciple of second Soka Gakkai president Josei Toda, Ikeda worked for more than a decade to develop the organization's peace, culture, and education movement. After Toda's death in 1958, Ikeda succeeded him as Soka Gakkai president, and in 1975 he became founding president of Soka Gakkai International. He is a prolific author and is the recipient of numerous awards, including the United Nations Peace Award and the International Tolerance Award of the Simon Wiesenthal Center. His annual peace proposals, issued each year on the anniversary of the founding of SGI, review the state of the world and suggest practical initiatives grounded in Buddhist philosophy.

China, the Japanese militarists had invaded the Chinese mainland causing the Chinese people untold suffering. I was also moved by the conviction that it is impossible to build peace in Asia while ignoring the 700 million citizens of China.

Just as I had expected, I became the subject of intense criticism. People asked why a religious leader was "flirting with the communists." I became the subject of personal threats.

Three months after that visit to China, I went to the Soviet Union to confirm the Russian leadership's intentions toward China, and another three months later I returned to China to explain what I had learned. Once again, I was ridiculed for going to communist countries.

Despite criticism, my stance as a Buddhist is always to see things from the standpoint of respecting and trusting in other human beings. I believe that mutual understanding is always possible when we conduct dialogue from the common ground of our shared humanity. This has been the spirit behind my citizen's diplomacy, and it was this same spirit that motivated my visit to Cuba in June of 1996.

The practice of Buddhism is based on compassion. The word compassion in Japanese is written with two Chinese characters, *ji* and *hi*. *Ji* corresponds to *metta* in Pali and *maitri* in Sanskrit, and conveys the meaning of "true friendship," while *hi* represents *karuna* in both languages, and conveys the meaning of "empathy" or "shared feeling."

Thus, in Buddhism, compassion signifies the sublime endeavor to share the suffering of another from the stance of our common humanity and to create an expanding network of genuine friendship and trust.

I perceive in Shakyamuni's compassion—elaborated and extolled in the Mahayana tradition as the Bodhisattva Way—a profound and unshakable humanism. The SGI is a body committed to developing activities in the areas of peace, culture, and education based on this Buddhist humanism.

HUMAN REVOLUTION

The bedrock of the Buddhist spirit of humanism is reverence for all life, which discerns an incomparably precious "Buddha nature" inherent not only in humankind but in all living beings.

In the *Lotus Sutra*, the Buddhist scripture most widely known, respected, and influential among the peoples of Asia, Shakyamuni elucidates "the one great reason" a Buddha appears in this world. In the Expedient Means (*Hoben*) chapter, he explains that his mission as a Buddha is to open the door of Buddha-wisdom to all beings and fulfill his pledge to raise all beings to his own enlightened life-state. Nichiren, who appeared in Japan in the thirteenth century and established an accessible, populist Buddhism, was seeking to realize this same commitment to enable all people to open for themselves the door of Buddha-wisdom.

Following the teachings of Nichiren, the members of the SGI recite the mantra *Nam-myoho-renge-kyo* derived from the title (*daimoku*) of the *Lotus Sutra* to the Gohonzon (or mandala) inscribed by Nichiren. Through this practice SGI members strive to reveal their own Buddha nature and create a life-state of supreme happiness that will endure throughout eternity. We refer to this process as "human revolution."

Although the actual modes of SGI activities vary in each country according to cultural and other conditions, the description of activities that follows may be considered typical. The prime opportunity for SGI members to encourage and learn from each other is the discussion meeting, a regular (usually monthly) gathering of members, their friends, and neighbors. This is not a one-sided affair where the ordained sermonize to the laity, nor is it an anonymous mass meeting: it is an intimate occasion where each participant can take center stage. The basic function of the discussion meeting is to enable the participants to stimulate each other toward further growth and transformation.

Ever since the Soka Gakkai was founded in 1930, the discussion meeting has been the central activity. Discussion meetings are held by local groups which determine the content of their meeting. And while there may be presentations about the principles of Buddhism or upcoming activities, the meetings always revolve around the experiences in faith of the members. More formal, in-depth study of Buddhist principles is supported by separate meetings. But the essence of the discussion meeting is revealed in the name originally given to the gathering at the time of the founding president of the Soka Gakkai, Tsunesaburo Makiguchi: *Discussion meeting offering experimental proof of the validity of the life of major good.*

The first key feature of the discussion meeting is that, with its basis in the members' experiences, it provides a link between the inner-motivated and the shared. A member relating his or her experience of faith is not describing knowledge imparted by others, but an actualized experience that comes from within, the outcome of an inner-motivated effort of self-transformation. Through a succession of experience testimonials, the members are able to both praise and encourage each other's efforts, developing a shared sense of confidence and empowerment. Through this experience, both speaker and listener can deepen their conviction of faith.

The second key feature of the discussion meeting is its egalitarian spirit. At a discussion meeting, concepts such as social standing, position, or personal advantage are irrelevant: the discussion meeting is an embodiment of cooperation between individual human beings on an equal basis. In that sense, it is a wellspring of democracy, an oasis for the heart where participants recharge their life force and quench their spiritual thirsts.

The powerful Buddha nature that emerges from the combination of chanting daimoku and the mutual inspiration achieved by attending the discussion meeting enables each individual to generate value in the forms of beauty, benefit, and goodness. Indeed, the word "soka" in Soka Gakkai means "the creation of value."

The Profound Meaning of the Lotus Sutra (*Hokke Gengi*) states: "No affairs of life or work are in any way different from the ultimate reality."[1] Each aspect of an individual's life—the challenges of work, family, study, health, finances, relationships, etc.—provides a venue for the creation of value by manifesting one's Buddha nature and the chance to experience actual proof of practice in the form of material and spiritual improvement and growth. Experiences of actual proof provide the content of the members' testimonials at discussion meetings. The discussion meeting, founded on dialogue and equality, is thus an excellent opportunity to build a culture of peace.

RESPONSIBILITY, COMPASSION, AND WISDOM

In *Abolishing War*, Elise Boulding defines peace culture in the following terms: "A mosaic of identities, attitudes, values, beliefs, and patterns that lead people to live nurturantly with one another and the Earth itself without the aid of structured power differentials—to deal creatively with their differences and share their resources."[2]

The Parable of the Medicinal Herbs (*Yakusoyu*) chapter of the *Lotus Sutra* contains a poetic depiction of a culture of peace. The parable describes a variety of plants watered by a cloud that envelops the Earth: "Though all these plants and trees grow in the same earth and are moistened by the same rain, each has its differences and particulars."[3] In terms of Buddhism, this image depicts how all people can benefit from the impartial Buddhist law and, like the three kinds of medicinal herbs and two kinds of trees, can attain a state of enlightenment that is expressive of their unique character and individuality. This image resonates with the view of peace culture defined by Elise Boulding.

Here the blessings of the sun and the rain depict equality under the heavens, while the earth that sustains the plants depicts equality on Earth. In Buddhism, this represents the true path of culture whereby we respect each other's differences and celebrate our diversity while equally sharing the life-sustaining gifts of Earth and the firmament.

The SGI aims to apply a philosophy of humanism, rooted in respect for the sanctity of life, in the fields of peace, culture, and education. In this way, we seek to foster a robust and universal culture of peace. These three fields correspond to the Buddhist concept of the "three virtues," those qualities inherent in humankind identified by Nichiren as most worthy of respect: a sense of responsibility, compassion, and wisdom.

The first of these three virtues, a sense of responsibility, refers to the responsibility to protect the right to life shared by humankind and all living things. It is a tenacious determination to work for the creation of peace. Nichiren spoke of his own determination to "block off the road that leads to the hell of incessant suffering."[4]

In 1957, my mentor Josei Toda, the second president of the Soka Gakkai, issued a declaration for the abolition of nuclear weapons and entrusted the younger members with the task of implementing this desire. "Nuclear weapons," he stated, "are an enemy of humankind; their use, an act that would deny humanity its fundamental right to live, must be judged an absolute evil."[5]

This declaration was made at the height of the Cold War and was a cry for peace founded in the Buddhist spirit of reverence for life. It sparked a wave of reaction throughout society. My mentor's peace proposal is the wellspring for the SGI's peace activities, which have developed into a series of movements to actualize peace among humankind and to protect the environment (thus realizing peaceful coexistence with the natural environment). I have also aimed to bring my mentor's principles to bear in the academic field by founding the Toda Institute for Global Peace and Policy Research.

The SGI has consistently supported the United Nations as the "Parliament of Humankind," and has cooperated with the UN Department of Public Information in organizing the "Nuclear Weapons—Threat to Our World" exhibition, which seeks to publicize the dangers of nuclear weapons and has been shown in 18 cities in 15 countries around the world.

We have jointly organized with the UN Department of Disarmament Affairs the "War and Peace" exhibition, which also covers environmental problems and has likewise been shown around the world. The Soka Gakkai in Japan has organized "The Environment Exhibition—Ecoaid." Our efforts to support human rights education include the exhibition "Toward the Century of Humanity: An Overview of Human Rights in Today's World" and, in conjunction with the Simon Wiesenthal Center, "The Courage to Remember—Anne Frank and the Holocaust" exhibition.

In addition, SGI conducts fundraising drives for refugees and has a medical project in Nepal where Soka Gakkai medical volunteers work in a refugee camp. SGI in Brazil, meanwhile, is collaborating with environmental NGOs in research on reforestation of the Amazon rain forest and also promotes projects to prevent deforestation and desertification.

I myself have been making peace proposals to mark SGI Day (January 26) since 1978, aiming to promote the ideal of the United Nations and call for reform of UN systems to expand the role of NGOs. A consistent theme of these proposals, written from a Buddhist standpoint, is the call for the abolition of war.

Turning to the second virtue, compassion, this is the inspiration for the fostering of culture. By cultivating the inner feelings of human beings, we can nurture such positive qualities as empathy, trust,

134

and friendship, bringing the uniquely fragrant blossoms of each culture to bloom. It is vital to the human future that we learn to respect each other's differences and peculiarities, feel empathy for, and learn from each other. I am confident that this will open the way for a new global culture for all humanity.

To provide opportunities for the peoples of the world to learn from each other's cultures, I have created such institutions as the Min-On Concert Association, the Fuji Art Museum, the Tokyo Fuji Art Museum, and the Victor Hugo House of Literature. The SGI also sponsors cultural exchange delegations to countries around the world to enable people to learn from each other's cultures. We hold cultural festivals in various countries, creating opportunities for the cultural expressions of different peoples to share the same stage.

In addition, I have also founded the Boston Research Center for the 21st Century and the Institute of Oriental Philosophy to promote intercivilizational dialogue and exchange and to conduct research into the world's religions, ideologies, and philosophies.

The third field is education and corresponds to the third virtue, wisdom. President Makiguchi wrote that the purpose of education is people's happiness. He advocated "value-creating education" that would allow all people to develop the infinite wisdom inherent within them.

In an effort to introduce Mr. Makiguchi's theory of value-creating pedagogy as widely as possible throughout the world, I have established a series of Soka schools: Soka junior and senior high schools, Soka University and Soka University of America, as well as Soka kindergartens in Hong Kong, Singapore, and Malaysia. Mr. Makiguchi's theories are now attracting attention in a large number of countries, noticeably Brazil, India, and the United States, and are gradually bearing fruit. The Soka Gakkai Education Division has organized counseling sessions where experienced educators make themselves available to students and parents on a volunteer basis, as well as meetings where teachers can share and learn from each other's experiences. In cooperation with the United Nations, meanwhile, the SGI has organized the "World Children and UNICEF" exhibition and the "World Boys and Girls Art" exhibition, which have toured the world.

The activities in the fields of peace, culture, and education summarized above are examples of SGI's efforts to give concrete form to the virtues of responsibility, compassion and wisdom, which constitute the actual content of a humanism rooted in reverence for life.

HUMANITARIAN COMPETITION

Early in the twentieth century (1903), President Makiguchi published *The Geography of Human Life* (*Jinsei Chirigaku*) which strongly advocated a shift to humanitarian competition at a time when imperialism and colonialism were still the prevailing modes of international relations. He analyzed competition among nations as consisting of the phases of: military competition, political competition, economic competition, and humanitarian competition. He stressed that humanity's aim should be humanitarian competition. In short, he said humanity needed to replace confrontational competition in the military, political, and economic spheres with the cooperative competition of humanism.

Cooperative competition, he wrote, was a process through which, working for the sake of others, one could benefit oneself even as others benefit. Cooperation between oneself and others, based on mutual respect, is the path of compassion.

I have regularly called for us to vie with one another in the fostering of world citizens as one form of humanitarian competition. By world citizens, I am referring to people who, while rooted in their own cultural tradition, dedicate the fruit of that culture to the cause of a lasting peace for humankind. In Buddhist terms, such people are referred to as *bodhisattvas*. My dream is to see all the world's religious and cultural traditions produce a continuous stream of such world citizens who will compete with one another to contribute to world peace.

The bodhisattva, as a world citizen, is someone who is constantly challenging egotism and is engaged in the race to transform what Buddhism refers to as deluded impulses (represented by the three poisons of greed, anger, and stupidity) into enlightenment. Bodhisattvas, refusing to be engulfed in the consumerism and materialism of contemporary society, embrace a noble spirit of serving others, and pledge to make this their mission in life. This process

136

sets in motion a fundamental change in life orientation—from egotism to the desire to create happiness for oneself and others.

I believe that every religion should be promoting, according to its own methods, this kind of fundamental change in life from our contemporary materialism to a highly spiritual and humanistic culture. I would like to suggest that the SGI's discussion meetings, in providing an opportunity for mutual enlightenment, serve as one example of this.

Finally, I strongly hope that the world's religions will use dialogue and exchange to resolve the multitude of problems that threaten the survival of humanity, and stress harmony and cooperation with the aim of creating a culture of peace. Of course each culture and religious tradition has its own characteristics and practices. This makes it natural that each tradition should respect the differences of others, but it is also essential to search for our common ground as human beings, to search for universality. It is vital that we together clarify core human ethics, elements of which would include love for humanity, reverence for all life, nonviolence, and compassion, as well as mutually beneficial modes of coexistence with nonhuman nature.

It is my greatest hope that each religion can base its actions on our common humanity and stress, above all, creative cooperation in our quest to resolve the grave problems facing our world. In this way, with mutual respect and learning from each other, we can work for the survival of the human race.

NOTES

1. Quoted in "The Gift of Rice," *Letters of Nichiren*, ed. Philip P. Yampolsy, trans. Burton Watson (New York: Columbia University Press, 1996), 516. See translator's explanatory note on page 517.

2. Elise Boulding and Randall Forsberg, *Abolishing War: Dialogue with Peace Scholars Elise Boulding and Randall Forsberg* (Boston: Boston Research Center for the 21st Century, 1998), 36.

3. *The Lotus Sutra*, trans. Burton Watson (New York: Columbia University Press, 1993), 98.

4. Nichirin Daishonin, *The Major Writings of Nichirin Daishonin*, vol. 4, translated and edited by the Gosho Translation Committee (Tokyo: NSIC, 1986), 272.

5. For a literary narrative, see Daisaku Ikeda, "Declaration 16 & 17," *The Human Revolution XII*, serialized in the *Monthly SGI Newsletter* 126 (June 1993), 62-65.

SUGGESTED FURTHER READINGS

Causton, Richard, *The Buddha in Daily Life* (London: Rider Books, 1995).

Ikeda, Daisaku, *A New Humanism: The University Addresses of Daisaku Ikeda* (New York: Weatherhill, Inc., 1996).

_____, *Toward a Culture of Peace: A Cosmic View* (1999 Peace Proposal - available from the SGI office in Tokyo).

Metraux, Daniel A., "The Soka Gakkai: Buddhism and the Creation of a Harmonious and Peaceful Society," in Christopher S. Queen and Sallie B. King, eds., *Engaged Buddhism: Buddhist Liberation Movements in Asia* (Albany: SUNY Press, 1996).

The *SGI Quarterly* - can be obtained from the SGI Office of Public Information (see below).

Toynbee, Arnold, and Daisaku Ikeda, *Choose Life: A Dialogue* (Oxford: Oxford University Press, 1976).

CONTACT INFORMATION

• Soka Gakkai International
Office of Public Information
15-3 Samoncho, Shinjuku-ku
Tokyo 160-0017, Japan
Tel: 81 + 3-5360-9830
Fax: 81 + 3-5360-9885
Website: www.sgi.org

Buddhist Leaders and Peacework Activities

Dhammachari Lokamitra

TBMSG hostel study class. *Courtesy: Dhammachari Lokamitra*

Acharn Sulak Sivaraksa.
Photo by Don Farber

Tzu Chi members deliver warm food during a 1998 flood in Xi-zhi, Taipei. *Courtesy: Tzu Chi Foundation*

Venerable Shih Cheng-yen

Venerable Karma Lekshe Tsomo (left) with Dr. Shih Heng-ching.

(I-r) Ch. Tsedendamba, Deputy Khambo Lama of Tashichoeling Monastery; Jebtsun Damba Khutuktu, Head of Mongolian Buddhism; Venerable Lama Bataa Mishigish.

141

President A.T. Ariyaratne leading a peace meditation on August 9, 1999.

Professor Stephanie Kaza.
Photo by Jonathan Wilson

Robert Aitken, Roshi, at his retirement as teacher of
the Honolulu Diamond Sangha, Palolo Zen Center,
December, 1996. *Photo by Tom Haar*

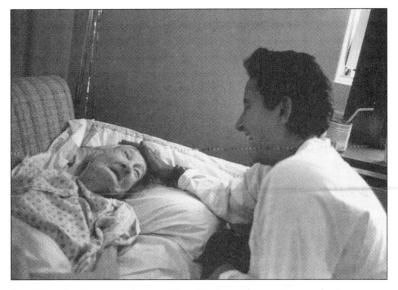

Zen Hospice Project volunteer Pam Weiss with a patient at the Laguna Honda Hospital Hospice Unit. Photo by A. Raja Hornstein

President Jeon Chong-yoon

Work is an important aspect of monastic training in the Korean Buddhist Chontae Order.

143
.
.
.
.
.

Tai Chi at Naropa University. *Courtesy: Naropa University*

Venerable
Kosan Sunim

Professor Judith Simmer-Brown. *Courtesy: Laurita Fotografía*

144
.
.
.
.
.

Venerable Kosan Sunim (left) and monks distributing campaign materials.

Soka Gakkai International
President Daisaku Ikeda.
Courtesy: SGI

Soka Gakkai International youth members in Hiroshima collect signatures in support of the Abolition 2000 campaign. *Courtesy: SGI*

Venerable Somdech Maha Ghosananda.
Photo by Don Farber

Venerable Thich Nhat Hanh (center) on a walking meditation. *Photo by*
Don Farber

Venerable Bhante Henepola
Gunaratana

Venerable Chan Master Shih Sheng-
yen. *Courtesy: Ch'an Meditation
Center*

José Ignacio Cabezón

His Holiness Tenzin Gyatso, the XIVth
Dalai Lama. *Photo by Don Farber*

Part III

INNER PEACE, OUTER KINDNESS

Chapter 13

THE HUMAN FAMILY[1]

Venerable Somdech Preah Maha Ghosananda

WE ARE OUR TEMPLE

Many Buddhists are suffering in Tibet, Cambodia, Laos, Burma, Vietnam, and elsewhere. The most important thing we Buddhists can do is to foster the liberation of the human spirit in every nation of the human family. We must use our religious heritage as a living resource.

What can Buddhism do to heal the wounds of the world? What did the Buddha teach that we can use to hear and elevate the human condition? One of the Buddha's most courageous acts was to walk onto a battlefield to stop a conflict. He did not sit in his temple waiting for the opponents to approach him. He walked right onto battlefield to stop the conflict. In the West, we call this "conflict resolution."

How do we resolve a conflict, a battle, a power struggle? What does reconciliation really mean? Gandhi said that the essence of nonviolent action is that it seeks to put an end to antagonism, not the antagonists. This is important. The opponent has our respect. We implicitly trust his or her human nature and understand that ill will is caused by ignorance. By appealing to the best in each other, both of us achieve the satisfaction of peace. We both become peace-makers. Gandhi called this a "bilateral victory."

We Buddhists must find the courage to leave our temples and enter the temples of human experience, temples that are filled with

VENERABLE SOMDECH PREAH MAHA GHOSANANDA was born in 1924 in Southcentral Cambodia, ordained into the Cambodian Buddhist Sangha in 1943, and received his doctoral degree from Nalanda University in 1969. Among his initiatives, he has worked to establish Buddhist temples in the refugee camps on the Thai-Cambodian border. Maha Ghosananda established the first Cambodian Buddhist temple in the United States and has led nine Dhammayietras, or Walks for Peace and Reconciliation, in Cambodia. He is a founder of the Peace Council at Windsor Castle and has worked unceasingly to ban landmines. He has been nominated for the Nobel Peace Prize annually since 1994.

suffering. If we listen to the Buddha, Christ, or Gandhi, we can do nothing else. The refugee camps, the prisons, the ghettos, and the battlefields will then become our temples. We have so much work to do.

This will be a slow transformation; many people throughout Asia have been trained to rely on the traditional monkhood. Many Cambodians tell me, "Venerable, monks belong in the temple." It is difficult for them to adjust to this new role, but we monks must answer the increasingly loud cries of suffering. We only need to remember that our temple is with us always. We *are* our temple.

WHO IS THE ENEMY?

In 1981, the United Nations held a conference to discuss the future of Cambodia. During that time, we held a Buddhist ceremony for peace. At the end of the ceremony, a Khmer Rouge leader came up to me, very cautiously, and asked if I would come to Thailand to build a temple at the border. I said that I would.

"Oh," thought many people, "he is talking to the enemy. He is helping the enemy! How can he do that?" I reminded them that love embraces all beings, whether they are noble-minded or low-minded, good or evil.

Both the noble and the good are embraced because loving kindness flows to them spontaneously. The unwholesome-minded must be included because they are the ones who need loving kindness the most. In many of them, the seed of goodness may have died because warmth was lacking for its growth. It perished from coldness in a world without compassion.

Gandhi said that he was always ready to compromise. He said, "Behind my noncooperation there is always the keenest desire to cooperate, on the slightest pretext, even with the worst of opponents. To me, a very imperfect mortal is ever in need of God's grace, ever in need of the Dharma. No one is beyond redemption."

I do not question that loving one's oppressors—Cambodians loving the Khmer Rouge—may be the most difficult attitude to achieve. But it is a law of the universe that retaliation, hatred, and revenge only continue the cycle and never stop it. Reconciliation does not mean that we surrender rights and conditions, but rather that we use love in all of our negotiations. It means that we see ourselves in the opponent—for what is the opponent but a being

152

in ignorance, and we ourselves are also ignorant of many things. Therefore, only loving kindness and right mindfulness can free us.

Gandhi said, "The more you develop ahimsa in your being, the more infectious it becomes, until it overwhelms your surroundings and, by and by, it might oversweep this world!" We are each individually responsible for our own salvation and our own happiness. Through our service, we find a road to salvation. This service is nothing but our love for all beings and the uplifting of ignorance into light.

PEACE IS GROWING SLOWLY

There is no self. There are only causes and conditions. Therefore, to struggle with others and ourselves is useless. The wise ones know that the root causes and conditions of all conflicts are in the mind.

Victory creates hatred. Defeat creates suffering. The wise ones wish for neither victory nor defeat. We can oppose selfishness with the weapon of generosity. We can oppose ignorance with the weapon of wisdom. We can oppose hatred with the weapon of loving kindness.

The Buddha said, "When we are wronged, we must set aside all resentment and say, 'My mind will not be disturbed. Not one angry word will escape from my lips. I will remain kind and friendly, with loving thoughts and no secret malice'." Peace begins in the mind. Yes, we show loving kindness, even for the oppressor.

After a great darkness, we see the dawning of peace in Cambodia. We are grateful for the Buddha's compassion and light, his realization of peace, unity, and wisdom. We pray that this unity, the heart of reconciliation, the middle path, will be present at every meeting and dialogue of Cambodia's leaders.

We seek to learn and teach the skills of peace. When we live the Dharma, we develop inner peace and the outer skills needed to make peace a reality. With peacemakers of all faiths, we can accept no victory except peace itself. We have no need for personal honor, title, or glory. Loving-kindness is alive in every heart. Listen carefully. Peace is growing in Cambodia, slowly, step by step.

During his lifetime, the Buddha lobbied for peace and human rights. We can learn much from a lobbyist like him. Human rights

153

begin when each man becomes a brother and each woman becomes a sister, when we honestly care for each other. Then Cambodians will help Jews, and Jews will help Africans, and Africans will help others. We will all become servants for each other's rights. It is so even in my tiny country. Until Cambodians are concerned with Vietnam's right to exist and be free, and with Thailand's rights, and even with China's rights, we will be denied our own rights.

When we accept that we are part of a great human family—that every man and every woman has the nature of Buddha, Allah, and Christ—then we will sit, talk, make peace, and bring humankind to its fullest flowering. I pray that all of us will realize peace in this lifetime, and save all being from suffering!

Peacemaking is at the heart of life. We peacemakers must meet as often as possible to make peace in ourselves, our countries, and the whole world. And real peace will not favor East, West, North, or South. A peaceful Cambodia will be friendly to all. Peace is nonviolent, and so we Cambodians will remain nonviolent toward all as we rebuild our country. Peace is based on justice and freedom, and so a peaceful Cambodia will be just and free.

Our journey for peace begins today and every day. Making peace is our life. We must invite people from around the world to join in our journey. As we make peace for our country and ourselves we make peace for the whole world.

NOTE

1. Reprinted from *Step by Step: Meditations on Wisdom and Compassion* (1992) by Maha Ghosananda with permission of Parallax Press, Berkeley, California.

SUGGESTED FURTHER READING

Maha Ghosananda, *Step by Step: Meditations on Wisdom and Compassion* (Berkeley: Parallax Press, 1992).

CONTACT INFORMATION

• Dhammayietra Center for Peace & Nonviolence
P.O. Box 144
Phnom Penh
Cambodia
Tel: 885-23-36-4205
E-mail: dmy@forum.org.Kh

Chapter 14

AHIMSA: THE PATH OF HARMLESSNESS[1]

Venerable Thich Nhat Hahn

The Sanskrit word *ahimsa*, usually translated "nonviolence," literally means "nonharming" or "harmlessness." To practice ahimsa, first of all we have to practice it within ourselves. In each of us, there is a certain amount of violence and a certain amount of nonviolence. Depending on our state of being, our response to things will be more or less nonviolent. Even if we take pride in being vegetarian, for example, we have to acknowledge that the water in which we boil our vegetables contains many tiny microorganisms. We cannot be completely nonviolent, but by being vegetarian, we are going in the direction of nonviolence. If we want to head north, we can use the North Star to guide us, but it is impossible to arrive at the North Star. Our effort is only to proceed in that direction.

Anyone can practice some nonviolence, even soldiers. Some army generals, for example, conduct their operations in ways that avoid killing innocent people; this is a kind of nonviolence. To help soldiers move in the nonviolent direction, we have to be in touch with them. If we divide reality into two camps—the violent and the nonviolent—and stand in one camp while attacking the other, the world will never have peace. We will always blame and condemn those we feel are responsible for wars and social injustice, without recognizing the degree of violence in ourselves. We must work on ourselves and also work with those we condemn if we want to have a real impact.

VENERABLE THICH NHAT HANH, poet, Zen master, and chairman of the Vietnamese Buddhist Peace Delegation during the war, was born in Vietnam in 1926 and became a monk at the age of 16. In Saigon in the early 1960s, Thich Nhat Hanh helped to found the "engaged Buddhist" movement, establishing the School of Youth Social Service, a Buddhist university, a publishing house, and a peace activist magazine. He was exiled from Vietnam in 1966, and in 1982 he founded Plum Village, a Buddhist community in exile in France. He currently resides at Plum Village where he continues his prolific writing and works to alleviate the suffering of refugees, boat people, political prisoners, and hungry families in Vietnam and throughout the Third World.

It never helps to draw a line and dismiss some people as enemies, even those who act violently. We have to approach them with love in our hearts and do our best to help them move in a direction of nonviolence. If we work for peace out of anger, we will never succeed. Peace is not an end. It can never come about through non-peaceful means.

When we protest against a war, we may assume that we are a peaceful person, a representative of peace, but this might not be the case. If we look deeply, we will observe that the roots of war are in the unmindful ways we have been living. We have not sown enough seeds of peace and understanding in ourselves and others, therefore we are co-responsible: "Because I have been like this, they are like that." A more holistic approach is the way of "interbeing": "This is like this, because that is like that." This is the way of understanding and love. With this insight, we can see clearly and help our government see clearly. Then we can go to a demonstration and say, "This war is unjust, destructive, and not worthy of our great nation." This is far more effective than angrily condemning others. Anger always accelerates the damage.

We know how to write strong letters of protest, but we must also learn to write love letters to our president and representatives, demonstrating the kind of understanding and using the kind of language they will appreciate. If we don't, our letters may end up in the trash and help no one. To love is to understand. We cannot express love to someone unless we understand him or her. If we do not understand our president or congressperson, we cannot write him or her a love letter.

People are happy to read a good letter in which we share our insights and our understanding. When they receive that kind of letter, they feel understood and they will pay attention to your recommendations. You may think that the way to change the world is to elect a new president, but a government is only a reflection of society, which is a reflection of our own consciousness. To create fundamental change, we, the members of society, have to transform ourselves. If we want real peace, we have to demonstrate our love and understanding so that those responsible for making decisions can learn from us.

All of us, even pacifists, have pain inside. We feel angry and frustrated, and we need to find someone willing to listen to us who is capable of understanding our suffering. In Buddhist iconography, there is a bodhisattva named Avalokitesvara who has 1,000 arms and 1,000 hands, and has an eye in the palm of each hand. One thousand hands represent action, and the eye in each hand represents understanding. When you understand a situation or a person, any action you do will help and will not cause more suffering. When you have an eye in your hand, you will know how to practice true nonviolence.

Imagine if each of our words also had an eye in it. It is easy to depict a hand with an eye, but how might an artist also put an eye into our words? Before we say something, we have to understand what we are saying and the person to whom our words are directed. With the eye of understanding, we will not say things to make the other person suffer. Blaming and arguing are forms of violence. When we speak, if we suffer greatly, our words may be bitter, and that will not help anyone. We have to learn to calm ourselves and become a flower before we speak. This is "the art of loving speech."

Listening is also a deep practice. The bodhisattva Avalokitesvara has a deep talent for listening. In Chinese, his name means "listening to the cries of the world." We have to listen in a way that we understand the suffering of others. We have to empty ourselves and leave space so we can listen well. If we breathe in and out to refresh and empty ourselves, we will be able to sit still and listen to the person who is suffering. When she is suffering, she needs someone to listen attentively without judging or reacting. If she cannot find someone in her family, she may go to a psychotherapist. Just by listening deeply, we already alleviate a great deal of her pain. This is an important practice of peace. We have to listen to our families and in our communities. We have to listen to everyone, especially those we consider our enemies. When we show our capacity of listening and understanding, the other person will also listen to us, and we will have a chance to tell him of our pain. This is the beginning of healing.

Thinking is at the base of everything. It is important for us to put an eye of awareness into each of our thoughts. Without a correct understanding of a situation or a person, our thoughts can be misleading and create confusion, despair, anger, or hatred. Our most important task is to develop correct insight. If we see deeply into the nature of interbeing, that all things "inter-are," we will stop blaming, arguing, and killing, and we will become friends with everyone.

These are the three domains of action—body, speech, and mind. In addition, there is nonaction, which is often more important than action. Without our doing anything, things can sometimes go more smoothly just because of our peaceful presence. In a small boat when a storm comes, if one person remains solid and calm, others will not panic, and the boat is more likely to stay afloat. In many circumstances, nonaction is fundamental to our well-being. If we can learn to live the way a tree does—staying fresh and solid, peaceful and calm—even if we do not do many things, others will benefit from our nonaction, our presence. We can also practice nonaction in the domain of speech. Words can create understanding and mutual acceptance, or they can cause others to suffer. Sometimes it is best not to say anything. This is a book on nonviolent social action, but we must also discuss nonviolent nonaction. If we really want to help the world, the practice of non-action is essential.

Of course, sometimes nonaction can be harmful. When someone needs our help and we refuse, she may die. If a monk, for example, sees a woman drowning and does not want to touch her because of his precepts, he will violate the most fundamental principle of life. When we see social injustice, if we practice nonaction, we may cause harm. When people need us to say or do something, if we don't, we can kill by our inaction or our silence.

To practice ahimsa, we must first learn ways to deal peacefully with ourselves. If we create true harmony within ourselves, we will know how to deal with family, friends and associates. Techniques are always secondary. Most important is to become ahimsa, so that when a situation presents itself, we will not create suffering. To practice ahimsa, we need gentleness, loving kindness, compassion, joy, and equanimity directed to our bodies, our feelings, and other people.

Real peace must be based on insight and understanding, and for this we must practice deep reflection—looking deeply into each act and each thought of our daily lives.

With mindfulness—the practice of peace—we can begin by working to transform the wars in ourselves. There are techniques for doing this. Conscious breathing is one. Every time we feel upset, we can stop what we are doing, refrain from saying anything, and breathe in and out several times. Aware of each in-breath and each out-breath. If we are still upset, we can go for walking meditation, mindful of each slow step and each breath we take. By cultivating peace within, we bring about peace in society. It depends on us. To practice peace in ourselves is to minimize the numbers of wars between this and that feeling, or this and that perception, and we can then have a real peace with others as well, including the members of our own family.

I am often asked, "What if you are practicing love and patience and someone breaks into your house and tries to kidnap your daughter or shoot your husband? What should you do? Should you shoot that person or act in a nonviolent way?" The answer depends on your state of being. If you are prepared, you may react calmly and intelligently, in the most nonviolent way possible. But to be ready to react with intelligence and nonviolence, you have to train yourself in advance. It may take ten years, or longer. If you wait until the time of crisis to ask the question, it will be too late. A this-or-that kind of answer would be superficial. At that crucial moment, even if you know that nonviolence is better than violence, if your understanding is only intellectual and not in your whole being, you will not act nonviolently. The fear and anger in you will prevent you from acting in the most nonviolent way.

To prevent war, to prevent the next crisis, we must begin right now. When a war or a crisis has begun, it is already too late. If we and our children practice ahimsa in our daily lives, if we learn how to plant seeds of peace and reconciliation in our own hearts and minds, we will begin to establish real peace and, in that way, we may be able to prevent the next war. If another war does come, we will know that we have done our best. Is ten years enough time to prepare ourselves and our nation to avoid another war? How much time does it take to breathe consciously, to smile, and to be fully present in each moment? Our real enemy is forgetfulness. If we nourish mindfulness every day and water the seeds of peace in ourselves and those around us, we have a good chance to prevent the next war and to defuse the next crisis.

IF YOU WANT PEACE, PEACE IS WITH YOU IMMEDIATELY[2]

Twenty years ago, I wrote four Chinese characters on a paper lampshade: "If you want peace, peace is with you immediately." A few years later, in Singapore, I had the chance to practice these words.

It was 1976, and several of us were conducting an operation to rescue boat people, in the Gulf of Siam. The project was called, "When blood is shed, we all suffer." At that time, not many people knew about the presence of the boat people, and the governments of Thailand, Malaysia, and Singapore would not allow them to land on their shores. The practice was to push the boat people back out to sea so they would die, and those on land would not have to deal with them.

We hired two large ships—the *Leapdal* and the *Roland*—to pick up refugees on the open sea, and two small ships—the *Saigon 200* and the *Blackmark*—to communicate between the larger ships and to transport water, food, medicine, and supplies. Our plan was to fill the two large ships with refugees and take them to Australia and Guam, where, on arrival, we would inform the press so that the world would take notice of their plight, and they would not be sent back. In Malaysia, Indonesia, and other countries, thousands of boat people had been sent back and many of them died in the sea. We had to do our work in secret, since the governments of the world did not want to acknowledge the plight of the boat people, and we knew we would be deported from Singapore if we were discovered.

We managed to rescue nearly 800 boat people from the Gulf of Siam. On New Year's Eve, I rode out to sea in the small *Saigon 200* to talk with refugees on the larger ships. Using a wireless telephone, I wished them a Happy New Year. After we said goodbye, I headed back to shore, and, in the darkness, a huge wave welled up and drenched me. I had the impression that the power of darkness was warning me, "It is the fate of these people to die. Why are you interfering?"

Sometimes we asked fishermen to pick these boat people up during the night, and then we took them by taxi to the French embassy. In the morning, they were discovered by the French ambassador, who was very kind. He called the police, knowing that because of his awareness of the presence of these people, they would get "illegal refugee" status. Even though they were put in prison, it was far better than being sent back to sea. Then we worked to help these people get accepted to go to France. We were trying to do many things to reverse the situation.

From time to time, we saw things you cannot believe. We met with a group of 60 people in a barracks. They had just destroyed their own boat so that Malaysian police would not send them back out to sea, but the police were trying to repair their boat in order to do just that. When we saw these people, the men were just staring into empty space and the women and children could not stop crying. One of them told us that they came in two boats. The Malaysian police had given them some water and told them to go to Singapore, where they would be welcomed, but this was not true—the Singaporeans always towed boats back out into the ocean no matter how dangerous it was for the boat people.

When the two boats tried to sail away from Malaysia, one capsized. The 60 people on this boat had witnessed the deaths of everyone on the other boat, right in front of their eyes, and there was nothing they could do to help. So they decided to return to the shores of Malaysia, and this time they destroyed and sank their own boat the moment they arrived. They did not want to be pushed out to sea again. We immediately went to the nearest town and called Reuters, AFP, and other media people to come and take photographs. Because of this, the police did not send them back out to sea, but instead brought them to prison and later to a refugee camp.

The suffering we touched doing this kind of work was so deep that if we did not have a reservoir of spiritual strength, we would not have been able to continue. During those days, we practiced sitting and walking meditation, and eating our meals in silence in a

161

very concentrated way. We knew that without this kind of discipline, we would fail in our work. The lives of many people depended on our mindfulness.

After we had rescued nearly 800 people from small boats at sea, the government of Singapore discovered us. We were close to succeeding in sending the *Roland* and the *Leapdal* to Australia, but because of a leak to the press, several reporters tracked us down and published a story about our project. The press is sometimes frivolous; they just want to write a story, even if human lives are at stake.

Because we had been exposed, the Singapore authorities gave the order for the police to surround our flat at two o'clock in the morning. Two policemen were at the front door, two at the back, and two came in to get me. They took my travel documents and ordered me to leave the country within 24 hours. I knew that two large boatloads of people were waiting for me to help bring them to shore. The police said, "We will return your travel documents at the airport tomorrow." Those policemen were not like human beings. They were unable to understand the suffering of the boat people or how we were trying to help them.

What could we do in such a situation? We had to breathe deeply and consciously. Otherwise we might panic, or fight with the police, or do something to express our anger at their lack of humanity. Knowing that in 24 hours we had to leave 800 people on two boats without food and water, what could we do? We could not go back to sleep.

At that time of the night, no one would answer phone calls. Even the French Embassy was not open. So all of us practiced walking meditation inside our small flat for the rest of the night. If you practice conscious breathing before some difficulty arises, you will be prepared.

We had to find a way for 800 people to travel safely to Australia or Guam. The *Saigon 200* and the *Blackmark* were not allowed to leave port to take food and water to the refugees on the *Leapdal* and the *Roland*. The *Roland* had enough fuel to reach Australia, but we needed to get food to them. Then its engine broke down. The day was very windy and the sea quite rough and we worried about their safety, even just drifting offshore. But the Malaysian government would not allow the ship to enter Malaysian waters. I tried to get permission to enter a neighboring country in order to continue the rescue operation, but the governments of Thailand, Malaysia, and Indonesia would not grant me an entry visa. Even though I was on land, I too was drifting on the sea, and my life was one with the 800 refugees on the ships. There were more problems than seemed possible to solve in just 24 hours.

I decided to practice the mediation topic, "If you want peace, peace is with you immediately," and I was surprised to find myself quite calm, not afraid or worried about anything. I was not just being careless. This was truly a peaceful state of mind, and in that state, I was able to overcome this difficult situation. The idea came to me to ask the French embassy to intervene on my behalf so that my visa would be extended for a few more days, enough time to tie up all of these loose ends. And at five minutes before noon, just as the Immigration Department was about to close for the weekend and I would have to leave the country, the extension was granted. As long as I live, I will never forget those seconds of sitting meditation, those breaths, those mindful steps during that night and that morning. Success came when I faced the problem directly. I vowed that if I could not have peace at that moment, I would never be able to have peace. If I could not be peaceful in the midst of danger, the kind of peace I might realize in easier times would not mean anything. Practicing the topic, "If you want peace, peace is with you immediately," I was able to resolve many problems one after another.

We had to hand the refugees over to the United Nations High Commissioner for Refugees, who kept them for months and years in the camps in Malaysia. It was very painful. Yet we had conducted our operation in prayer and meditation because we knew that everything depended on our mindfulness. We did sitting mediation late into the night every night, then recited the *Heart Sutra*, as if we were in a monastery.

Our work did bring the cries of the boat people to the attention of the world. In 1977, the U.S. government increased the quota for Vietnamese refugees to 7,000 per year, then 15,000, then 100,000. Australia and other countries followed suit. If we do our best, in full awareness and with a heart free from anger, we cannot worry about results.

NOTES

1. Reprinted from *Love in Action: Writings on Nonviolent Social Change* (1993) by Thich Nhat Hahn with permission of Parallax Press, Berkeley, California.

2. "If You Want Peace, Peace Is With You Immediately" is originally from *The Sun My Heart* (Berkeley: Parallax Press, 1988). Reprinted with permission of Parallax Press.

SUGGESTED FURTHER READINGS BY THICH NHAT HAHN

Being Peace (Berkeley: Parallax Press, 1987).

The Heart of the Buddha's Teaching (Berkeley: Parallax Press, 1998).

Old Path White Clouds: Walking in the Footsteps of the Buddha (Berkeley: Parallax Press, 1991).

Peace is Every Step: The Path of Mindfulness in Everyday Life (New York: Bantam Books, 1991).

The Miracle of Mindfulness: A Manual on Meditation (Bantam Books, 1975).

See also: King, Sallie B., "Thich Nhat Hanh and the Unified Buddhist Church: Nondualism in Action," in Christopher S. Queen and Sallie B. King, eds., *Engaged Buddhism: Liberation Movements in Asia* (Albany: SUNY Press, 1996).

CONTACT INFORMATION

• Plum Village
  13 Marineau
  33580 Dieulizol
  France
  Tel: 33-556-616688
  Fax: 33-556-616151
  E-mail: NH-OFFICE@plumvillage.org

Chapter 15

THE HAPPINESS OF PEACE

Bhante Henepola Gunaratana

Although it is societies that make war, each society is made up of individuals. If individuals learn to live together with one another in peace and harmony, the society will be in peace and harmony. Individuals are like the nucleus and society is like the atoms. The molding of our character takes place as individuals. However, an individual cannot separate from the rest of the individuals. All have to live together. Human beings are social animals and they are always drawn to the society of other human beings. Individuals influence other individuals.

If an individual has an idea and keeps it a secret, then that idea does not benefit anybody. Ideas have to be expressed to become effective. So long as they remain in an individual's mind, nobody but that individual benefits. When that individual dies, the ideas also expire without society having any chance to experiment with them.

Ideas are not generated in emptiness. The brain does not manufacture ideas out of nothing. Ideas must have raw materials to grow. The "conditioning" and influences that occurred during our childhood provide the raw material for our ideas. We are all affected by parents, teachers, friends, associates, books, media, culture, religion, and the atmosphere around us. We think and behave according to the way we have been influenced.

BHANTE HENEPOLA GUNARATANA was born in 1927 in Sri Lanka and ordained as a Buddhist monk at the age of 12. He worked as a teacher and missionary in India, Malaysia, and Kuala Lampur before coming to the United States in 1968 to serve as General Secretary of the Buddhist Vihara Society of Washington, D.C.. He later became president of the society, teaching courses in Buddhism, conducting meditation retreats, and lecturing widely throughout the United States and Canada. He has taught at numerous universities and has published books and articles in Malaysia, India, Sri Lanka, the USA, England, and France. Ven. Gunaratana is currently president of the Bhavana Society in West Virginia and continues to teach meditation on every continent.

THE IMPORTANCE OF RESPECTING ALL RELIGIONS

Religion plays a major role in this influencing or "conditioning" process. In some societies, the role religion plays is, in fact, the determining factor of that society's politics, economics, social structure, harmony, and peace.

Buddhism in the past played a major role in promoting peace and harmony among people. This does not mean that Buddhists are totally non-violent. Buddhist societies are not free from violent crimes, bribery, corruption, and killing. However, no Buddhist can justify their killing, violent crimes, bribery, and corruption by quoting the Buddha.

This means that if individual Buddhists observe true Buddhist principles, there can be very peaceful Buddhist societies. Buddhists have a reputation for peace. When we were trying to establish the Bhavana Society in West Virginia, however, we encountered numerous problems. One family tried to organize opposition to our establishing the meditation center. The lady of that house telephoned her immediate neighbor and asked her to sign a petition "to drive away these devil worshippers from our neighborhood."

The woman who received the telephone call responded by saying, "Thank you for calling me to sign the petition against this new society in our neighborhood. I will not only *not* sign the petition, but I will also call all our neighbors and ask them not to sign it because Buddhists are peaceful people. We need them in our neighborhood. We should be ashamed of ourselves if we even think of driving these peace-loving people away."

The Buddha emphasized that in his teaching there is only one taste—the taste of the peace of happiness *(Upasamasukha)*. The peace of happiness is what each and every one of us seeks. If I ask you what you want in your life, you may say without any hesitation, "I am looking for peace and happiness." I don't think there can be a single right-minded individual who does not want peace and happiness. This urge for peace and happiness does not have a religious label; it is universal. It shatters all boundaries—artificial or concrete.

We should learn, without being hypocritical, to think and to speak about other religions and cultures in private and in public with loving-friendliness, compassion, and appreciative joy—whole-

166

hearted rejoicing in another's good fortune. We should learn to act towards other religions and cultures, in private and in public as well, with loving-friendliness, compassion, and appreciative joy.

We sincerely enjoy hearing people say, "I was educated in a Christian school or in a Catholic school. The school gave me a very good education. I respect others and their religions. However, I remain a Buddhist, a Hindu, a Jew, or a Muslim. Because I have intentionally learned about other religions, I have a great appreciation of them." We are delighted to hear people say, "We live in a neighborhood where almost everyone belongs to a religion different from ours, and they respect our religion. They never troubled us asking us to accept theirs. They respect our religion as I respect theirs." We enjoy seeing people living harmoniously in pluralistic cultures with many races, nationalities, and ethnic origins, using different languages, eating different foods, wearing different clothes, and enjoying their own music and games.

This same neighbor with the petition gave us a lot of trouble when we moved in. The father had encouraged his children to bother us. We didn't complain but sent our loving and friendly thoughts to that family five times a day. We noticed that they had several small children so, even though they hated us, one particularly harsh winter we invited them to come get free firewood from our land in order for them to warm their home. The man came and got firewood without even looking us in the face, let alone thanking us. But we did not expect thanks from him.

Several years later, however, the oldest son returned from the Navy and apologized to us for the unkind behavior toward us when they were children. That really touched our hearts. He said that he learned in the Navy that Buddhism is a peaceful religion. Therefore, he has found respect for Buddhism. Now the family is very quiet.

In addition to teaching children moral, ethical, and religious values, all religious institutions, temples, churches, synagogues, mosques, monasteries and religious schools should take the lead in educating children to respect *other* religions and cultures, for religion and culture are a vital part of many people's lives. Even people who are not very visibly religious become defensive when their traditional religion is criticized.

167
.
.
.
.

In keeping with the Buddha's wise and compassionate advice, most Buddhist parents teach their children that if they respect their own religion they should also respect the religions of others because when you respect others they in turn respect you. If you insult them, they in turn insult you. This has been demonstrated in the history of Buddhism. The emperor Asoka of India was well known for following this principle of mutual respect. At the same time that he was erecting monuments, he was advising his subjects to honor and respect all the religions practiced in India at his time. Perhaps because of these instructions, the period of Asoka's rule is considered to be the most peaceful time in all of Indian history. All leaders should take the initial step to promote peace among people.

OBSERVATIONS ON PEACEMAKING

All noble religious principles are universal. Generosity, patience, compassion, appreciative joy, loving friendliness, and equanimity, for example, are all taught in Buddhism. But all religions advocate them. Even without religious affiliations, people can practice them.

The Buddha has pointed out how poverty can lead to crimes and violence. In many societies, as poverty increases, rich people increase the height of the walls around their homes and place broken bottles and electric wires on top of them. They put bigger padlocks on their iron gates and build still stronger gates. They get vicious dogs and armed guards, then buy more expensive insurance, all to protect themselves against thieves and burglars. No matter how much protection they have, however, crimes are not going to decrease as long as poverty continues to grow. The Buddha recommended that people be more and more generous and compassionate and learn to share what they have with poverty-stricken people. The more compassionate you are, the more generous you can be. The more generous you are, the more loving-friendliness you cultivate to help the world.

Adopting the practice of generosity and loving-friendliness one day a week or once a month or once a year or periodically is not enough. We should practice these virtues throughout our lives in order to help ourselves and others have peace. This practice is not restricted to saints, far and above the hearts and minds of human beings. These practices are the guidelines for peaceful living among ordinary people.

If the poverty, ill health, discrimination, and indifference to our fellow human beings continues to increase, violence, crimes, and even war are to be expected. The moment we forget our commitment to ourselves and to our society, we become involved in fights, wars, and criminal activities. Buddhist countries have ample examples of this. Furthermore, "Kill the enemy to protect religion," does not preserve any religion. The moment you think of killing someone, you have already killed the most basic Buddhist principle. If you discriminate against others, you violate the Buddha's compassionate teaching of loving-friendliness, compassion, and appreciative joy.

"One who protects the Dhamma (the Buddha's teachings about the fundamental truths of existence) is indeed protected by the Dhamma like one who carries an umbrella in a heavy rain is protected by the umbrella. This is the advantage of well-practiced Dhamma. One who lives by the Dhamma does not go to a woeful state of existence."[1]

If you have an umbrella that protects you from sun, rain, and wind, you like it and you will want to protect it. If you put it in a cupboard and lock it up after returning from outside on a rainy day, can you protect it? No, definitely not. Your umbrella will be destroyed by mildew, insects, dust, mice, and ants. Or, if you simply lock it up in a cupboard and never touch it again for years, can you protect it? Keeping it in one place does not serve the purpose of the umbrella either. As an intelligent person, what you should do to protect your umbrella is take care of it properly. Dry it well when it is wet. Mend or repair it if it is torn or broken, and use it carefully as necessary.

Similarly, the happiness that comes from peace protects you if you protect peace. Memorizing, reciting, and studying words are not enough, you should also learn to live peacefully in your own daily life. You should experience peace yourself. One who abides in peace, delights in peace, meditates on peace, and remembers to maintain peace does not fall away from the happiness of peace. This advice applies to clergy and laity.

What is to be done to protect peace? There can be many responses to this question. As the Buddha said, one who preaches peace gives ambrosia to people, or "The gift of peace excels all other

169

gifts." One way to help preserve peace is to publish the message of peace, to spread it by word of mouth, or to memorize numerous passages describing peace.

However, if we spend all our time in teaching, preaching, writing, or memorizing, we will not have any time to actualize this message. You may listen to millions of words of peace millions of times, and still you cannot bring peace to the world. If you do not pay close, undivided attention to the message of peace within you, without any biases and prejudices, you may never learn to promote peace. It never makes any sense in your mind. Why? Because you are not listening to your own inner voice of peace with undivided attention, with the intention of bringing peace to the world. You listen to it with some doubt in your mind. Or your body is here and your mind is somewhere else. You should listen to your own heart, thinking, "How can I share the happiness of peace with my neighbor?"

As you become more interested in peace, you begin to lose your interest in greed, hatred, and delusion. Conversely, those who are consumed by greed, hatred, and ignorance are not interested in peace. You can be interested either in peace or in greed, hatred, and delusion. If you are interested in knowing the way obsession comes about and how it causes violence, destruction, and despair in you and others, you are on the right track of promoting and protecting peace.

In order to protect peace we must not only learn, teach, recite, and investigate peace, but we must also completely realize the functions of peace within us. When we say that we should be totally involved in promoting peace, you might think that you should give up everything and spend your entire life in a solitary place, enjoying peace. No, not at all. You don't have to do that. You must learn to look into your own mind with 100 percent honesty, without any biases, to understand how much ignorance, hatred, greed, jealousy, and fear you have in your mind.

Most of the time you are unaware of how much peace you can generate within you and how much of it you can share with others. You may remember how uncomfortable and irritable you become when someone attacks or criticizes your opinions, ideas, and beliefs. Arousing the happiness of peace becomes much easier if you have this awareness when you have conversations with other people. This very understanding is the beginning of putting peace into practice in your life.

Being generous with material things is very easy for some people and very difficult for others, but being generous about others' opinions, beliefs, or concepts is the most difficult thing of all for human beings. Human history is full of wars waged to protect ideas and opinions. Letting go of ideas is more difficult than letting go of material things.

PERSONAL STEPS TOWARD GENERATING PEACE

The first step toward bringing peace to the whole world is looking at your own mind very closely and thoroughly. Watch your body and speech mindfully. Look at them every moment, every day. When you make a decision, look at your mind very closely, sincerely, and squarely, to see whether you are dishonest and if your mind is trying to trick you. Before you talk, see whether you are going to say something that will hurt your listener. See whether your speech will bring harmony and peace, or disharmony and suffering.

If your decision or your speech is dictated by the thought of letting go of your own prejudices, biases, greed, hatred, delusion, and jealousy, then you will experience thoughts of loving-friendliness, compassion, appreciative joy, equanimity, wisdom, understanding, mindfulness, and penetrating insight. If your mind is full of greed, hatred, delusion, jealousy, fear, tension, anxiety, worries, confusion, and doubts, you will not enjoy peace. When your actions are synchronized with the reality of the peaceful nature within yourself, you protect yourself and you protect others.

The happiness of peace is not a hypothetical theory but a reality of life. It is the wish to experience in your own life at every moment the heritage of our intrinsic nature. The moment you become aware of it, you must make a firm wish to share it with others. As long as you are full of violent thoughts, you cannot build peace for or with others. Cultivate peace within yourself first, and then share it with others.

A Buddhist who does not appreciate and promote the improvement of the spiritual, moral, and ethical life of all human beings is not really practicing Buddhism. When the Buddha, out of compassion and loving-friendliness, sent the first 60 Buddhist missionaries in 60 directions to teach the Dhamma, he instructed them to never exert any force to get someone to accept these teachings. In so doing, he exhibited his sensitivity towards other people's beliefs. Among the most vital birthrights of human beings is their religion. If we violate others' religion or we force others to neglect their religion, in the name of protecting our own, all religious practice suffers. By honoring the rights of others to practice their religion as they choose, we encourage them to respect our right to do the same.

The happiness of peace is a collective experience. Whenever someone violates the rights of another, a hole is drilled in the happiness of peace of the entire society. Buddhists are taught to remember this. Buddhists do not think only of other Buddhists when they practice loving-friendliness, compassion, appreciative joy, and equanimity; they don't exclude anybody or any being. This practice is boundless and unlimited.

As a matter of principle, we never ask anybody's religion when they come to our centers to learn Dhamma or to practice meditation or to ask us questions. We answer their questions and teach the Dhamma, or we give meditation instructions without asking them about their religious background. We want to cultivate the universality of human nature, the components of which we all are made. We see physical form, feelings, perceptions, thoughts, and consciousness as the common denominators for all of us. In that respect, we all are one. We recognize our differences in beliefs, ideas, and opinions, and we agree to disagree. We learn to disagree without becoming *disagreeable.* This helps us to integrate peacefully into society and to live in harmony with others.

Because of this attitude, when we found centers anywhere in the world, people belonging to other religions, already well established in those communities, generally come forward to support us. When we started the first temple in America, for example, there were very few traditional Buddhists available to support us. Nor did we have the funds we needed. Most of our support came from Americans, and most of those who supported us did not know anything about Buddhism. They simply saw us as peaceful people who did not cause anybody any trouble.

Later on we found out, through trial and error, that most of the people who supported us weren't even particularly interested in whether we believed this or believed that. They simply supported us out of their own generosity, compassion, appreciative joy, and equanimity. We were not surprised in the least to note that they had these wonderful, universal human qualities. When we allow all people to manifest their own noble qualities, we create and promote peace.

NOTE

1. Dhammo have rakkhati dhammacari - chattam mahantam yathavassakale Dhammo sucinno sukhamavahati - naduggatim gacchati dhammacarı (Theragatha V. 303).

SUGGESTED FURTHER READINGS

Bhante Henepola Gunaratana, *Mindfulness in Plain English* (Boston: Wisdom Publications, 1994).

Bhikkhu Nanamoli, *The Life of Buddha; According to Pali Canon* (Seattle: Vipassana Research Publications of America, 1992).

Ven. Nyanaponika, *Heart of Buddhist Meditation* (York Beach: Samuel Weiser Incorporated, 1973).

Ven. Piyadassi, *The Buddha's Ancient Path* (Seattle: Vipassana Research Publications of America, 1996).

Ven. Walpola Rahula, *What the Buddha Taught* (New York: Grove/Atlantic Incorporated, 1986).

U Silananda, *Four Foundations of Mindfulness* (Boston: Wisdom Publications, 1995).

If you can't find these books at your local bookstore, contact:

* Buddhist Book Service
Bhante Uparatana
2600 Elmont Street
Wheaton, Maryland 20902-2760
Tel: (301) 946-9437
E-mail: uparatana@aol.com

CONTACT INFORMATION

* Bhavana Society
Route 1 Box 218-3
Highview, West Virginia 26808
Tel: (304) 856-3241
Fax: (304) 856-2111
E-mail: bhavana@access.mountain.net
Website: http://www.bhavanasociety.org

Chapter 16

A PURE LAND ON EARTH

Venerable Chan Master Sheng-yen

PEACE—FROM THE BUDDHIST'S POINT OF VIEW

The Buddhist approach to fostering peace grows out of wisdom cultivated in meditation and shared with others in a wide range of activities, among which teaching and exemplary behavior are paramount. Buddhism teaches us that the causes of conflict and war lie within ourselves; it also teaches us how to constructively temper our own tendency to generate conflict. Underlying this is the Buddhist idea that peace in society begins with peace within oneself. This cultivated inner peace numerically expands from one person to the next until we can truly say that we both act and think locally as well as globally. Simply by sharing our inner peace on a one-on-one basis, we can have a staggering effect on global peace.

THE CAUSES OF CONFLICT AND WAR

When nations engage in war, when factions are in conflict, ordinary people caught in the middle experience suffering. Their hopes for peace and a fulfilling life are often dashed on the rocks of political or economic expediency. Contradictory as it may seem, leaders often resort to war to end war. In the name of peace, war is waged. The history of mankind has evolved along this self-destructive pattern. Ironically, this rule applies as well to smaller group dynamics. Ostensibly, everyone desires peace, but often a group uses force to control dissidents within its ranks. Again violence is used to suppress violence, even within the family.

Born on a farm near Shanghai, **VENERABLE CHAN MASTER SHENG-YEN** became a monk at thirteen and spent his formative years following the traditional path of Buddhist monks. After the Communist revolution, as an expatriate, Master Sheng-yen was conscripted into the Taiwanese Army. Returning to civilian life, he entered solitary retreat in the mountains for six years. His next career path took him to Japan where he earned a doctorate in Buddhist studies. Master Sheng-yen has received transmission in both the Linji (Rinzai) and Caodong (Soto) schools of Chan/Zen, and currently shares his time between Taiwan and the United States.

Using violence to enforce peace often works, but at great cost. The ensuing peace is fragile and temporary. Soon, war breaks out again and often on a larger scale. In this way, throughout history, a durable peace has eluded the human race.

INNER PEACE

To achieve social peace, Buddhism begins with a program of inner peace, believing that long-lasting peace derives from the ability of each person to calm his or her own mind and to temper actions controlled by the mind. Thus empowered, individuals can encourage those in their immediate sphere of influence to also understand the need for peace and to begin calming their minds. In such a widening circle of influence, more and more people will be included. Step by step, people throughout the world can be at peace with themselves and with others. Like a pebble thrown into a pond, causing expanding ripples to reach the far shore, a single person can positively influence many others toward peaceful modes of thinking and acting.

SANGHA—THE MEDITATIVE COMMUNITY

The *meditative community* is the peace program and the means we advocate and practice. It is not a community of individuals acting alone, but a community of meditators bonded by an attainable ideal. A good model is perhaps the Buddhist monastic community, or *Sangha*, which we call a *Harmonious Society*. The word *harmonious* encourages members to maintain a peaceful attitude toward others, to adjust their behavior to accommodate others, and to offer themselves for the benefit of others. Accepting the role of peacemaker is more direct than requiring that others wage peace. Following this harmonious model, a larger society can attempt to influence disharmonic elements in its midst through peaceful means.

History reveals that Buddhists, as a community, have never initiated a religious war. On many historical occasions Buddhists have worked to alleviate the pain and suffering of warfare. In the time of Shakyamuni Buddha, there were many warring factions in India. Many stories tell of the Buddha advising a king to govern his country with virtue and compassion; he admonished leaders to forswear force and to influence neighboring countries through virtue and compassion. This advice is as valuable today as it was then.

176

The Buddhist Practice of Peace: Gratitude and Compassion

In many *sutras* the Buddha teaches lay practitioners to treat their parents, children, spouses, and colleagues with understanding and compassion. These *sutras* teach that each person has many roles in society and that each role dictates specific responsibilities and duties. Rather than putting blind faith in rituals and worship, the Buddha tells us that we should strive to mindfully undertake the responsibilities and duties of our normal lives. If everybody does so, the world will enjoy enduring peace. You can say that the Buddha was the first advocate of "engaged Buddhism."

Other *sutras* teach us to treat our parents, our country, our teachers, and all sentient beings with heartfelt gratitude for their generosity to us. If our parents do not need our help, we can show our gratitude by offering and dedicating ourselves to the benefit of our families, society, and all sentient beings.

Going one step farther, the Mahayana tradition advocates the Bodhisattva Way, urging us to treat everyone as our parents, or as our good and virtuous friends who lead us to the Bodhisattva Way. Such friends help us in every possible way. Some help us in their positive influence. Others challenge our patience and equanimity through their negative influence, thereby indirectly making us improve our minds and actions. One who practices the Bodhisattva Way must show the utmost gratitude to everyone and vow to help them. In this sense it can be said that Buddhists have no enemies. Even when a person wants to hurt us, or succeeds in hurting us, we seek to influence him so that his harmful disposition will be limited in its effects. When there are no enemies, there are no wars.

Causes and Conditions: The Influence of Few on Many

The course of history can be changed radically by a zealous, dedicated individual or by a minority. A small group of people may greatly impact the ideals, ethos, philosophy, and behavior of the majority. The impact can be either negative or positive. When the impact is negative, the minority leads the society into war and destruction. When the impact is positive, they lead the society into prosperity, stability, and happiness, and may even bring about a

new civilization or culture. In these ways, great or infamous historical eras are made.

As a starting point, then, Buddhism believes that each person
should cultivate compassion in their own mind so that they will
not be disposed to harm. In turn they will influence others to desist
from harmful acts. Gradually, in this simple way, world peace can
be achieved.

THE TRANSFORMATION OF THE MIND

The conventional view of peacemaking is to focus on changing
the environment to achieve peace. Such a view advocates the use of
institutions, laws, economic structures, military power, etc., to create an environment in which peace can flourish. Buddhists do not
oppose such a view, but stress the greater urgency of transforming
the mind of the individual.

To transform our minds, we must understand the intimate relationship between the environment and the mind. Buddhists believe that if a person's mind is not pure and calm, whatever ad-
vanced technology he may possess, however pleasant the environment he may enjoy, he will not be happy. On the other hand, if a
person's mind is pure and calm, even in a tumultuous and confusing environment, he or she can ride out the storm without losing
composure. In the midst of disaster, he or she will not suffer, and
will be able to help others.

Furthermore, if our minds are compassionate, we will tend to
see the environment as deserving of our concern, and take steps to
purify it through activism. The Buddha said, "The world changes
according to our state of mind." In this way, environmental activism can be seen as an indirect result of cultivating meditation.

A PURE LAND ON EARTH: PRACTICE AND TEACHING

In the not too distant past, Buddhists believed that to practice
Buddhism, you had to devote your entire life to a monastic style of
practice. You had to stay in a remote place and devote your entire
life to reading the *sutras*, prostrating before the Buddha's statue,
and meditating. In modern times we have returned to the way
Shakyamuni Buddha practiced Buddhism. The Buddha left home
to become a monk because he saw sentient beings fighting among

themselves and with themselves. Conflict existed in the inner mind and spread through words and action to the world beyond. All suffered from these fights, conflicts, and confusion. The Buddha vowed to find a way to help sentient beings alleviate this suffering.

Having attained enlightenment, a mind of peace, wisdom, and compassion, he found five disciples and shared his attainment, experience, and method with them. This was the original Buddhist *Sangha*. With his teachings, the five disciples attained enlightenment in a very short time. He exhorted the five disciples to travel the world over to spread the message and means of liberation. He cautioned them not to travel together so that they could disperse in five directions and cover more territory.

Until his *parinirvana* at the age of 80, the Buddha never stopped travelling and teaching. Even at the very end of his life, he did not forget sentient beings. The Buddha devoted his entire life to spreading the teachings of peace. This tradition of peace teaching continues today in all Buddhist communities.

The notion of "a Pure Land on Earth" is particularly emphasized in the Mahayana tradition of Buddhism. The *Hua-Yen Sutra* (*Avatamsaka Sutra*) [Taisho.9, 449] states: "The moment you give rise to the sincere and earnest intention [to attain enlightenment], you have attained enlightenment." This means that, as soon as you give rise to the aspiration to attain the Buddha's mind of compassion and wisdom, you have become a Buddha. Although you are not yet a perfect and complete Buddha, your mind is in harmony with the enlightenment of all Buddhas. As long as you are a Buddha, the world you see is a Pure Land, for when seen through the Buddha's eye of wisdom and compassion, every place in the world *is* a Pure Land. In other words, peace is created in and with a mind at peace.

A similar idea can be found in the *Mahaprajnaparamita Sutra*, which teaches that in helping others accomplish their enlightenment you accomplish your own. Where do we find people to help? In this world, and in every world in the ten directions, but mostly right in your immediate surroundings—your family, friends, colleagues, and especially, your adversaries, whom you should regard as bodhisattvas. Thus may the Pure Land exist on earth.

179
.
.
.
.

HOW TO ESTABLISH PEACE OR A PURE LAND ON EARTH— THE METHOD

We have talked about the concept of a Pure Land on Earth, but how shall we accomplish it? The method we use we call the Three Practices, which consist of precepts (morality), meditation (concentration), and wisdom. I will discuss them in turn.

The precepts are the vows you take to lead a peaceful way of life through regulating your own behavior of body, thought, and speech. In the passive sense, upholding the precepts means vowing not to commit any wrongful acts. In the active sense, it means vowing to engage in as many acts as possible that benefit yourself as well as others; it means taking responsibility.

The purpose of practicing meditation is to create inner peace by calming the mind and stabilizing your emotions. If you practice meditation well you are less likely to become angry or agitated in your every day life. By meditation, we do not mean just sitting with concentration; we also mean bringing mindfulness to all your waking activities. Thus your emotions and behavior will be more stable, and conflicts with others will lessen. In these simple ways we can establish peace in the lives of individuals and societies.

The simpler methods include contemplating your thoughts, your breath, or counting your breaths. As soon as you begin to contemplate, your mind will calm down quickly. When you practice precepts and meditation together, wisdom naturally arises in your mind, which means that you will be able to see everything more objectively, and your mind and behavior will not be adversely affected by the environment. By practicing precepts, meditation, and wisdom, your mind and actions will be at peace. You will be able to live peacefully with others at all times.

THE "PURE LAND ON EARTH" MOVEMENT

The Dharma Drum Mountain Buddhist Association, with headquarters in Taiwan and the United States, actively promotes the Movement of the Pure Land on Earth. We teach these concepts and methods of practice to all practitioners, whatever their cultural or educational background. Our slogan is: "Everywhere is a meditation hall; everywhere is a Buddhist temple." Every family is encouraged to set up a meditation space, a place where together and singly, family members can compose their minds and experience genuine peace. We believe that "engaged Buddhism" begins by engaging one's own mind, in one's own space.

We promote this peace movement wherever we go. In Taiwan, Europe, and America we have conducted more than 150 seven-day meditation retreats. Those who continue their meditation practice become our worldwide "Ambassadors of Peace." We have founded a university in Taiwan, which will provide undergraduate and graduate education in social and humanitarian subjects geared toward the development of the individual and the peaceful transformation of society. We hold annual international conferences at the Institute of Chung-Hwa Buddhist Culture in Taipei, focusing on a global understanding and spread of Buddhist principles and practice of peaceful living. Our professional seminars spread the message and practice of peace to professionals in all fields, including prominent military and political leaders. Ordinary Buddhists around the world promote this idea and ideal of peace, sharing with and encouraging others.

In July of 1997 we sponsored the Third Chung-Hwa International Conference on Buddhism in Taiwan, with the conference topic being: "The Earthly Pure Land and Contemporary Society." With a subtopic of "Building a Pure Land on Earth," scholars from 11 countries representing Asia, America, and Europe presented 48 papers on ways the vision of the Pure Land may have practical relevance today and in the future.

The keynote of the conference was expressed in this way: "Neither the diverse Buddhist traditions, nor fields of scholastic discipline, nor any religion can assert that only its faith or tradition is superior. It is essential that in the process of mutual acceptance and learning, we work toward the vision of 'Building a Pure Land on Earth.'"

THE WORLD AS SANGHA

If the *Sangha* is the community of Buddhists, then true Buddhists see the world as their *Sangha*. This is not to say that we should see all people as Buddhists, but that we should see them as parents, brothers, sisters, and children, all deserving of our compassionate care. And it all starts within the small circle of earth that each one of us inhabits at any given moment. This is where peacework begins—within our own bodies, hearts, and minds. It is concrete, it is direct, it is simple, and it is the way of the Buddha.

181

SUGGESTIONS FOR FURTHER READING

Dalai Lama, *Ethics for the New Millennium* (New York: Riverhead Books, 1999).

Eppsteiner, Fred, ed., *The Path of Compassion: Writings on Socially Engaged Buddhism* (Berkeley: Parallax Press, 1988).

Fu, Charles Wei-hsun, and Sandra A. Wawrytko, eds., *Buddhist Ethics and Modern Society* (Connecticut and London: Greenwood Press, 1991).

Kraft, Kenneth, ed., *Inner Peace, World Peace: Essays on Buddhism and Nonviolence* (Albany: State University of New York, 1992).

Shantideva, *A Guide to the Bodhisattva's Way of Life,* translated by Stephen Batchelor (Dharamshala: Library of Tibetan Works and Archives, 1979), 3-9.

Sheng-yen, "On the Temporal and Spatial Adaptability of the Bodhisattva Precepts, with Reference to the Three Cumulative Pure Precepts," in *Buddhist Behavioral Codes and the Modern World: An International Symposium,* ed. Fu, Charles Wei-hsun, and Sandra A. Wawrytko (Connecticut and London: Greenwood Press, 1994), 3-50.

_____,"Buddhist Tradition and Modernity" in *Buddhist Ethics and Modern Society,* ed. Fu, Charles Wei-hsun, and Sandra A. Wawrytko (Connecticut and London: Greenwood Press, 1991), 3-4.

_____,"The Relationship between Buddhist Vinaya and Building a Pure Land on Earth" in *Chung-Hwa Buddhist Journal,* Vol. 10, 1997 (in Chinese).

Sivaraksa, Sulak, *Seeds of Peace: A Buddhist Vision for Renewing Society* (Berkeley: Parallax Press, 1991).

Thich Nhat Hanh, *The Heart of the Buddha's Teaching: Transforming Suffering Into Peace, Joy & Liberation* (Berkeley: Broadway Books, 1999).

_____, *Interbeing: Commentaries on the Tiep Hien Precepts* (Berkeley: Parallax Press, 1987), 72.

_____, *Being Peace* (Berkleey: Parallax Press, 1988).

_____, *Peace Is Every Step: The Path of Mindfulness in Everyday Life* (Berkeley: Parallax Press, 1992).

CONTACT INFORMATION

- Dharma Drum Mountain Buddhist Association
Nung Ch'an Monastery
89, Lane 65, Ta-Yeh Road
Pei-Tou, Taipei, Taiwan
Tel: (02) 2893-3161

- Ch'an Meditation Center
90-56 Corona Avenue
Elmhurst, NY 11373
Tel: 718-592-6593
718-595-0915
Fax: 718-592-0717
E-mail: DDMBAny@aol.com
Website: http://www.chan1.org

Chapter 17

THE UNESCO DECLARATION: A TIBETAN
BUDDHIST PERSPECTIVE

José Ignacio Cabezón

The *Declaration on the Role of Religion in the Promotion of a Culture of Peace* is an important document, and I am grateful for the opportunity to think through some of the issues that it raises. I write from the perspective of the Tibetan Buddhist tradition, a tradition with which I have identified, first as a monk, then as a lay person, for almost 25 years. Most readers are probably aware of the fact that the Tibetans lost their independence in the wake of the violent Chinese occupation of their homeland in 1959. In that year His Holiness, the fourteenth Dalai Lama, the political and religious leader of the Tibetan people, left Tibet together with approximately 100,000 Tibetans, and sought political asylum in India. Based in the small Himalayan hill station of Dharamsala in northern India, the Dalai Lama and the Tibetan government in exile have been involved in a 40-year nonviolent effort to regain Tibetan independence. For his unswerving commitment to the Tibetan people's peaceful struggle for independence, the Dalai Lama was awarded the Nobel Peace Prize in 1989.

What was for the Tibetans a tragedy—namely, the loss of their homeland, and, especially after the cultural revolution, the continuous and systematic destruction of their religion and culture—has represented for the rest of the world an opportunity to become acquainted with their unique religious heritage. The form of

JOSÉ IGNACIO CABEZÓN is Professor of Buddhism and Comparative Thought at the Iliff School of Theology in Denver, Colorado, USA. He has a B.S. with an emphasis in physics from the California Institute of Technology and a Ph.D. in Buddhist Studies from the University of Wisconsin-Madison. He was a monk in the dGe lugs order of Tibetan Buddhism for almost a decade, living for six of those years among Tibetan refugees in the monastery of Sera in south India. He is the author or editor of numerous books and scholarly articles on Buddhism including *Buddhism, Sexuality and Gender; Buddhism and Language; Scholasticism: Cross Cultural and Comparative Perspectives;* and, with Roger Jackson, *Tibetan Literature.*

Mahayana Buddhism practiced in Tibet, in particular, has now spread throughout the world, and its principles have, for the Dalai Lama and for Tibetans generally, come to serve as the foundations on which to build a philosophy of nonviolent political resistance and response to injustice. (See Cabezón in the Suggested Further Readings.) In the remarks that follow I would like to respond to the UNESCO declaration by drawing on the doctrinal foundations of Tibetan Buddhism in general and on the thought of the Dalai Lama in particular.

The Tibetan Buddhist tradition, and especially the Dalai Lama, its leader, emphasizes the importance not only of nonharming, but also of actively helping others. There is a clear resonance between these foundational Buddhist principles and many of the sentiments expressed in the declaration. Not only are many of the ideas contained in the text appealing, but the very structure of the document—emphasizing, after the preambles on the world situation and on peace, the *commitment* and *responsibility* that we as religious persons must have—gives the document an air of practicality and relevance that is welcomed.

The declaration not only reinforces for Buddhists principles that are familiar, it also challenges us to think about issues and themes that, while perhaps more central to other religions, are less emphasized in Buddhism. I am thinking here especially of the themes of repentance and forgiveness (sec. 6) that, while certainly not unknown to the Buddhist tradition, are not frequently found in Buddhist writings on peace. By drawing our attention to these important themes, the document challenges Buddhists to give serious thought to the harm that we as individuals and as a collective have done to others and to the world, to acknowledge and to take responsibility for such harm, to make it known publicly (what Tibetan Buddhists call "confession," *so sor bshags pa*). It encourages us to seek, where appropriate, to provide restitution for such harm, to seek forgiveness, and to use this as an opportunity to renew our commitment to the welfare of others.

The emphasis on peace as a process (sec. 10) is also a welcomed reminder that even if peace is somehow innate to who we are as individuals and as a society—our natural condition, if you will—it is not something that comes naturally to us, requiring instead a

184
.
.
.
.
.

long-term commitment that must be continually cultivated and renewed.

While both reinforcing and challenging Buddhists in the ways just mentioned, it is also true to say that Buddhist principles raise questions about the declaration. Mahayana Buddhism in general and the philosophical school known as the "Middle Way" (*Madhyamaka*, Tib. *dBu ma*) in particular have a long tradition of questioning and even deconstructing all concepts, including those that it holds as ideals. In this regard, it is perhaps worth noting that the very notion of peace is no more immune from the deconstructive critique of the Mahayana than is any other worthy goal. What insight might such a critique bring in its wake?

First, it puts peace into perspective by refusing it the status of an ultimate. Both individual/inner peace and social/world peace, although clearly goals worth pursuing, are not ends in themselves. It is all too easy to put peace on a pedestal, to idolize it, to allow it to become the God of an age that has otherwise lost its sense of spiritual meaning and direction. In its most extreme forms this tendency to lose perspective on peace leads to a kind of idolatry in which social peace comes to act as a substitute for lost religious ideals, and inner peace as a kind of self-absorption whose main result is the reinforcement of narcissism. For Indo-Tibetan Mahayana Buddhists, putting peace into perspective entails avoiding two extremes that in each case reduce religion to something that it can and should not be: social activism on the one hand, and an individualistic, self-centered spirituality on the other.

Over and above this, however, the Mahayana critique of the notion of peace reminds us that peace has no intrinsic self-existence; that, like all virtues, and indeed all phenomena, it has no independent mode of being; that it is a conventional thing that depends upon other things for its emergence. Peace cannot arise simply by wishing it into existence, but only by the cultivation of its causes. Viewing peace in this way has the salutary effect of shifting the emphasis of peacework from result to causes. To work for peace is not to work for some vague and abstract pie-in-the-sky ideal but to toil in the ground of its causes: to cultivate the causes and conditions for its emergence. Shifting the emphasis of peacework from result to causes also diminishes the tendency to make of peace

185

a fetishized object. It acts as a counter-measure to the all-too-prevalent commercialization and commodification of peace in our time, a commodification that has led to the marketing of this ideal in everything from books to musical concerts to clothing and jewelry.

Viewing peace as a conventional phenomenon dependent on causes further encourages the *identification* of those causes, as we find in the declaration's sections 13-18. Indeed, the declaration is, within the limits of its brevity, quite sophisticated in this regard, realizing both the complexity of those causes and the role that religion plays (or has failed to play) in this regard. The document also presents us with a nuanced view of the way in which that nexus of causes will vary from one cultural context to another. Cultivating the causes of peace is a slow and gradual work with no ready-made formulas for its execution. It is situational and contextual, tentative, more like an art than a science. All of this is to say that the work of peace should be envisioned as a bottom-up process, proceeding from causes to result, from the local to the global. Indeed, I would go so far as to say that the top-down model, which seeks to make peace descend into our midst from the heaven of ideals, is doomed to failure. This is not only because such a model often disregards the causal process, but also because it encourages a kind of unhealthy clinging to the ideal of peace. Peace, in the top-down model, becomes imagined (a more accurate term would be "reified") and then clung to as an absolute that is independent, not only of causes, but of time, place, cultures, and the beings that inhabit these. In the end, peace becomes reified/deified as a transcendent and ultimately unattainable absolute, and our proper relationship to it devolves into one of worship and awe. The deleterious side effects of such an attitude should be obvious.

While aware of the fact that peace can only be achieved by cultivating its causes, Buddhists in recent years have tended to stress a single aspect of the nexus of those causes by emphasizing the importance of inner spiritual cultivation to the work of peace. (See also sec. 11 of the declaration.) Such a move has clearly served an important function, one might almost say corrective, to the dominant Western, especially secular, discourse that has tended to see world peace in strictly *external* terms, reducing it to socioeconomic-political factors. More important, stressing the spiritual dimension—the cultivation of inner peace—has brought to the forefront of the discussion the question of the role that a proper *motivation* can and should play in socially oriented peacework. Doing that work for the right reasons and with the right frame of mind not only has moral implications for the work itself (for Buddhists the virtuous/nonvirtuous character of action is inextricably linked to motivation), it also has practical ones. A motivation that is other-, rather than self-, centered simply has more staying power, more ability to withstand the hardships it encounters. It is perhaps to the detriment of the document under discussion that it contains little if any mention of the importance of altruism as a motivation for the work of peace.

At the same time, it is possible to overemphasize the role that the inner life plays in achieving world peace or in motivating peacework and social activism. It is both unrealistic and morally problematic to postpone dealing with issues of social justice until the inner life has been perfected. Systemic injustice often calls for forms of analysis and action that cannot be reduced, at least in the short run, to questions of spiritual development. Moreover, the abject living conditions of a vast portion of the people of the world make the reduction of peace to inner peace at best naïve and, at worst, a kind of implicit collusion with the forces of injustice.

A final word might be in order concerning the practical value of the declaration. How can this document, and the work that went into crafting it, avoid the fate of so many similar undertakings? How can it avoid becoming ignored as yet another irrelevant homily in the archives of peace studies? Interreligious statements of this sort have often suffered from the fact that specificity and "bite" are sacrificed in the interest of achieving interreligious consensus. This is certainly a potential problem in the case of the declaration. However, it is precisely in fleshing out in religiously specific terms the implications of the declaration that that document, and the work of the Barcelona conference, will bear fruit. The present volume goes a long way to achieving this in the Buddhist case, which is, perhaps the greatest tribute that can be paid both to the declaration and to the women and men who were responsible for it.

SUGGESTED FURTHER READINGS

Cabezón, José Ignacio, "Buddhist Principles in the Tibetan Liberation Movement," in Christopher S. Queen and Sallie B. King, eds., *Engaged Buddhism: Buddhist Liberation Movements in Asia* (Albany: SUNY Press, 1996).

H. H. the Dalai Lama and Jean-Claude Carrière, *Violence and Compassion* (New York: Doubleday, 1994).

H. H. the Dalai Lama, *Kindness, Clarity and Insight,* ed. J. Hopkins and E. Napper (Ithaca: Snow Lion, 1984).

H. H. the Dalai Lama, *The World of Tibetan Buddhism* (Boston: Wisdom Publications, 1995).

"Nobel Lecture by His Holiness Tenzing Gyatso, the Fourteeenth Dalai Lama of Tibet." *News Tibet,* vol. 23, no. 2 (1989) 4-6.

CONTACT INFORMATION

The Tibetan freedom struggle, the Tibetan people's response to the Chinese overthrow of their government in 1959, is headed worldwide by His Holiness the Dalai Lama who, in 1989, was awarded the Nobel Peace Prize for his commitment to the peaceful and nonviolent struggle for Tibetan independence. The Dalai Lama and the Tibetan government in exile are based at Tekchen Kyishong, Dharamsala, District Kangra, H.P., India. The International Campaign for Tibet, the nongovernmental organization that represents the Dalai Lama in matters related to Tibetan independence, is based in Washington, D.C.:

* International Campaign for Tibet
  1825 K St., N.W., Suite 520
  Washington, D.C. 20006

Chapter 18

DIALOGUE ON RELIGION AND PEACE*

His Holiness Tenzin Gyatso, the XIVth Dalai Lama

Since the very beginning of human civilization, everyone is try-ing to achieve a happy life. I think that the very aim of science, of technology, and also of man is good; its aim is not destruction, not killing, not more suffering...that is clear.

But in spite of our high material development, we still face a lot of problems. In tackling the problems it is important to distinguish two levels: the one of the existing problems (how to solve them) and the one of the preventive measures (which is still more important).

In every event there are processes and conditions concerning the existence of the problem. Of course we have to deal with these prob-lems and to make every effort to solve them but sometimes it is rather difficult. For example, Bosnia is in crisis. It seems that human emo-tion gets out of control and the best part of the human brain which can judge or which can use reason cannot function properly when your emotion becomes out of control. That is what is happening in Bosnia and some other areas. Therefore it is extremely important to take preventive measure, paying attention to the time, causes, and conditions. That is the prime time to handle or to intervene.

Transcript of a discussion held at the December, 1994 UNESCO seminar on "The Contribution by Religions to the Culture of Peace." These remarks are reprinted with permission of H.H. the Dalai Lama and the Centre UNESCO de Catalunya.

TENZIN GYATSO was born in 1935 in northeastern Tibet. At the age of two, he was recognized as the XIVth Dalai Lama of Tibet, and was formally installed in the capital of Lhasa at the age of four. In 1950, he assumed political leadership of the country, and struggled to peacefully resist the threat of a Chinese Communist invasion. In 1959 he was forced to flee Tibet after the Chinese crushed a popular uprising, killing more than 87,000 people. Since then, His Holiness has lived in exile in Dharamsala, a small town in northern India, the seat of the Tibetan gov-ernment-in-exile. In 1989, he was the recipient of the Nobel Peace Prize for what the Nobel Committee called "his constructive and forward-looking proposals for his solution of international conflicts, human rights issues, and global environ-mental problems." He advocates peaceful solutions to the world's problems based upon tolerance and mutual respect, and works to preserve the cultural heritage of the Tibetan people.

189
.
.
.
.
.

As a Buddhist monk, I feel that the human motivation is the prime thing; this is the ultimate mover, whether destructive or constructive, good or bad.

In general people pay more attention to work or action and less to motivation. When we talk about the future of humanity or our concern about the future, every human being has responsibility. Talking about motivation I think that religious people have a special responsibility and a special role to play. At that level, which I usually describe as *internal disarmament*, you try to reduce negative emotions such as hatred, anger, jealousy, extremism, and greed, and promote compassion, human affection, tolerance, these things. That is extremely important.

When the human being is born, ignorance is part of his mind. But through training and education the amount of ignorance can eventually reduce, and similarly hatred, anger. Through proper education we can increase human compassion, human tolerance.

In that respect the various religious traditions have a great potential to help and to contribute; not necessarily in order to make more believers... My attitude or belief is Buddhist and I also practice as much as I can although my practice is very limited. My good excuse is that I'm too busy. Anyway I do my best to implement these noble ideas, but my attitude is to wonder how much can I contribute from my tradition for humanity. I'm not thinking about how to propagate Buddhism, but how much I can contribute from my practice, experience, and my tradition. If I try to propagate Buddhism, the other sides will also propagate and eventually there will be a border and a clash will be possible. These things are really not easy.

After all, religion is a personal matter. The different religious traditions are good houses, have good methods, messages, and potentials. You realize this potential to serve humanity. This means to reduce negative emotion and to promote positive emotion.

Spirituality can be at two levels: one is spirituality with faith and another is spirituality without faith. The nonbeliever first tries to be a good human being, a 'whole-hearted' person. The eyes of that person should naturally see the other as a fellow human being. Then naturally a sense of respect, of concern, will automatically come. Individually, there is a sort of inner necessity, inner feeling.

I'm quite sure that each major religion has great potential to serve, to help humanity.

We human beings are, after all, not a machine product. If a human being is a machine product, then it is ultimately logical and could fulfill all human requirements by machine. But since we are not machine products, the human requirements cannot be fulfilled by machines alone. Particularly in those societies where material comfort is highly developed, there are still quite a number of people who under the beautiful surface have some kind of mental unrest. This shows the limitation of material development. I am quite sure that even in the next century, despite the material comfort or development, humanity in general will still need religions.

Now the next question: in order to serve humanity from various different religious traditions more effectively, first the relations between religions should be good ones. In the very name of religion sometimes blood has been shed in the past and even today. This is the first thing we have to eliminate. Nowadays the idea of religious pluralism is present among the different religious communities. This is a very healthy sign.

A relation of genuine harmony among different religious traditions is essential. For some time I have been making attempts to promote the genuine spirit of harmony among the different religious traditions. According to my own little experience I feel that there are a few methods. One of them is meeting scholars from various religious traditions in order to dialogue with them on the differences and similarities in the areas of doctrine.

Another method is to meet genuine practitioners of different religions. Here you cannot really say "no" to the value of other religious traditions. According to my own religious experience and through personal contacts, my appreciation and knowledge about the deeper value of Christianity grew. These kinds of meetings can give a really powerful understanding about the value of other religious traditions.

And third, religious leaders must occasionally come together, like some time ago at Assisi where all major religious leaders came together and prayed. That is also very useful, particularly in the eyes of the public.

Then, fourth, the joint pilgrimage. We visited the different religious holy places. If possible we prayed together, if not we did silent meditation. This year I visited Jerusalem with this spirit. One morning I went to the Holy Wall with that small cap [a yarmulke]. My friend arranged one red small hat, so that went very well with this color [of my robe]. And while my Jewish brothers prayed, I meditated; I got a feeling of energy. Then, next I went to the main Christian temple in Jerusalem and to the Muslim Rock. The local Muslim people welcomed you with sensitive feeling but very religiously hesitated to allow my scarf to be put on that rock. But that didn't matter. I did appreciate to stand in front of the rock and did meditation. Through such occasions I really got some kind of strange feeling, of course positive, particularly last year in Lourdes, in France. I visited it as a pilgrim rather than a tourist. So, although I failed to get a vision of Mary, I really felt a vibration in front of this image of Mary. I prayed on that spot for millions of people, for brothers and sisters who seek some inner strength. I prayed on this holy place that served or helped millions of people, so that in the future also it should continue, I prayed. So this I feel is a very powerful experience. I hope that in the future the followers of different religious traditions go to these different holy places in joint pilgrimage, and get a deeper experience.

Then another thing. Some of my friends in the environmental movement have expressed their complaints that perhaps there is not enough attention being paid and enough contributions being made on the part of the religious practitioners. The concern about environment is also a responsibility for all humanity. All human beings have a responsibility, so naturally religious believers have a responsibility to take a more active role in that field. I think this is very useful.

So therefore, thank you.

Questions:

Q: Could you be more specific about the environmental question?

A: Firstly, this matter to me is very new. When I was in Tibet, I had no idea about such problems. But after some environmental scientists gave me a clear explanation, it seemed really a very serious matter. If we look at this blue planet from space, it is a very small, tiny beautiful planet. This is our only home, and we have no alternative to go to. The environment is damaged without us noticing it obviously. Bloodshed is obvious and immediately strikes our mind; the response comes also more immediately. It is very important that every individual member of the human society is aware of the fragility of the environment and of the fact that when damage occurs, it is very gradual and unnoticeable. Since environmental scientists do all their best to try to raise public awareness, it is also important that followers of religious traditions contribute in terms of raising further public awareness.

Q: During the last three days this seminar has been deliberating on how to move from a culture of war to a culture of peace. At the end of the seminar we hope to have a declaration which all of us can sign. Would you say something about this?

A: I always believe basic human nature is gentleness, compassion. My reasoning is quite simple: anger and hatred are of course also part of our mind, but the dominant force of our mind is affection. And, according to the medical science, a peaceful mind is better for the body than an agitated mind. A more compassionate, calm mind affects the body in a very positive way. Constant anger, constant fear is very bad for the health. Therefore, a more peaceful mind, a more compassionate mind, suits the body better. Therefore, we can say that the basic human nature is gentleness. This is our real hope. Sometimes I think that today, because of excessive coverage of violence by media, which is always reported on the front page, eventually people get the impression that all human nature is aggressive and negative. That eventually leads to discouraging oneself. But why do the bloodshed and the negative things become news? Since human nature is gentleness, killing and bloodshed move people so deep down that it becomes news. When we hear that thousands of children are taken care of with compassionate love, we take it for granted. This is normal, nothing new. To some extent, it is this excessive and unbalanced portrayal of the negative aspects of human nature which perhaps may give rise to people having a negative conception of human beings. So, as I stated earlier, it is important to be told that the fundamental human nature is gentleness and that human nature is closer to the wholesome

193

states of mind and emotion. Once that is realized, it may be possible for us to try to develop an environment, a climate, and a culture where we can learn to live in a way which is much closer to the fundamental goodness of human nature.

Q: Your Holiness, one sentence of our draft declaration talks about the protection of all forms of life. Within my tradition (the Catholic tradition), human life deserves special attention because the human person is created in a major code. I would like to know what is the position of your religion on the point of the human life of the unborn child because in our vision the protection of human life starts from the moment of its conception.

A: If you look at the Buddhist definition of killing of a human being, it is quite clear that it embraces not only fully the human being but the unborn fetus as well.

Q: In South Africa, as you know, the religions together played a very important role in resolving the apartheid problem. I hope I don't put you on the spot, and I speak as an individual. But what do you think, your Holiness, the religions could do together that could help Tibet? What could they do together that would put the issue of Tibet forward to a solution?

A: I'm sure that religions together can play an important role. One of the aspects of the issue of Tibet is that the fate of Tibet is not just the fate of six million Tibetans alone, but it also involves the well-being of many people in that region because of the geographical situation between India and China, the two most populated nations. In searching for genuine peace and friendship between these population giants, Tibet can play an important role also, to some extent, for the other newly independent republics. In the heartland of Asia, Tibet can play an important role.

And then there is the Tibetan culture, which is essentially a peaceful culture, based on a compassionate and harmonious relationship not only with fellow human beings, animals, and other forms of life but also with the natural environment itself. I feel that the Tibetan issue is related more with culture rather than with national political struggle. Of course, political freedom is also very, very important. But my main concern is the cultural heritage in that part of the world. If the Tibetan culture survives, it can be a source of

194

benefit not only to the six million Tibetans but also to the North, to the whole Mongolian area, and to the South, and to China. Millions of young Chinese at the moment have lost their deeper human values. They are simply thinking about money and face a lot of corruption and scandals. Once the politically rigid system controlled that fate. Now with more economic liberalization there is no way to reduce the corruption or scandal anymore. Without deeper cultural values and self-discipline, it will be very difficult. The Tibetan culture has the potential to help. Therefore, the preservation of Tibetan culture is important and the following of different religious traditions can do more. For me, the major issue is the preservation of that kind of peaceful nature culture. It would be very helpful if the people who think about peace and the environment can contribute more toward resolving the problem.

Q: Your Holiness, you mentioned visits to places of pilgrimage not as tourist but as pilgrim. Would you welcome visits to Tibet by people of other religions in this spirit, and if so, what advice would you give to these pilgrims?

A: If such things could be organized, on my part I would express my warm welcome. Unfortunately, my welcome will have to be expressed not from Tibet but from India. First, you need some kind of permission from the Chinese government. In fact, in Central Tibet there are several Muslims who have been living there through several centuries, at least a few thousand Muslims. In Dharamsala, my place, there is one Christian.

Q: You placed very well the question of Tibet in the geostrategic consideration, which is very important. Myself, as well as the organization I am associated with, are involved in questions that violate culture from the human rights perspective. My questions to you, Holiness, would be how do you see it in terms of self-determination of the Tibetan people when we talk about preserving a culture of peace, because the perspectives change; because you stated very well that actions alone are not important, but assumptions and motivations are important. So how do you view, given this rare opportunity we have, the question of the self-determination of the people of Tibet in all aspects, preserving a culture of peace, preserving a culture of religious heritage as well as to be able to develop themselves?

A: Actually two resolutions have been passed at the United Nations recognizing the Tibetan people's right for self-determination. I think that the second resolution mentioned human rights, including the right of self-determination. However, my approach during the last 15 years has been, as I usually call it, a 'middle level of approach': the only practical way is to negotiate with the Chinese government in the spirit of compromise, in the spirit of reconciliation. The last 15 years my whole approach was trying to have negotiations and to reach through negotiation a kind of mutual agreeable solution.

Q: It has interested me quite a lot to hear that the Dalai Lama has been worshipping across religious borders, and we have also seen that the Pope has been making travels all over the world, and other church leaders. In our own position in Cameroon, we have always been on good terms and in working relationships with other Church leaders, but it has always been rather strange to me, and those I have talked to, to find that although the major religions are based on monotheism there is nevertheless quite a barrier to coming together to create what we might call a big gathering in the name of God. On the contrary, as you rightly said, there has been quite a lot of violence in God's name. My question now is, what in your impression—and I'm not asking for a panacea that is a solution for everything—is the cause of this intolerance on the part of human beings that are worshipping the one and only God? What stops them coming together and feeling like a people from one family under one roof and not emphasizing too much their different relations? This has been a teasing question, and I thought I should use this opportunity to ask your Holiness.

A: My own personal feeling is that often people fail to appreciate truly the real essence of religion. I personally see religion as a method to bring about an inner positive transformation. But people often use religion rather as a base of identity, something to make yourself feel that you belong to something, rather than understanding its true nature, as a spiritual guideline. So when that happens, given that human beings have emotions like anger, hatred, jealousy, then sometimes religion is used to further these negative emotions.

Q: Since this is a group representing many different religious and spiritual traditions, as well as people interested in peace and nonviolence, is there something we could do to support and recognize the struggles of the Tibetan people and their commitment to live by nonviolence and compassion, and would this be helpful in your view?

A: Definitely it would be of tremendous help.

SUGGESTED FURTHER READINGS BY H.H. THE DALAI LAMA

The Art of Happiness: A Handbook for Living (New York: Riverhead Books, 1998).

Ethics for the New Millennium (New York: Riverhead Books, 1999)

Freedom in Exile: The Autobiography of the Dalai Lama (New York: Riverhead Books, 1991).

The Good Heart: A Buddhist Perspective on the Teachings of Jesus (Boston: Wisdom Publications, 1996).

Opening the Eye of New Awareness (Boston: Wisdom Publications, 1999).

The World of Tibetan Buddhism: An Overview of Its Philosophy and Practice (Boston: Wisdom Publications, 1995).

CONTACT INFORMATION

• His Holiness Tenzin Gyatso, the XIV Dalai Lama
Thekchen Choeling
McLeod Ganj
176219 Dharmasala (HP)
India
Tel: 91-1892-21343
Fax: 91-1892-24213
Website: www.tibet.com

Conclusion

BUDDHIST PEACE PRINCIPLES

David W. Chappell

Peace is a blessing and a mystery, and much like happiness or enlightenment, it often becomes elusive when we seek it. But the many conditions necessary for peace are better understood than they have ever been. Buddhists have always emphasized inner mindfulness work, but social mindfulness is increasingly important in Buddhist peacework and is the focus of this concluding reflection.

The outstanding leaders in this volume offer resources from their Buddhist communities to support building cultures of peace. Even more than their writings, their lives constitute the best responses to the UNESCO *Declaration on the Role of Religion in the Promotion of a Culture of Peace*. Their cultivation of inner peace and their support of religious diversity embody the goals of the declaration. However, the commitments outlined in the declaration (#13-18) entail social, economic, political, and demilitarizing actions that involve new challenges since they extend beyond Buddhist practices for individuals and require Buddhists to develop social roles. The essays in this volume contribute greatly to clarifying social guidelines for Buddhists and deserve a final reflection to prepare us all to work with others in creating cultures of peace.

THE SOCIAL IMPERATIVE

Buddhist peace is not primarily a solitary quest, and only at times did the Buddha wander lonely as a rhinoceros. We have heard about, and some may have tried, practicing alone, living in caves or as forest renunciants. This is a special vocation, or for special times, or for unusual people. The peacework of the writers in this book is different and involves both monastics and laity.[1]

Everyone agrees that Buddhist peacework must exist in the mind, in mindfulness training, in noticing the different parts within ourselves and their interactions. A single soul does not exist, said the Buddha, for we live and breathe and have our being as a multitude.

Peace comes when we recognize the many voices within us, and discover their willingness to try new tunes, or wait their turn.

The inner dialogue that constitutes mindfulness work was a new discovery by the Buddha, and history has not been the same since. However, today there is a new urgency for that peacework to be manifest socially, ecologically, and materially. The effort to extend peacework into these various spheres is at the heart of this book.

In the past such insistence on social dialogue was the interest of a few. But the acceleration of modern technology has given affluence for some, but a population explosion and depletion of resources for most, that requires a heightened awareness of our actions and their consequences, and a constant openness to possible alternatives, to avoid driving headlong and at high speed into the devastation of our world.

The inner dialogue that is mindfulness training can be manifest socially as a group practice involving regular and frequent "time out" from daily pressures for mindful dialogue in whatever social nexus we find ourselves. The patterns of this social mindfulness work, and its connections with earlier forms of Buddhism, require further analysis.

SOCIAL ACTION AS FOUNDATIONAL TO BUDDHISM

In ancient India, the Buddha discovered that individual human happiness and misery were determined not primarily by physical abundance, but by inner mindfulness. Buddhist peacework began with the actions of the Buddha who taught both personal and group practices. While right mindfulness and wisdom could be cultivated in private, social checks and balances occurred twice a month on the new moon and the full moon days when his disciples gathered to recite the social rules of practice (*uposatha*). If problems arose concerning practice, the disciples were to resolve them by unanimous agreement. This pattern of regular and frequent meetings to monitor moral actions, and the process of resolving problems by discussion and consensus, has been a Buddhist social model of dialogue and accountability from its earliest days.

While the fortnightly meeting of the Buddhist community (*sangha*) dealt mostly with internal matters, the 45-year teaching career of the Buddha was filled with other kinds of social interaction at all levels of society. The Buddha taught kings and untouchables, brahmins and bandits. Similar to the Buddha, the authors in this present volume share a foundation of Buddhist mindfulness training, but they also engage their societies in a variety of ways.

While *dhyana* and *prajna* (meditation and wisdom), or *samatha* and *vipassana* (calming and insight), are two legs of the Buddhist chair, it cannot stand without social action. Traditional Buddhist morality (*sila*) was codified in the vinaya scriptures and included several hundred prohibitions, but four applied to all Buddhists: no killing, stealing, lying, or sexual misconduct. While these are universal moral values, the additional rules of the monastic life were foundational to the Buddhist community by marking its distinctive identity, vision, and constancy of purpose through time and across cultures, and they have contributed to peacework in several important ways.

Because Buddhist monastics were strictly nonviolent and offered no direct challenge to local governments, the Buddhist order was able to spread and coexist with other societies in a nonthreatening way. As a result, it survives as one of the oldest enduring religious orders and was innovative in providing a religious and social alternative to people in a variety of cultures. For over a millennium in East Asia the Buddhist nunnery was the only escape for women from a sometimes brutal, male-dominated social order. Also, most of the time monastics were excused from being drafted into the army because political leaders came to recognize the monastic rule of nonviolence for monks.

The rules of nonviolence, voluntary poverty, and chastity were exceptional also because the Buddha's definition of purity was universal: the rules applied equally to everyone regardless of caste and social distinctions. The Buddha insisted that these moral standards were more important social criteria than birth or power or knowledge, that character counted more than caste. Although the Buddha did not overtly challenge the idea of caste as a social hierarchy, he did challenge its membership criteria based on birth. Instead, he substituted an emphasis on character, and claimed that his followers were the "true brahmin."[2]

The *Dhammapada* is an early summary of Buddhist teaching that has become a classic for all Buddhists. The opening verses of the Pali version begin by focusing on the mind of the individual. However, an alternative *Dhammapada* text in Prakrit, found in Gandhara, has a different arrangement of its verses and does not begin with a focus on mind, but with a social critique:

> Not by matted hair, nor by family, nor by birth does one become a brahmana; but in whom there exist both truth and righteousness, pure is he, a brahmana is he.

> What is the use of your matted hair, O witless man! What is the use of your antelope garment? Within you are full (of passions), without you embellish.

> If from anybody one should understand the Doctrine preached by the Fully Enlightened One, devoutly should one reverence him, as a brahmana reveres the sacrificial fire.[3]

These verses represent a social revolution in ancient India by rejecting the criteria of religious posturing and birth for the caste system. Instead, the new measure of worthiness, the new criteria for respect and sanctity, were inner understanding and purity based on the Buddhist morality of noninjury and nonattachment. This same effort to rank people by their moral quality and understanding rather than by their birth or posturing was taught by Socrates in the West and by Confucius in China, who also challenged the established criteria for their social structures.[4] The emphasis on universal morality, instead of family and clan connections, was an important advance in human culture in the development of peacework.

Even though the Buddha emphasized inner, spiritual achievements within his own community (sangha), internal group decisions were to be based on consensus and equality, not on authority or tradition or lineage or spiritual attainment. As a result, the Buddhist sangha represents one of the earliest examples of radical democracy in which decisions were final only when everyone agreed.[5] With his disciples, the Buddha formed a new kind of society, an alternative community, that transcended cultural and social distinctions.

The Buddha was also a social activist beyond his community of monastics. In the first years of his teaching career, the Buddha made a point of visiting the kings of the two most powerful states in his region, Bimbisara and Pasenadi. These kings became the Buddha's disciples, and as a result influenced thousands of their citizens toward the Buddha's path.[6] While enjoying the privacy of forest retreats, the Buddha also traveled into outlaw territory to pacify the most notorious mass murderer of the day, Angulimala.[7] Also, it is well known that when the Sakya clan and the Koliyas were about to go to war over the use of water from the Rohini River, the Buddha intervened on the battlefield to avoid conflict.[8]

The basic principle underlying Buddhist social activism is dependent origination, meaning that "We are all interdependent and share an inescapable responsibility for the well-being of the entire world" (Ven. Kosan). The sangha not only was open to all castes, but actively went out into society to help others. In the first year of his teaching when the Buddhist community was just beginning and consisted of only 60 monks, the Buddha sent them forth:

> Go forth, monks, for the good of the many, for the happiness of the many, out of compassion for the world, for the benefit, for the good, for the happiness of gods and men. (*Mahavagga, Vinaya* 1.11.1)[9]

NON-MONASTIC BUDDHIST ORGANIZATIONS (NMBOS) AND VIOLENCE

The Buddha himself was not free from controversy and was called a widow-maker and son-stealer for attracting men to leave their family life to take up his homeless path. Although the Buddha left his family and many of his followers became monks, not all became homeless. The Buddha gave considerable advice to laity, and the early scriptures record the names of 21 householders who were enlightened without ever becoming monks.[10] The Buddha required the cultivation of inner freedom, not monasticism, and lay followers have always played important roles.

The Buddha also planned ahead for the social continuity of his community. When a wealthy banker, Anathapindika, donated a park to the Buddha that had formerly been owned by the son of King Pasenadi, the Buddha did not take personal ownership but asked that it be made available to members of his order in the present and future. By accepting property, the Buddha encumbered his followers with new social and economic responsibilities in managing the land. The political and economic arrangements made by the Buddha furthered his influence and provided support for the

203

members of his community, but also led to other organizations not defined by the monastic rules.

After the death of the Buddha, lay devotion at stupas (reliquaries of saints) became a major form of Buddhist practice as seen in later Mahayana Buddhist scriptures. Stupas evolved into temples whose major role was to provide opportunities for lay devotionalism. Buddhism involved not only individual behavior, such as meditating, teaching, healing, and removing suffering in a one-to-one encounter, but also social arrangements. Even though the temple services were led by monks or nuns, their organization was often in the hands of laity. While early Buddhism laid down explicit rules for monastics, there were no uniform guidelines for stupas and temples, and their styles, practices, and organizations differed greatly across cultures.

In China, the common practice involved a few, large monasteries that trained monastics who then served in the far more numerous temples scattered across the country in villages and on private estates.[11] Traditional Buddhist practice impacted society not just through the monasteries and temples, but also through a diversity of auxiliary organizations that arose in connection with local temples. In every Buddhist society practice evolved into temples and charities, hospitals and schools, orphanages and pawnshops. However, non-monastic Buddhist organizations (NMBOs) lacked uniform codes in the vinaya and differed across cultures because of different cultural influences and heavy government controls.

Until recent times, governments in Asia have tightly restricted religious organizations. Since monastics and monasteries were visible and easily controlled because of their strict vows of poverty, celibacy, nonviolence, distinctive dress, and shaved heads, governments have tolerated them. The opposite is true of independent lay Buddhist movements (NMBOs) in society, which have been perpetually suppressed in Asia as politically threatening. Lay Buddhist organizations have survived only when they served as supporters of monasteries or as devotional groups led by priests in local temples.

Buddhist practice in the monastery was designed to bring peace to individual monastics. By limiting Buddhist organizations to the monastery, governments prevented Buddhism from developing social institutions that could challenge them politically, although there were exceptions.[12] By outlawing monastic activities outside the monasteries and restricting lay organizations, the state maintained its power, but greatly limited Buddhist peacework.

During the last millennium, an increasing number of independent lay Buddhist associations (NMBOs) emerged in East Asia based on devotion to Amida Buddha, Guanyin Bodhisattva, and the *Lotus Sutra*. In China they were known as People of the Way or White Lotus Buddhism and were marked by social inclusivism.[13] Religious practice was combined with vegetarianism and charity work, such as building hostels, famine relief, and the repair of roads, canals, and bridges. Sometimes leaders such as Nichiren (1222-1282) in Japan and Luo-qing (1443-1527) in China were openly critical of state-supported monastic Buddhism.

Not unlike the emergence of Protestant groups in Europe that sometimes were violently persecuted, lay Buddhism in East Asia also suffered violence, and sometimes even responded in kind. In the sixteenth century in Japan, there was a series of uprisings by Pure Land practitioners (*Ikkoo ikki*) and Lotus devotees (*Hokke ikki*),[14] and White Lotus uprisings in China in the sixteenth to nineteenth centuries.[15] The lack of a strong grounding in Buddhist social principles for all NMBOs meant that lay Buddhists sometimes deviated from their nonviolent origins and became embroiled in the power struggles of their society like everyone else.[16]

Only in this century as new constitutional governments and separate legal systems spread in Asia, have Buddhists been able to greatly increase NMBOs and peacework. It is striking how many new Buddhist organizations are developing in recent times when government restrictions have been relaxed, but it is also important to remember that many Buddhists still live in dangerous situations. In Vietnam, Burma, Tibet, and mainland China, Buddhists are censured, some Buddhist activities are outlawed, and some leaders imprisoned. In the last 60 years, most Buddhist cultures have suffered invasion, revolution, and civil war, so that most Buddhists have experienced the denial of their human rights at one time or another. It is important to remember, therefore, that many of the Buddhist programs presented in this volume are still in the stage of recovering from suppression and have not evolved out of the safety of generations of religious freedom as enjoyed by Christian groups in the West.

205

Based on Buddhist principles, violence is not an option for NMBOs. In 1967, after a four-month period in which six members of the School of Youth for Social Service (founded by Thich Nhat Hanh) were killed and others wounded, the staff and students read this pledge at a funeral:

> Now, once again, we solemnly promise never to hate those who kill us, above all never to use violence to answer violence, even if the antagonists see us as enemies and kill until they annihilate us. We recall our pledge that people, no matter what their origins, never are our enemies.... Help us to keep steadily this nonviolent mind in our social work by love that asks nothing in return.[17]

Thich Nhat Hanh emphasizes that the enemies of Buddhists are not other people. The enemies are greed, anger, and ignorance. The enemies are patterns of denial and structures of privilege. The enemies are silence and fear. The enemies are not other people.

BUDDHIST SOCIAL PRINCIPLES

The *Mahaparinibbana Sutta* (*Digha-nikaya* 16.1) records that the Buddha used seven criteria to evaluate the social strength of the Vajjian society by asking if they:

1. held regular and frequent assemblies;

2. met, dispersed, and conducted their business in harmony;

3. did not authorize what had not been authorized by their ancient tradition;

4. respected, revered, and saluted the elders among them and valued their words;

5. didn't forcibly abduct wives and daughters of others nor take them captive;

6. respected, revered, and saluted the shrines at home and abroad, and didn't withdraw the proper support given before;

7. gave proper provisions for the safety of Buddhist Arhats so that they could live in comfort, and so that other Arhats might come to live there in the future.[18]

Certain of these rules are to be expected—such as, support for the sangha, respect for elders, and respect for women in other families—but there is a remarkable insistence on maintaining traditions, both secular and religious. This principle reinforces the exceptional nonsectarian nature of early Buddhist teaching.[19] In

206

addition, there is the insistence on regular and frequent assemblies conducted in harmony and leading to harmonious settlements. A similar norm was applied to sangha meetings that used the rule of consensus for all decisions, making the sangha the epitome of democracy since everyone had a voice and everyone had to agree on all decisions.

Compassion is a gift of the human heart and cannot be manipulated. However, social processes are necessary, and some are better than others, in helping people evolve a sense of trust and universal responsibility. The Buddha recommended "regular and frequent meetings" that are convened, conducted, and concluded with consensus. The modern code words for this activity are nurturing diversity and dialogue. Compromise can be another word for consensus.

The practice of suffusing the four directions with compassion was an early Buddhist practice. Kindness arises not just through inner mindfulness, but requires human interaction. Empathy develops first in the family, then among friends, and then with a wider range of humans and other beings. Empathy does not depend on organizations, but it does depend on the processes of our interactions. Compassion arises when the ego boundaries are softened in trust and sharing, when others trust their pain to you and you are open and able to feel it. This process is not a solitary event.

The Buddha's teachings always occurred in a social setting that involved question and answer, but not dialogue. The interchange was always unequal and the Buddha is presented as the authoritative teacher. Nevertheless, the arrangements he recommended for others were very different. The inner processes of mindfulness are to be balanced and inwardly transforming. Similarly, his advice to hold regular and frequent assemblies that are to be conducted in harmony, and his requirement of biweekly uposatha meetings of the sangha where decisions are to be made by consensus, imply transforming dialogue. Only through careful and penetrating discussion, sharing of motivations, and mutual adjustment of participants to the values and needs of each other, can consensus arise and harmony result for the benefit of the common good.

Very few people have as much experience with interreligious dialogue as Hans Ucko, who was responsible for facilitating and over-

207

seeing Jewish-Christian-Muslim dialogue for the World Council of
Churches in Geneva. Yet the Buddhist-Christian Symposium held
in July 1994 in Switzerland[20] came as a big surprise to him. I have
described his response as follows:

> He commented to me that in most dialogue meetings between
> Christians and Jews, or between Christians and Muslims, the part-
> ners came with clearly articulated theological positions and attempted
> to persuade the others of the validity of their viewpoints. In con-
> trast, the technique used by the directors of the 1994 Symposium,
> Pia Gyger and Niklaus Brantschen, was to break the Symposium
> into small groups which began with personal sharing by each per-
> son of their inner thoughts on that day. Instead of being challenged
> by the others, the response invariably was an empathetic sharing of
> similar or complementary inner experiences by others in our group
> that clarified and expanded the inner experience by placing it in an
> interfaith context. Hans Ucko found this group of interfaith seek-
> ers and sharers to be in profound dialogue, but unusual because of
> its mutual sympathy and support.[21]

It is no accident that the conference directors, Sister Pia Gyger and
Father Niklaus Brantschen, are ordained Catholics, but also Zen
practitioners and teachers. The process of dialogue did not focus
on comparing doctrine, but was a sharing of the concerns of people.
Dialogue in the Buddhist mode requires awareness and mindfulness that is mutually transforming and integrating, and is very different from discussion and debate. As the factors and relationships
in personal reflections are revealed, absolutes are left behind, new
interpersonal connections become possible, and integration in the
midst of diversity can arise.

Mindfulness training was the method developed by the Buddha
to develop inner peace, but regular and frequent dialogue leading
to consensus was his method for social well-being.

DIALOGUE AS THE PRACTICE OF SOCIAL MINDFULNESS

Dialogue takes Buddhist mindfulness practices into the social
sphere. It is a way to become aware of the different social factors
involved in our shared world to develop a more inclusive understanding and to create new choices for action.

Buddhist mindfulness has two dimensions: calming and focusing
one's mind (*samatha*) and seeing the interdependent and transitory

nature of all things (*vipassana*). *Samatha* temporarily mutes external factors so that people can see the role of their mental and emotional habits in shaping their perception and creates a psychic space where people can experiment with alternative ways of viewing and reacting to the world. For the Buddhist, these alternative ways of thinking must involve *vipassana*, namely, recognizing the interdependency and impermanence of each external object and inner personal experience. Seeing our interconnectedness and impermanence naturally leads to a sense of our common ground that leads in turn to empathy and compassion.

The Buddha's meditation methods consisted of recognizing a plurality of forces that shape our expectations, our habits, and our decisions. He challenged his culture's emphasis on a permanent, controlling ego (*atman*) that should be in charge. Rather, he demonstrated how our inner self was constructed through many factors in the learning processes that work together to construct a moment of consciousness. He showed how these processes inevitably lead to conflict and misery when a single factor becomes dominant, but that conflict can be dissolved through noticing the different elements shaping our consciousness and recognizing that attachment to only one way of perceiving inevitably leads to misery.

The good news is that by developing this inner transparency and inner dialogue about our perceptions, we discover that there are choices about how to construct our awareness, and that there are peaceful and nonpeaceful ways to perceive and respond to our world. Mindfulness training is a method to defuse our ego, our hurts, and our attachments, and a way to find sympathy and compassion with others, and an arena for discovering creative new options.

The Buddha taught that by taking time out from reacting to events and by using the disciplines of morality, mindfulness, and wisdom, his followers could discover that peace depends not so much on what happened to them, but on what attitude, understanding, and reaction they give to these events. The discovery that inner peace depends on our choices about our interpretation and attitude toward external events constituted a major turning point in human history and continues to constitute a major turning point in individual lives.

Just as mindfulness training requires stopping normal activities (*samatha*) to see the factors that make up our awareness (*vipassana*), so developing compassion requires taking time out to become aware of beings other than oneself. To be effective rather than indulgent, compassion needs to be facilitated, nurtured, and guided by "regular and frequent" dialogue.

Today in business management, the old command model of top-down management has been replaced by an emphasis on teamwork and nurturing horizontal relationships. When a group has a controlling person, inevitably conflict will arise. In the political sphere, dictatorships in the twentieth century have killed more people than all the killing in previous human history.[22] Peace requires checks and balances, participation in decision making, and the recognition of diversity. Inner peace requires seeing the pluralism within, and social peace requires recognizing and collaborating with the pluralism without.

The mindfulness practices of Buddhism remain the major form of peacework and shape everything else. One reason that the Dalai Lama received the Nobel Peace Prize was his unusual reaction to the Chinese brutalization of his people. Instead of anger and violence, the Dalai Lama found common ground with the Chinese. He emphasized that the Chinese are just like him, they want to get rid of suffering and to find happiness. His capacity to find alternative ways of understanding and responding to the hurts of the world have convinced him that all people can develop a heart of compassion.

Dialogue is mindfulness training at the social level. It is not a discussion about external issues, but a sharing of personal experiences that opens awareness to the range of human factors involved in social decisions. In that way, dialogue requires an exploration of one's motivations and the motivations of others.

Robert Aitken says that "enlightenment is an accident, but meditation helps one to be accident prone." Similarly, compassion is a gift, but dialogue is an invitation for gift exchange.

210   **HUMAN RIGHTS AND BUDDHIST SOCIAL MORALITY**

Dialogue is not enough. Dialogue requires mutual respect, equality, and willing partners. So long as governments or corporations control the media, communication technology will not bring peace, parity, and freedom. Modern technology in this century has facilitated the brutality of dictators as well as the compassion of peacemakers. Dialogue is a practice that needs a suitable context. Note, for example, that Jiang Zemin has refused to meet with the Dalai Lama. Aung San Suu Kyi is still under police restrictions. Willing dialogue partners are not there.

Buddhist morality is not enough. The Buddhist precepts apply to individual purity and the Mahayana bodhisattva precepts offer only general encouragement for universal compassion, caring for the sick, and treating all people, including enemies, as family relatives. However, the special problems of organized society, of structural violence, of social oppression and environmental degradation, are not adequately addressed.[23] In his acceptance speech for the 1989 Nobel Peace Prize, the Dalai Lama said:

> Peace, in the sense of the absence of war, is of little value to someone who is dying of hunger or cold. It will not remove the pain of torture inflicted on a prisoner of conscience. It does not comfort those who have lost their loved ones in floods caused by senseless deforestation in a neighboring country. Peace can only last where human rights are respected, where the people are fed, and where individuals and nations are free....

> Responsibility does not only lie with the leaders of our countries or with those who have been appointed or elected to do a particular job. It lies with each of us individually....What is important is that we each make a sincere effort to take seriously our responsibility for each other and for the natural environment.[24]

The Dalai Lama is very aware of the complex problems of our globe and urges each person to develop a sense of universal responsibility. Daisaku Ikeda similarly encourages and tries to prepare members of Soka Gakkai to be world citizens. But both the Dalai Lama and Daisaku Ikeda do much more. They offer concrete proposals and guidelines for governments to adopt. And they both appeal to and support the United Nations and the Declaration of Human Rights.

Scholars have argued that Buddhism has no doctrine of human rights and, technically, they are right. At a metaphysical level, Buddhist teaching has always rejected the concept of an unchanging, substantial self. But the Buddha warned not to take doctrines too seriously. At a practical level, human rights have been strongly affirmed by contemporary Buddhists such as the Dalai Lama, Sulak Sivaraksa, Maha Ghosananda, Daisaku Ikeda, and others. Human rights were not written in the heavens by gods, but constructed in history by mortals. They have no more, and no less, authority than the growing consensus of the human community about political limits to protect each of us, and social goals for all of us. As a metaphysical doctrine they are inadequate, but as social norms they are an invaluable and necessary tool for Buddhist peacework.

Most Buddhists in Asian countries have suffered invasion, civil war, or oppressive political regimes in recent times. The Buddhist leaders in this book make clear the classic Buddhist social teaching of the inherent dignity and spiritual equality of all people, the importance of having compassion for the suffering of others, and the necessity of including all people in the decision-making process. Human rights may not be inherent in people in a metaphysical sense, but they are strongly supported by Buddhist leaders as a negotiated social contract based on fairness and respect since everyone wants freedom from arbitrary arrest and imprisonment, health, food, self-esteem, and education.[25]

Human progress has not been biological, but technological and institutional. While as consumers we are well aware of technological advances, none of our authors has mentioned the remarkable advances in legal safeguards for people in this century that have given new freedom to Buddhists to develop social programs. Although Buddhist thinkers have been critical of all absolutes, including legal ones, the practical benefits of law as social contract are an important part of peacework by stabilizing social compromise. Although the Buddhist tradition has been very good in its prohibitions and very idealistic in its emphasis on universal responsibility, it has been rather weak in the intermediate steps of social responsibility—education, health, employment, welfare, and cultural development. This "middle path" needs much more attention by Buddhists. Fortunately, it is in this middle area where many of the new contributions of Buddhist peacework are being made, especially as seen in this book.

The 30 articles of the *Universal Declaration of Human Rights* have a remarkable parallel to the threefold morality of Mahayana

Buddhism: do no evil, cultivate good, and save all beings. The French jurist Karel Vasak saw the three values of the French Revolution (liberty, equality, and fraternity) as representing three levels or "generations" of human rights. The human rights articles consist of prohibitions that protect individuals from governments (2-21), those that nurture individuals in their economic, social, and cultural relationships (22-27), and those that affirm the need for a global order (28-30). This structural affinity with Mahayana ethics, as well as the importance of human rights in Buddhist liberation movements and peacework, and the global spread of human rights as a shared standard, is making the *Universal Declaration of Human Rights* an essential new pillar of social ethics for contemporary Buddhists.

When the Diem regime outlawed public celebration of Wesak in Vietnam in 1963, thousands of Buddhists resisted nonviolently in public gatherings. The resulting arrests, torture, and killing of practitioners were detailed in a 45-page report on human rights violations submitted to the government by a Buddhist delegation. The appeal to human rights as a standard that is recognized worldwide has been a major advance of human civilization in the twentieth century. But it is the picture of Thich Quang Duc enveloped in flames at a Saigon intersection in 1963 that has seared itself into our collective global consciousness. Nonviolent political protest reported widely by the media has transformed our cultures. Legal protection of individuals is the first level of human rights and Buddhist morality. But the second and third levels of human rights and Buddhist morality require mutual responsibility and global awareness that involve personal and cultural transformation that are emphasized by Buddhist peacework.

SMALL GROUPS AND SOFT POWER

Today we are at an historic turning point when telecommunications is awakening a global consciousness and people are realizing that peace is both individual and social, that our inner life connects with social processes, and many problems cannot be handled adequately by individual efforts alone.

But Buddhist peacework is different from Internet buddy groups or interest groups where people are linked by common threads. Peacework is also different from most religious groups, Buddhist

213

and otherwise, which are formed along ethnic, economic, or doctrinal lines. Instead, the Buddhist peace groups described by our authors emphasize the cultivation of trust and caring in the midst of differences, the building of common ground with those who act as enemies. This process requires openness to the other and trusting the other, which brings about personal and social transformation. The Internet may entertain and extend one's contacts, but it does not challenge and transform people, nor does it build trust.

A recurring pattern in the responses to the UNESCO declaration is the emphasis on small group experiences. Lokamitra describes the growing emergence of Buddhist social activities among the Dalit peoples of India that include hostels where poor children can stay when going to school, each run by local Buddhists. The three practices of Dalit Buddhists are: (1) to take responsibility to apply Buddhist teaching for economic independence and self-reliance; (2) to trust in spiritual friendship, Kalyana Mitrata, with other Dalit Buddhists for emotional support through hard times; and (3) to work as a team, not under a boss, toward a common goal. Ven. Karma Lekshe Tsomo also reports on the many activities in the emerging Buddhist women's movement involving local discussion groups, small conferences, and training of women leaders. Sulak Sivaraksa plants "seeds of peace" by forming small groups when there is a need or an opportunity for supporting orphaned children, or ecology, or single mothers, or interreligious cooperation for social relief, or "spirit in education."

Even though the medical relief work of the Tzu-chi Foundation of Ven. Cheng-yen has grown into the largest charity organization in Taiwan, its finances are open for all to see. It is based on volunteers who pay their own way to each relief site, and it encourages a pure mind and peaceful attitudes in each situation as the foundation of its work. "Our doctors and nurses are taught to treat patients as they would their own relatives, and to heal them in both body and mind." Ven. Cheng-yen comments that her book *Still Thoughts* was written "in order to plant the seeds of compassion and great love in every student." Her attitudes of humility and modesty, and her sharing of power, encourage personal attention and caring in all interactions. The activities of the Buddhist Peace

Fellowship, the Naropa Institute, the retreats of the Ven. Joen's Chontac Buddhist Order, or of Ven. Sheng-yen's sangha as a "meditative community," all emphasize the quality of one's attitudes in action. "We believe that 'engaged Buddhism' begins by engaging one's own mind, in one's own space," writes Ven. Sheng-yen. This "grassroots Buddhism" emerges in whatever situation arises, whether in a factory, school, family, or neighborhood.

The work of Sarvodaya is now expanding to include micro enterprises and more than 300 micro banks, soon to become 3,000 micro banks, to encourage villages to develop interdependence across racial, religious, and ethnic lines. To get a loan from a Village Development Bank, five or six others have to be the guarantors. There is no collateral required for the poor, and their guarantors may be Buddhists, Hindus, Christians, or Muslims or Sinhalese or Tamils. Dr. Ariyaratne writes in his essay about the role of micro banks in community building:

> By this process an immense trust and personal bond is created among different communities. Instead of having conflicts between them, together they can now confront other basic issues like poverty, exploitation, environmental degradation, crimes, alcoholism, the drug problem, and other social ills. This means a cooperative effort cutting across race and religious divisions.

Economics is an essential tool of modern life, and the Sarvodaya Movement is making it an instrument of individual and social integration, rather than fragmentation.

Daisaku Ikeda emphasizes that the heart of his Soka Gakkai International organization is the monthly district meeting of 20 to 40 members who share their experiences, discuss their difficulties, and offer mutual support. The remarkable ethnic diversity achieved by SGI is based on the small, caring support groups that give daily attention to new members and who make up the district meetings. Through their Buddhist practice and small group support, members find a source of interpersonal caring that often exceeds their family experience. But districts group together as areas, regions, and national organizations so that in 50 years the membership of SGI has grown to more than 10 million in 128 countries.

Daisaku Ikeda has talked about the importance of cultural

215

changes, developing new awareness through institutions of art and education, and building new friendships, as "soft power." Even though it may not seem as dramatic and substantial as armies, economics, and political legislation, Ikeda believes that soft power can change the world. And so does the Dalai Lama. In recent decades, a vivid example of the importance of soft power is the women's movement that began as persuasion and consciousness-raising through cultural events and the media, but which now has resulted in legislation and the restructuring of corporations and governments.

The primary area of Buddhist peacework is soft power, and it has three main forms: individual mindfulness, organized social development, and nonviolent resistance to structural violence. The traditional emphasis of Buddhist peacework has focused on improving human mindfulness and compassion for others—such as described by Ven. Kosan, Maha Ghosananda, Stephanie Kaza, José Cabezón, and H.H. the Dalai Lama. [26] But the most radical practice of social transformation has been inspired by the nonviolent resistance against oppression pioneered by Gandhi. Nonviolent resistance has been adopted by the Dalai Lama in exile, by the Dhammayatria monks in Thailand to protect the environment, in the civil disobedience of members of the Buddhist Peace Fellowship, and in the lives of Sulak Sivaraksa, Maha Ghosananda, and Thich Nhat Hanh. However, the most characteristic practice advocated by the new Buddhist movements has been the founding of new NMBOs to enhance human development—such as those organized by Thich Nhat Hanh, Daisaku Ikeda, Jeon Chong-yoon, Judith Simmer-Brown, Shih Cheng-yen, A.T. Ariyaratne, Robert Aitken, Shih Sheng-yen, Dhammachari Lokamitra, Karma Lekshe Tsomo, and Sulak Sivaraksa.

Since the constitutional separation of church and state in several Asian countries has meant new freedom for Buddhist social activities in recent decades, Buddhist peacework has experimented with a wide variety of new social programs. Perhaps the most successful modern example of Buddhist social renewal has been the work of A.T. Ariyaratne in the Sarvodaya Movement. Through energy sharing (*shramadana*), more effective ways have been developed to meet the collective needs of villages. In order to learn how to cooperate as a village, Sarvodaya has developed the method of a Shramadana Camp. In breaks from the common work for village needs, the participants sit in a circle and conduct "family gatherings." Ariyaratne describes these in his article:

> All religious, caste, race, linguistic, class, national or political differences are of no importance in these family gatherings. Instead meditations on loving kindness for all beings, songs, dances, and other cultural items that promote the concept of 'one world, one people' occur. Discussions related to the constructive work at hand, learning on a variety of useful subjects such as health and sanitation, and the practice of nonviolence in everyday life form the agenda of family gatherings.

Inclusion of ethnic and religious minorities is given special attention in Sarvodaya. Ariyaratne notes in his essay that in a Family Gathering "the first opportunity to observe their religion is given to the minority religious groups before the majority performs their recitation or rituals. Then together they do a common meditation."

This constant effort to be *inclusive of all voices in a balanced way* is a basic principle of Buddhist mindfulness, the foundation of social dialogue, and the basis for a shramadana camp. However, it is also a necessary practice to transform unjust power structures in daily life and a primary method for social and cultural development. For example, the practice of including diversity in a shramadana camp is extended back into village life by recognizing and organizing six different groups, called formations—children, adolescents, youth, mothers and women, farmers and craftsmen, and elders—to ensure that each constituency is heard and that leaders can develop among peers. Also, the Sarvodaya Shramadana Society of a village is formed around an executive committee that must include 25 members, including three children 7-15 years of age, three youths, and three women. As Ariyaratne observes in his essay, "In this way vested interests and domination of the society by self-centered adults are eliminated and the pursuit of the highest codes of ethics is encouraged."

Like cells in the body, however, local small groups can also be effective when clustered and networked together to form larger groups. Dr. Ariyaratne describes in his essay how local small groups become a national organization.

The initiative to build a culture of peace through people's self development at the grassroots has reached horizontally to every part of the country. Networking these villages in clusters of ten (a pioneering village, four intermediary villages and five peripheral villages) and then getting these clusters to network at divisional and district levels with a national headquarters has been accomplished. This network is active today trying to tackle people's secondary needs like those pertaining to education, health, economy, and a livable environment. Sarvodaya is also anxious to do whatever it can do to turn around the economy and technologies to promote a nonviolent society and finally to take up the issue of crimes in the country including the unnecessary war that is going on in the Northern and Eastern Provinces.

As leadership skills and methods of cooperation are developed in each formation, and integrated through the executive committee, the village can advance to legal incorporation. At that point, soft power becomes hard power.

DIALOGUE AND HARD POWER

"Hard power" means government legislation, financial corporations, and armies. The impact of hard power over all forms of life has increased dramatically in the twentieth century. New organizations have increased cultural diversity and human potential, but also offer increased opportunity for exploitation, greed, and ignorance. How the principles of the early Buddhist sangha and those applied by the Buddha to the Vajjians, and by the Sarvodaya Movement, can be implemented in global politics and economics is now a major challenge.

The challenge is to constitute a "council of all beings" that embodies global dialogue involving individuals, groups, and nonhuman species. Plant and animal life need a voice if our ecosystem is to survive, if we are to survive. Institutions are also new life forms, and are even treated as "fictive persons" in American law. Corporations and governments must also speak and listen if our globe is to evolve into a mindful community. Dialogue, transparency, accountability, and democracy are instruments of recent history that facilitate mutual participation and nourish community. But individuals need to be educated into social mindfulness to give life to these community support systems.

The market economy is an economic form of democracy where people vote with their dollars, but it also can become too centralized. It is not just Communist central planning that has failed. The massive failures of the World Bank in trying to achieve social development over the last half century reveal that a top-down approach of central economic control cannot work.[27] Only through mutual dialogue between the rich and the poor who have become the objects of centralized policies can better ways be found to build cultures of peace.

Social dialogue requires more than inner motivation; it needs new structures. For example, television licenses should require free airtime to enable people to engage in dialogue with leaders who are running for election (and who have received a substantial number of signatures of support) or with leaders in office to ensure public discussion free from financial requirements.

Corporations reluctantly take time out for meetings of shareholders, and often corporate executives try to manipulate such meetings to avoid dialogue. Governments reluctantly take time out to share information and involve the public, and often officials try to restrict information or to shape it for their own protection. Corporations cannot survive without public approval and consumer trust. Governments cannot survive without the support of their citizens. We as individuals cannot live without the love and friendship of others. We cannot be happy alone, but to maintain our togetherness, we as individuals have to be open to dialogue. Since governments and corporations need our support to survive, we can insist that they be open to dialogue. And to be open to dialogue means to be open to change.

Dialogue goes beyond discussion and brings about mutual transformation. Dialogue shares not just information, but uncovers the processes that are shaping us and the struggles we are having, and leads to mutual respect and a sense of solidarity. In dialogue we not only reveal ourselves to others, but also discover ourselves in new ways. Through dialogue we are changed.[28]

To be happy together means to be mindful, to be open to dialogue, and to be open to change. Only when we dialogue within ourselves, and among ourselves, can we get new input, find new options for action, discover new understandings, adopt new attitudes, and make new decisions for a better way. Rather than finding change to be painful, mindfulness and dialogue enable change to be joyful by providing a safe context and a way to share in the adventure of creating a better world. By helping others, we are helped. Mindfulness and dialogue offer personal cleansing and enrichment that lead to happiness as a byproduct of working together to create cultures of peace.

Even while people disagree about their lifestyles and goals, for our common good we must agree to "hold regular and frequent assemblies" and to "meet, disperse, and conduct our business in harmony." As Sulak writes, peace is a process of "finding common ground through open communication and putting into practice a philosophy of nonharm and sharing resources." This task of constant dialogue, transparency, accountability, and democracy—both as an inner mindfulness practice and as a social procedure for global survival—is at the heart of Buddhist peacework.

Several non-monastic Buddhist organizations (NMBOs) have institutionalized guidelines such as we have discussed. For example, the phrase "engaged Buddhism" was coined by Thich Nhat Hanh and became embodied in his School of Youth for Social Service and the Order of Interbeing founded during the Vietnam War. The Chontae Order in Korea was revived in 1966 and expressed the new priorities of Buddhism for society, for daily life, and for everyone. The Sarvodaya Movement was begun in Sri Lanka 41 years ago by A.T. Ariyaratne and is dedicated to the principles of nonviolence and energy sharing (*shramadana*) for social renewal. In the last 40 years, Daisaku Ikeda has transformed Soka Gakkai from an exclusivistic movement under Nichiren Shoshu to one dedicated to dialogue. To build a community of concern, he has published many books on meetings with world leaders dedicated to building peace. He has also established institutes and schools to ensure that his peaceful ideals become translated into helping people become world citizens.

There are many other groups not represented in our book. Won Buddhism began in 1916 in Korea as a reform movement and now is active with the UN and in interfaith dialogue. The Rissho Koseikai (RKK) is a lay Buddhist group founded in Japan in the 1930s by

Nikkyo Niwano that now has several million members dedicated to dialogue. In response to an initiative by Christian Unitarians, the RKK jointly sponsored the World Conference on Religion and Peace (WCRP) that first met in 1970 in Kyoto. RKK has become the main institutional support for several other interfaith organizations, such as the International Association for Religious Freedom (IARF) and the Federation of New Religious Organizations of Japan (Shinshuren). Several members of the WCRP in Europe were active in shaping the UNESCO declaration. Each year RKK presents a Niwano Peace Prize, frequently to non-Buddhists. But dialogue is also encouraged on economic issues as seen in the WCRP/ Europe Assembly held in Budapest in 1997 on "Religions for a Just Economic Order." Followup events included a seminar with British government officials on debt relief for poorer nations (September 22, 1998) and a meeting with European officials in Brussels (October 14-16, 1998) that led to the WCRP/International President being appointed to represent WCRP's moral and ethical concerns to the European Commission on a regular basis. These and other activities are reported in the main English-language journal of RKK, *Dharma World*, that is subtitled *For Living Buddhism and Interfaith Dialogue.*

BUDDHIST INSTITUTIONAL REFORM?

The two greatest instruments affecting the well-being of society and the planet are governments and corporations, but the three major collections of Buddhist bodhisattva precepts do not deal with political and economic institutions.[29] If Buddhists are motivated by compassion for others and wish to develop Buddhism for everyday life and for everybody, then the institutional structure of politics and economics are two important areas that need Buddhist attention.

Politics. Buddhists have organized themselves for political power in several countries in this century (Sri Lanka, Japan, and Tibet), but today most Buddhists affirm that peace is best served by the institutional separation of religious groups from government. Many Buddhists today enjoy freedom of practice under the legal protection of the separation of religious groups and government, although

221

.
.
.
.

Buddhists in Vietnam, Burma, North Korea, and the People's Republic of China are still suppressed. To my knowledge, Buddhists have never held international meetings to work together against repressive regimes. Instead, nonsectarian human rights groups such as the Campaign for Tibet work for political change. Only four Buddhist groups are even registered as NGOs with the United Nations,[30] and Buddhist groups have generally avoided political activity.

Rudolph Rummel has estimated that 203 million people have been killed in the twentieth century, the vast majority (169 million) not from war, but at the hands of nondemocratic governments, more than all those killed in previous human history. After this century of butchery, the evidence is clear that dictatorships are deadly: "Totalitarian communist governments slaughter their people by the tens of *millions*; in contrast, many democracies can barely bring themselves to execute even serial murderers."[31] Since Buddhists are committed to peace and nonviolence, and since violence is prevented by democracy and the sharing of power, it seems clear that Buddhists ought to support democracy whenever they can.

Rather than working to gain control of the government, Buddhist groups now generally accept their role as promoting the social and cultural development of people, and encourage them to be responsible citizens who individually assume political and economic roles. But one area where Buddhist organizations do have political responsibility is in the structure of their own organizations. Based on the social principles of early Buddhism, and on the nonviolence of democratic government, certain institutional guidelines emerge. (1) Buddhists must be committed to democracy. (2) To make democracy effective, Buddhists must support open access to information (transparency) and the sharing of power. (3) If Buddhists are committed to democracy and transparency in politics, then they also must nurture democracy and transparency in their own Buddhist organizations to cultivate democratic methods in their practitioners. Since many Buddhist organizations still follow traditional Asian cultural patterns rather than the principles recommended by the Buddha, a task for the future is to increase internal dialogue, transparency, accountability, and democracy within Buddhist organizations themselves.

Economics. Today nations have been replaced by transnational corporations (TNCs) as the source of life or devastation for large numbers of people. The income of the top 200 TNCs is greater than the personal income of 80 percent of the world's population, and their wealth is greater than the combined economies of 182 countries.[32] And TNCs are growing. Between 1980 and 1995, the number of TNCs increased from 7,000 to more than 40,000. "Today, 50 of the top 100 economies in the world are TNCs, 70 percent of global trade is controlled by just 500 corporations, and a mere one percent of the TNCs on this planet own half the total stock of foreign direct investment."[33] The quality of life of people is affected by the global economy more than by any other single factor. And a small number of corporations are becoming the dominant lifeforms of our age.

The challenge for all of us is whether corporations as organisms can develop peaceful cultures based on internal and external dialogue, or whether they will be driven by greed and ignorance. The complexities of corporate law and institutional procedures are bewildering and often parasitic. Learning how to apply Buddhist mindfulness, wisdom, and morality to corporate lifeforms in order to promote economic fairness and compassion are challenges that are crucial for the future well-being of society and the environment. The Dalai Lama recently observed:

> Economic inequality, especially that between developed and developing nations, remains the greatest source of suffering on the planet. Even though they will lose money in the short term, large multinational corporations must curtail their exploitation of poor nations. Tapping the few precious resources such countries possess simply to fuel consumerism in the developed world is disastrous; if it continues unchecked, eventually we shall all suffer. Strengthening weak, undiversified economies is a far wiser policy for promoting both political and economic stability. As idealistic as it may sound, altruism, not just competition and the desire for wealth, should be a driving force in business.[34]

As the Buddhist sangha spread across Asian cultures, it became one of the world's first transnational corporations. The study of Buddhist economics has been sporadic,[35] but as Buddhist organizations become freed from government interference, a major task will

223

be to evaluate their own corporate social responsibility. Several consumer groups monitor corporations, such as the Council on Economic Priorities (CEP) that was founded in 1969 as a nonprofit research organization, to analyze the social and environmental records of corporations. The assumption is that consumers who have a choice of products will choose to buy from those corporations which are the most responsible in supporting the common good. The criteria used to rate corporations include their environmental records, their charitable giving back to the community, their outreach to support community programs, the support of equality for women in training, promotion, and salaries, the encouragement of ethnic diversity and minorities, family benefits, workplace safety, and open disclosure of information about policies and finances. In 1994 the CEP published a book called *Shopping for a Better World* that compared 2,000 products from more than 200 companies in terms of their record of social responsibility.[36] In addition, since 1986 CEP has publicly recognized those corporations that are seeking to benefit the common good by giving them Corporate Conscience Awards that are widely publicized. In collaboration with *Fortune*, a leading business magazine, CEP researched and published a list of the "50 Best Companies for Asians, Blacks, and Hispanics."[37] In its March/April 1999 "Research Report," CEP also published a study of "Japan's Best Companies," based on a list of ten categories for social responsibility. How would Buddhist organizations rate if the CEP conducted a similar survey on them?

Another peace activity for Buddhist institutions could be to use its wealth to influence corporations. The Interfaith Center on Corporate Responsibility (ICCR) was formed almost 30 years ago and today includes 275 Protestant, Roman Catholic, and Jewish institutional investors worth an estimated US $90 billion, largely representing pension funds. As a result, ICCR representatives can attend meetings of stockholders and request that corporate policies be changed to be more socially responsible. For example, in 1998 ICCR representatives presented 209 social responsibility resolutions to 143 companies. Their list of resolutions is circulated as a model for other concerned citizens, and they conduct fact-finding reports on various industries.[38] A few Buddhist efforts are beginning, such as the

Alternatives to Consumerism project of Sulak Sivaraksa, but ICCR is still waiting to have its first Buddhist member.

Another means of influencing social consciousness is by providing community information on the working conditions of laborers in poorer countries who are suppliers for TNCs like Sears, Wal-Mart, Nike, Reebok, and so on. In the past, industries were localized and could be held accountable. Today, the international social network of Buddhists is starting to monitor and advertise virtuous and exploitative companies through its periodicals such as *Turning Wheel, Seeds of Peace,* and *Tricycle,* but much more needs to be done.[39]

A stimulus to develop new forms of Buddhism has often come from openness to other religions. Shih Cheng-yen began her medical relief programs partially in response to a question by Christian nuns asking why Buddhists were not more socially active. Sulak Sivaraksa was influenced by Christian schools. Buddhist hospice work follows the lead of Christian hospice efforts. Recently Bataa Mishigish, a Mongolian Buddhist monk, was able to study English in the United States and win a fellowship at the East-West Center because of initial support from Mormons. Since 1989 when Buddhism was freed from Communist suppression in Mongolia, the number of monasteries and temples has grown from one to more than 140, but recently the interest in Buddhism from young people has dropped since the traditional Buddhist practices are not meeting the emerging social needs of Mongolia. Bataa was helped through the program of mission service that sent Mormon youth to Mongolia. Perhaps a Buddhist Peace Corps is needed to provide avenues for the idealism and energy of Buddhist youth to go to places like Mongolia and for Mongolians to travel abroad in the international arena. Crosscultural experience is another form of dialogue that is needed to develop world citizens and a balanced global community.

Most Buddhist writings give a great deal of attention to peace through meditation and compassion by individuals. However, given the impact of governments and corporations on the well-being of the planet, Buddhist organizations now have an important responsibility to help others by developing Buddhist social principles for our institutional structures.[40]

CONCLUSION

In medieval China, Tiantai Zhiyi (538-597) summarized the path of the Buddhist practitioner in four vows, known today as the Great Bodhisattva Vows. Some have said that the first and third are to help others, and the second and fourth are to benefit oneself:

Beings are infinite in number,
I vow to save them all.
Obstructions are endless,
I vow to end them all.
The opportunities are innumerable,
I vow to learn them all.
Buddhahood is supreme,
I vow to embody it fully.

Today the innumerable opportunities for creating a peaceful world include specific social practices of dialogue, transparency, consensus building, mutual accountability, and democracy. Based on the essays in this book, a set of ten Buddhist peace principles emerge:

1. Buddhist morality is based on three principles: avoiding harm, cultivating good, and taking responsibility for freeing all beings.

2. Not harming means not hurting others; it also means actively protecting the integrity of each person and species in the ecosystem in accord with the Declaration of Human Rights and the Earth Charter.

3. Cultivating good means creating inner peace and outer compassion by seeing the diversity within ourselves and our interdependence with others which defuses the ego and finds common ground.

4. Freeing all beings means nurturing the well-being of others based on eco-social mindfulness developed by "regular and frequent" meetings conducted fairly and harmoniously.

5. Social harmony is built on small group dialogue where diversity can be expressed and common ground found by sharing the inner factors and conditions that lead to decisions and actions, not by primarily focusing on the decisions and actions themselves.

6. Harmonious meetings require procedures in which authority is shared, responsibility is distributed, participation is balanced, and decisions are democratic.

7. The sharing of power in society requires legal structures of checks and balances and open communication of information to monitor structural violence.

8. A just world requires a fair distribution of resources based on regular and accessible reports on financial and ecological resources locally, globally, and institutionally.

9. Institutions—governmental, economic, and religious—are new life forms and must participate in these same processes of open communication to find common ground and to support diversity, as well as to create and monitor a fair sharing of resources.

10. Creating a peaceful culture requires constantly learning from the diversity of oneself and others in a council of all beings to spark creativity for developing new possibilities.

This volume reflects the new Buddhist emphasis on social processes for bringing peace that extends the traditional monastic practice of inner mindfulness. In the 1930s in India, Mahatma Gandhi emphasized eradicating the caste system through "a change of heart," but the former untouchable, B.R. Ambedkar, worked for legal safeguards to effect change. Institutional changes were important to him both politically and personally. Ambedkar publicly burned those parts of the Hindu *Code of Manu* that mandated the caste system and vowed: "I was born a Hindu, but I won't die a Hindu." Later Ambedkar was chairman of the drafting committee for the constitution of India (1947-1948), and as a member of Nehru's cabinet he proposed that the Buddhist *dharmacakra* (wheel of the law) be on the Indian flag. In 1956 he publicly converted to Buddhism, followed by several million others in the next few years. Ambedkar argued for the end of social violence by making legal changes as well as changing individual attitudes.

Dhammachari Lokamitra is continuing Ambedkar's social revolution in the Trailokya Bauddha Mahasangha, Sahayaka Gana (TBMSG) founded in 1978. As Buddhist disciples did so many centuries ago, TBMSG members are dedicated to the liberating teaching of the Buddha, but today they are supported through new structures: legal protection, education, social development, and international support. Yes, there are innumerable opportunities for benefiting others that we must learn. Yes, Gandhi was right, the caste system will not disappear without a "change of heart." But

DAVID W. CHAPPELL

Ambedkar was also right: new legal safeguards and specific social structures are needed to encourage opportunities and support this change. In creating cultures of peace, inner peace must be balanced by eco-social mindfulness and social cooperation as the heart of Buddhist peacework.

NOTES

1. For a helpful analysis of these three kinds of Buddhist models, laity, monastics, and forest renunciants, see Regninald Ray, *Buddhist Saints in India* (New York: Oxford University Press, 1994).

2. While the Buddha taught and accepted everyone regardless of caste (see Schumann, *The Historical Buddha*, 187-193), he did spend most of his time teaching the Brahmin priests, reforming and replacing them with his own disciples as the "true brahman" (see the pioneering work of Peter Masefield, *Divine Revelation in Pali Buddhism* [London: George Allen & Unwin, 1986], 1-36, 147-161, and 164-170).

3. Verses 1-3 in the Gandhari Dharmapada are equivalent to verses 393, 394, and 392 respectively in the Pali Dhammapada. See John Brough, *The Gandhari Dharmapada* (London: Oxford University Press, 1962), 290.

4. However, Buddhism also challenged Confucianism because of the Buddhist idea of rebirth in various levels of existence, from animals to gods. As a result, the Confucian focus on family and clan was broadened to apply to people and animals alike. Not eating animals has become a hallmark of Chinese and Korean Buddhism, and temple lands often served as wildlife preserves.

5. See Phramaha Chanya Khongchinda, *The Buddha's Socio-Political Ideas* (New Delhi: Navrang, 1993) and Gokuldas De, *Democracy in Early Buddhist Sangha* (Calcutta: University Press, 1955).

6. See H. W. Schumann, *The Historical Buddha*, trans. M. O'C. Walshe (London: Penguin-Arkana, 1989), 88-93 and 105-112.

7. If we rely on the surviving historical records, the Buddha's encounter with Angulimala was one of the most popular stories of early Buddhism since it survives in more versions that almost any other single early text. See the cross-index of Chinese and Pali Scriptures by Chizen Akanuma, *The Comparative Catalogue of Chinese Agamas & Pali Nikayas* (Tokyo: Hajinkaku-shobo, 1958), 168.

8. See John A. McConnell, "The Rohini Conflict and the Buddha's Intervention," in Sulak Sivaraksa et al, ed., *Radical Conservatism: Buddhism in the Contemporary World* (Bangkok: Thai Inter-Religious Commission for Development, 1990), 200-208.

9. Prayudh Payutto, "Sangha: The Ideal World Community," in Sulak Sivaraksa et al., ed., *Buddhist Perspection for Desirable Societies in the Future* (Bangkok: Thai Inter-Religious Commission for Development, 1993), 276.

10. H.W. Schumann, *The Historical Buddha*, trans. M.O'C. Walshe (London: Penguin-Arkana, 1989), pp. 190-191.

11. See Holmes Welch, *The Practice of Chinese Buddhism, 1900-1950* (Cambridge: Harvard University Press, 1967).

228

12. For some studies of Buddhism as a social institution, see Peter A. Pardue, *Buddhism: A Historical Introduction to Buddhist Values and the Social and Political Forms They Have Assumed in Asia* (New York: Macmillan, 1968), R.A.L.H. Gunawardana, *Robe and Plough: Monasticism and Economic Interest in Early Medieval Sri Lanka* (Tucson, Arizona: University of Arizona Press, 1979), Yoneo Ishii, *Sangha, State, and Society: Thai Buddhism in History*, trans. Peter Hawkes (Honolulu: University of Hawaii Press, 1986), Stanley Weinstein, *Buddhism Under the Tang* (Cambridge: Cambridge University Press, 1987) and Jacques Gernet, *Buddhism in Chinese Society: An Economic History from the Fifth to the Tenth Century*, trans. Franciscus Verellen (New York: Columbia University Press, 1995). There were some exceptions to government-supervised monastic control—such as the growth of the Judo Shinshu movement of married priests in Japan and the military uprisings in the sixteenth century by Pure Land groups (*Ikkoo ikki*) and Nichiren groups (*Hokke ikki*), or the rule of the government of Tibet by the Dalai Lamas since 1642—but these exceptions prove the rule. See Tsepon W.D. Shakabpa, *Tibet: A Political History* (New Haven: Yale University Press, 1967), chapter 7.

13. See Daniel Overmyer, *Folk Buddhist Religion* (Cambridge: Harvard University Press, 1976).

14. See Joseph Kitagawa, *Religion in Japanese History* (New York: Columbia University Press, 1966) and Michael Solomon, "Honganji under Rennyo: The Development of Shinshu in Medieval Japan," in James Foard, Michael Solomon, and Richard Payne, eds., *The Pure Land Tradition: History and Development* (Berkeley: Berkeley Buddhist Studies Series, 1998), 399-428.

15. For the most thorough review of the different activities and interpretations of the White Lotus movements, see B.J. ter Haar, *The White Lotus Teachings in Chinese Religious History* (Leiden: E.J. Brill, 1992, reprinted by the University of Hawaii Press, 1999).

16. A classic example of the wedding of Buddhism and violence is the book of strategy by a Buddhist samurai, Miyamoto Musashi, entitled *The Book of Five Rings* (New York: Bantam Doubleday Dell, 1992) which describes how to successfully kill your opponent in sword fighting.

17. James H. Forest, *The Unified Buddhist Church of Vietnam: Fifteen Years for Reconciliation* (Hof van Sonoy, The Netherlands: International Fellowship of Reconciliation, 1987), 7. For a full account of the Buddhist peacework led by Ven. Thich Nhat Hanh in response to the war in Vietnam, see Chan Khong (Cao Ngoc Phuong), *Learning True Love: How I Learned and Practiced Social Change in Vietnam* (Berkeley: Parallax Press, 1993).

18. The sutta then reports that the Buddha recommended the first four principles to his monks, but replaced the last three with the following:

5. Do not fall prey to desires;
6. Be devoted to forest-lodgings;
7. Preserve personal mindfulness so that good companions will be attracted and will remain.

This discourse then gives several other lists focused on maintaining positive individual mental habits. Since the oral texts were preserved by monastics, it is natural that they would remember advice on their personal practices, while it is striking to see a list to prevent the decline of the Vajjin state.

19. See David W. Chappell, "Buddhist Interreligious Dialogue: To Build a Global Community," in Paul Ingram and Sallie King, *Memorial Volume for Fred Streng* (Surrey, England: Curzon, 1999), 3-35, and "Six Buddhist Attitudes Toward Other Religions," in Sulak Sivaraksa et al., ed., *Radical Conservativism: Buddhism in the Contemporary World* (Bangkok: Thai Inter-Religious Commission for Development, 1990), 443-458.

20. For a description of this event, see my report in *Buddhist-Christian Studies* 15 (1995), 239-240.

21. David Chappell, "Response to Winston King," in Sallie B. King and Paul O. Ingram, eds., *The Sound of Liberating Truth* (Surrey, England: Curzon, 1999), 58.

22. See Rudolph Rummel, *Death by Government* (New Brunswick: Transaction, 1994), 2.

23. See my "Searching for a Mahayana Social Ethic," *Journal of Religious Ethics* 24.2 (Fall 1996), 351-376 and my forthcoming "Universal Bodhisattva Ethics," in a volume honoring Ven. Jeon Un-deok of Korea, for an analysis of three major Mahayana precept scriptures.

24. Dalai Lama, "The Nobel Peace Prize Lecture, Oslo, Norway," in Sidney Piburn, ed., *The Dalai Lama: A Policy of Kindness* (Ithaca, New York: Snow Lion, 1990), 17-18.

25. See Stig Toft Modsen, *State, Society and Human Rights in South Asia* (New Delhi: Manohar, 1996), for a fuller discussion of the idea of negotiated human rights that arise out of political negotiations, rather than philosophical absolutes.

26. The Dalai Lama writes that he does not think that the problems in the world are based on faulty "social architecture" or inadequate technology, but on wrong motivation. The problem is not organizations or machinery, but within: "we have neglected to foster the most basic human needs of love, kindness, cooperation, and caring." Also, the Dalai Lama does "not believe in creating movements or espousing ideologies" or "the practice of establishing an organization to promote a particular idea." See his "Global Community and the Need for Universal Responsibility," in His Holiness the Fourteenth Dalai Lama and Fabien Ouaki, *Imagine All the People* (Boston: Wisdom Publications, 1999), 144-145.

27. See such books as Susan George and Fabrizio Sabelli, *Faith and Credit: The World Bank's Secular Empire* (San Francisco: Westview Press, 1994) and Catherine Caufield, *Masters of Illusion: The World Bank and the Poverty of Nations* (New York: Henry Holt, 1996).

28. The classic description of this process is by John Cobb, *Beyond Dialogue: Toward Mutual Transformation* (1982).

29. Even though the life of a bodhisattva is dedicated to saving all beings, the three most popular sets of bodhisattva precepts in East Asia – the Universal Bodhisattva Precepts in the *Da fangdeng tuoloni jing*, the Lay Precepts in the *Youposai jie jing*, and the Brahma-net Precepts in the *Fan-wang jing* – do not include any recommendations for institutional life. See my article on "Universal Bodhisattva Social Ethics" in the forthcoming commemorative volume for Ven. Jeon Un-deok.

230

30. The four Buddhist groups registered as NGOs with the United Nations are Rissho Koseikai, Won Buddhism, Soka Gakkai International, and the Associa-

tion of American Buddhists. The Hawaii Association of International Buddhists has applied for NGO status.

31. See Rudolph Rummel, *Death by Government* (New Brunswick: Transaction, 1994), 2. Some democracies have committed mass murder, such as the British starvation of Germans during and after World War I, or American atomic bombing of Japan, and the massacres of Filipinos during U.S. colonization at the beginning of the century. But in each case, "the killing was carried out in a highly undemocratic fashion: in secret, behind a conscious cover of lies and deceit, and by agencies and power holders that had the wartime authority to operate autonomously." (Ibid., 16)

32. These and other helpful statistics can be found in Charles Derber, *Corporation Nation* (New York: St. Martin's Press, 1998). See also David Korten, *When Corporations Rule the World* (West Hartford, CT: Kumarian Press, 1995).

33. Tony Clarke, *The Emergence of Corporate Rule and What to Do About It: A Set of Working Instruments For Social Movements* (San Francisco: International Forum on Globalization, 1996), 5.

34. The Dalai Lama, "Global Community and the Need for Universal Responsibility," in His Holiness the Fourteenth Dalai Lama and Fabien Ouaki, *Imagine All the People* (Boston: Wisdom Publications, 1999), 146.

35. For example, see Jacques Gernet, *Buddhism in Chinese Society: An Economic History from the Fifth to the Tenth Centuries* (New York: Columbia University Press, 1995).

36. The Council on Economic Priorities, *Shopping for a Better World* (San Francisco: Sierra Club Books, 1994). Membership in CEP can be obtained by writing to CEP, 30 Irving Place, New York, New York 10003-2386, Fax: 212-420-0968; e-mail cep@echonyc.com or through the internet at: http://www.accesspt.com/CEP.

37. *Fortune* (July 19, 1999).

38. The Interfaith Center on Corporate Responsibility is located at 475 Riverside Drive, Room 550, New York, New York 10115, Fax: 212-870-2023, e-mail: info@iccr.org.

39. A good source to network with various watchdog groups who track the destructive side of corporations is the monthly magazine *Multinational Monitor* founded by Ralph Nader and published by Essential Information, Inc., 1530 P Street, N.W., Washington, D.C. 20005; fax: 202-234-5176; e-mail: monitor@essential.org.

40. Representing Roman Catholic conscience, the University of Notre Dame in the United States has established a Center for Ethics and Religious Values in Business, and its co-directors, John W. Houck and Oliver F. Williams published *Is the Good Corporation Dead? Social Responsibility in a Global Economy* (Lantham, Maryland: Rowman & Littlefield, 1996). Similarly, the Harvard Divinity School has established a program on Religion & Values in Public Life that publishes regularly as an insert in the Harvard Divinity Bulletin that can be obtained free of charge from the Harvard Divinity School, 45 Francis Avenue, Cambridge, Massachusetts 02138.

REFLECTIONS ON THE *DECLARATION ON THE ROLE OF RELIGION IN THE PROMOTION OF A CULTURE OF PEACE*

Janusz Symonides

The making of peace is a topic of the utmost importance, a topic with which we have contended as long as human records have been kept. The Boston Research Center makes a significant contribution to the ongoing dialogue among religious people everywhere by making available, on this the cusp of the millennium, *Buddhist Peacework: Creating Cultures of Peace.*

Editor David Chappell has brought together representatives from all of the major Buddhist traditions to reflect on the achievement of both inner peace and global harmony. Many of the authors assembled here have suffered—and continue to suffer—greatly for their religious and political convictions. It is an ironic fact that great spiritual leaders are often the focus of sustained attack. The opportunity to hear them address directly their view of the social obligations of Buddhists carries extraordinary weight because, as Dr. Chappell indicates in his introduction, their words have moved beyond the realm of the theoretical.

In July 1989, the UNESCO International Congress, "Peace in the Minds of Men," was held in Yamoussoukro, Côte d'Ivoire. It called for the construction of "a new vision of peace by developing a peace culture." It seemed then that the end of the Cold War and of ideological confrontation between East and West created new possibilities for the United Nations' systems and for the whole of the international community to actually move toward a culture of peace.

The *Declaration on the Role of Religion in the Promotion of a Culture of Peace*, signed by so many spiritual leaders in 1994 and specifically addressed in this book, emphasizes that the present culture of war and violence based on distrust, suspicion, intolerance, discrimination, and hatred, must be replaced by a new culture based on nonviolence, tolerance, mutual understanding, solidarity, and on the ability to solve disputes and conflicts peacefully.

JANUSZ SYMONIDES is the director of UNESCO's Department of Peace, Human Rights, Democracy, and Tolerance.

In the new international atmosphere of the 1990s, UNESCO—on the initiative of its director-general Federico Mayor—has undertaken a series of activities aimed at the promotion of a culture of peace. An initial program was prepared in 1993. It provided for the elaboration of country projects aimed at the construction of a climate conducive to reconciliation in countries torn by war or civil strife. A decisive step forward was taken in 1995 when the twenty-eighth session of the General Conference adopted the Transdisciplinary Project, "Towards a Culture of Peace."

The United Nations General Assembly recognized the importance of the UNESCO project in its resolutions adopted in 1995 and 1996. In 1997, it called for the promotion of a culture of peace based on the principles of the United Nations Charter and respect for human rights, democracy, development, tolerance, and on equality between women and men. It also proclaimed the year 2000 the International Year for the Culture of Peace and the period 2001-2010 as the International Decade for a Culture of Peace and Nonviolence for the Children of the World.

A culture of peace can be constructed only through a global coalition and alliance of partners from states, the United Nations system, governmental and nongovernmental organizations, civil society, and individuals. The participation of religions and religious traditions is of vital importance. Dialogue between religions and cultures is one of the basic ingredients for any peace-building strategy because, as is often stated: "There is no peace without peace among religions."

Through the past several years, UNESCO has undertaken various initiatives in order to reflect on the possible contribution of religions to a culture of peace. The first meeting on this subject took place at the Catalunya Centre in Barcelona, Spain. During the second meeting, in 1994, the *Declaration on the Role of Religion in the Promotion of a Culture of Peace* was adopted.

The declaration acknowledges the world's cultural and religious diversity. It stresses that each culture represents a universe in itself and yet it is not a closed universe. Cultures give religions their language and religions offer ultimate meaning to each culture. No peace is possible without the recognition of pluralism and respect for diversity. Religions have contributed to the peace of the world, but they have also led to divisions, hatred, and war. The declaration speaks about the religious responsibility to promote dialogue and

234

harmony between and within religions. Participants called upon the different religious and cultural traditions to join hands together in this effort and to cooperate in spreading the message of peace. They condemned violence wherever it occurs, in particular, violence perpetrated in the name of religion.

The Barcelona declaration was endorsed by thousands of individuals and organizations, including many belonging to Buddhist, Christian, Hindu, Jewish, and Muslim religions. It is worth noting that, among the first signatories, were the Dalai Lama and the director-general of UNESCO. The declaration was widely disseminated. The text was published and favorably commented on in many journals and discussed during numerous international conferences.

Since the adoption of the Barcelona declaration, the contribution of religions to the culture of peace and interreligious dialogue has continued to receive attention in UNESCO's programs and actions. In June 1995, for example, the Organization held a meeting of experts on the Roads of Faith Project which took place in Rabat (Morocco). In June 1997, followers of three monotheistic religions and of the spiritual traditions of Hinduism, Buddhism, and Sikhism met in Malta with a view to promoting interfaith dialogue. A year later, in 1998, an important seminar on the dialogue between the three monotheistic religions took place—again in Rabat—and the Third UNESCO Seminar on the Contributions by Religions to the Culture of Peace was held in Granada (Spain). It was dedicated to the specific issue of religious education in a context of pluralism and tolerance and it built upon the principles of the Barcelona declaration.

The UNESCO-approved Programme and Budget for 1998-1999 underscores the need for strengthening the partnership with religious leaders in the framework of activities designed to promote tolerance and to encourage dialogue among religions, and the draft Programme for 2000-2001 also foresees, under the project "Spiritual Convergence and Intercultural Dialogue," the development of initiatives aimed at encouraging interreligious dialogue. A Consultative Committee for Interreligious Dialogue has also been created.

The Declaration and Programme of Action on a Culture of Peace, adopted by the United Nations General Assembly on 13 September 1999, lists religious bodies and groups among the main partners for the promotion of the culture of peace. Religious education

235

as well as religious practice and rituals provide a great potential for the rejection of violence and the promotion of a positive peace based on such values as justice, tolerance, solidarity, sharing, and love. They give a chance to develop skills of dialogue, negotiation, and nonviolent resolution of conflicts and differences. Religions may help to prevent conflicts and may also contribute greatly, through compassion, understanding, and forgiveness, to reconciliation and postconflict peace building.

Because religions may also be misused and exploited for political purposes and may lead to discrimination and violence, religious leaders and followers should stand up against aggressive nationalism and violation of the rights of religious minorities. The human family needs not only tolerance and recognition of cultural and religious diversity but also a unity, a confirmation of a common system of values, in fact, a global ethics. Religions have an extremely important role to play in this context. All faiths have a unique, irreplaceable role encouraging and guiding human beings toward the achievement of inner peace, which may well be seen as an ultimate guarantee of nonviolent stands and behavior.

The transformation of a culture of war and violence into a culture of peace and nonviolence demands the participation of everyone. Bearing this in mind, a group of Nobel Prize laureates drafted in March of 1999 at UNESCO the *Manifesto 2000 for a Culture of Peace and Nonviolence*. It contains six pledges: to respect life and human dignity; to reject violence in all its forms; to share with others; to defend freedom of expression and cultural diversity; to preserve the planet; and to rediscover solidarity. *Manifesto 2000*, which reflects so many Buddhist values, can be espoused and signed by every individual.[1] All the signatures on *Manifesto 2000* will be presented to the General Assembly of the United Nations for the millennium in September 2000.

It is highly appropriate, then, that *Buddhist Peacework*, which presents Buddhist reflections on the creation of a culture of peace and which promotes both inner peace and global harmony, is appearing during the International Year for the Culture of Peace, which was solemnly launched all over the world on 14 September 1999.

236

NOTE

1. The text of *Manifesto 2000* can be found on UNESCO's website: www.unesco.org.

Declaration on the Role of Religion in the Promotion of a Culture of Peace

We, participants in the meeting, "The Contribution by Religions to the Culture of Peace," organised by UNESCO and the Centre UNESCO de Catalunya, which took place in Barcelona from 12 to 18 December, 1994,

Deeply concerned with the present situation of the world, such as increasing armed conflicts and violence, poverty, social injustice, and structures of oppression;

Recognising that religion is important in human life;

Declare:

OUR WORLD

1. We live in a world in which isolation is no longer possible. We live in a time of unprecedented mobility of peoples and intermingling of cultures. We are all interdependent and share an inescapable responsibility for the well-being of the entire world.

2. We face a crisis which could bring about the suicide of the human species or bring us a new awakening and a new hope. We believe that peace is possible. We know that religion is not the sole remedy for all the ills of humanity, but it has an indispensable role to play in this most critical time.

3. We are aware of the world's cultural and religious diversity. Each culture represents a universe in itself and yet it is not closed. Cultures give religions their language, and religions offer ultimate meaning to each culture. Unless we recognise pluralism and respect diversity, no peace is possible. We strive for the harmony which is a the very core of peace.

4. We understand that culture is a way of seeing the world and living in it. It also means the cultivation of those values and forms of life which reflect the world-views of each culture. Therefore neither the meaning of peace nor of religion can be reduced to a single and rigid concept, just as the range of human experience cannot be conveyed by a single language.

5. For some cultures, religion is a way of life, permeating every human activity. For others it represents the highest aspirations of

human existence. In still others, religions are institutions that claim to carry a message of salvation.

6. Religions have contributed to the peace of the world, but they have also led to division, hatred, and war. Religious people have too often betrayed the high ideals they themselves have preached. We feel obliged to call for sincere acts of repentance and mutual forgiveness, both personally and collectively, to one another, to humanity in general, and to Earth and all living beings.

PEACE

7. Peace implies that love, compassion, human dignity, and justice are fully preserved.

8. Peace entails that we understand that we are all interdependent and related to one another. We are all individually and collectively responsible for the common good, including the well-being of future generations.

9. Peace demands that we respect Earth and all forms of life, especially human life. Our ethical awareness requires setting limits to technology. We should direct our efforts towards eliminating consumerism and improving the quality of life.

10. Peace is a journey—a never-ending process.

COMMITMENT

11. We must be at peace with ourselves; we strive to achieve inner peace through personal reflection and spiritual growth, and to cultivate a spirituality which manifests itself in action.

12. We commit ourselves to support and strengthen the home and family as the nursery of peace.

In homes and families, communities, nations, and the world:

13. We commit ourselves to resolve or transform conflicts without using violence, and to prevent them through education and the pursuit of justice.

14. We commit ourselves to work towards a reduction in the scandalous economic differences between human groups and other forms of violence and threats to peace, such as waste or resources, extreme poverty, racism, all types of terrorism, lack of caring, corruption, and crime.

15. We commit ourselves to overcome all forms of discrimination, colonialism, exploitation, and domination and to promote

institutions based on shared responsibility and participation. Human rights, including religious freedom and the rights of minorities, must be respected.

16. We commit ourselves to assure a truly humane education for all. We emphasise education for peace, freedom, and human rights, and religious education to promote openness and tolerance.

17. We commit ourselves to a civil society which respects environmental and social justice. This process begins locally and continues to national and transnational levels.

18. We commit ourselves to work towards a world without weapons and to dismantle the industry of war.

RELIGIOUS RESPONSIBILITY

19. Our communities of faith have a responsibility to encourage conduct imbued with wisdom, compassion, sharing, charity, solidarity, and love; inspiring one and all to choose the path of freedom and responsibility. Religions must be a source of helpful energy.

20. We will remain mindful that our religions must not identify themselves with political, economic, or social powers, so as to remain free to work for justice and peace. We will not forget that confessional political regimes may do serious harm to religious values as well as to society. We should distinguish fanaticism from religious zeal.

21. We will favour peace by countering the tendencies of individuals and communities to assume or even to teach that they are inherently superior to others. We recognise and praise the nonviolent peacemakers. We disown killing in the name of religion.

22. We will promote dialogue and harmony between and within religions, recognising and respecting the search for truth and wisdom that is outside our religion. We will establish dialogue with all, striving for a sincere fellowship on our earthly pilgrimage.

APPEAL

23. Grounded in our faith, we will build a culture of peace based on non-violence, tolerance, dialogue, mutual understanding, and justice. We call upon the institutions of our civil society, the United Nations System, governments, governmental and nongovernmental organisations, corporations, and the mass media, to strengthen

their commitments to peace and to listen to the cries of the victims and the dispossessed. We call upon the different religious and cultural traditions to join hands together in this effort, and to cooperate with us in spreading the message of peace.

Signed by the chairpersons of the session

JOAQUIM XICOY, President of the Parliament of Catalonia
FEDERICO MAYOR, Director General of UNESCO

and the following participants

MASAO ABE, Kyoto School of Zen Buddhism
SALEHA ABEDIN, Institute for Muslim Minority Affairs
ANTOINE ABI-GHANEM, Centre de Recherché sur les Droits de
    l'Homme et de las Famille, Faculté de Droit de Byblos, Liban
JOAN ALBAIGÉS, Centre UNESCO de Catalunya
AHMED SIDQI AL-DAJANI, Arab Organisation for Human Rights
M. ARAM, World Conference on Religion and Peace
EHUD BANDEL, Rabbis for Human Rights
JO BECKER, Fellowship of Reconciliation
JOAN BOTAM, Centre Ecumenic de Catalunya
ELISE BOULDING, International Peace Research Assembly
HANS BÜHLER, Pädagogische Hochschule Weingarten
JOAN CARRERA, Bishop of Barcelona
MARIANI DIMARANAN, Task Force Detainees of the Philippines
ALI ELSAMMAN, Association pour le Dialogue International Islamo-
    Chretien
JOAN ESTRUCH, Centre de Recerca de Sociologia de la Religió
ANGELO FERNANDES, Archbishop Emeritus of New Delhi
VICENÇ FISAS, Centre UNESCO de Catalunya
SIMONE FUOSS, Pädagogische Hochschule Weingarten
GANYONGA III, Fon of Bali
GÜNTHER GEBHARDT, World Conference on Religion and Peace
MAHA GHOSANANDA, Dhammayietra Centre for Peace and Nonviolence
LAMAR GIBBLE, World Council of Churches
DANIEL GOMEZ IBAÑEZ, Peace Council
LINDA GROFF, California State University
SOM RAJ GUPTA, Kirori Mal College, University of Delhi

TENZIN GYATSO, H.H. the Dalai Lama
DAG HEDIN, Life and Peace Institute
SOHAIL INAYATULLAH, World Futures Studies Federation
JOSEPH JOBLIN, Pontificia Universita Gregoriana
ALEXANDER KOJA, Moscow Patriarchate, Interreligious Relations
MIRTA LOURENÇO, UNESCO, Culture of Peace Programme
FÈLIX MARTÍ, Centre UNESCO de Catalunya
GERALD MISCHE, Global Education Associates
PATRICIA MISCHE, Global Education Associates
MAXIMILIAN MIZZI, Ecumenism and Interreligious Dialogue
MAURICIO MOLINA, Pax Romana
MARY MWINGIRA, Pax Romana
RAIMON PANIKKAR, Fundació-Vivarium
LOUIS-EDMUND PETTITI, Cour Européenne des Droits de l'Homme
JOSEPH RAJKUMAR, Pax Romana
HELGA RIEDL, Plum Village
KARL RIEDL, Plum Village
SAMDHONG RINPOCHE, Central Institute of Higher Tibetan Studies
BAIDYANATH SARASWATI, Indira Gandhi National Centre for Arts
JACOBUS SCHONEVELD, International Council of Christians and Jews
PATARAPORN SIRIKANCHANA, The World Fellowship of Buddhist
KISHORE SINGH, UNESCO, Human Rights Unit
PAUL SMOKER, International Peace Research Association
MARIE-LAURE SOREL, Association pour le Dialogue International
    Islama-Chretien
JANUSZ SYMONIDES, UNESCO Human Rights, Democracy and Peace
    Division
JOHN B. TAYLOR, World Conference on Religion and Peace
WAYNE TEASDALE, Council for a Parliament of the World's Religions
SUSANNA VILLARAN, Instituto Barlomé de las Casas
ANTE VICKOVIC, Theology College in Makarska
ANDREZEJ WIELOWIEYSKI, Member of the Polish Parliament
MAHMOUD ZAKZOUK, Faculty of Theology of Al-Azhar University

Parliament of Catalonia, Barcelona, 16/XII/1994

Glossary of Terms

ahimsa. Literally, nonviolence, a virtue first recognized by the shramana subculture of ancient India that gave birth to Jainism and Buddhism. Recently popularized as a method of political activism by Gandhi.

Bahujan Hitay. Literally, for the welfare of all, a phrase used by the Buddha to indicate the goal of his community and adopted by Trailokya Bauddha Mahasangha, Sahayak Gana (TSMSG) as a name for their social welfare and educational projects that are open to all people.

bodhisattva. Literally, a being (dedicated and destined) for enlightenment, who demonstrates great wisdom and compassion.

Buddha nature. An affirmation of the worth of each being as having the potential to attain enlightenment in this lifetime or inherently embodying enlightenment.

Buddha-wisdom. The liberating wisdom that sees the emptiness of all mental constructions and the interdependence of things. Manifest as infinite compassion.

Council of All Beings. A group practice created by John Seed in which some people don the masks of different animals and plants to speak for their needs in the current ecological crisis, while unmasked humans are placed in the center of the circle and asked to account for their actions.

daimoku. The invocation of "nam-myoho-renge-kyo" (literally, "I place my trust in the *Lotus Sutra*") which enables participation in the universal and saving power of enlightenment.

dalit. Literally, those who are oppressed, the name chosen for themselves by those in India who were designated as outcaste or "untouchable" by the established classes according to Hindu law in the *Code of Manu.*

Dhamma (Skt., **Dharma**). One of the Three Refuges (Buddha, Dhamma, Sangha); a core Buddhist term with various levels of meaning: morality, teachings, components of existence, and saving truth.

Dhammachari (fem., **Dhammacharini**). Literally, someone who is living the teaching (Dhamma) of the Buddha, a term used by Sangharakshita for members of the Friends of the Western Buddhist Order and Trailokya Bauddha Mahasangha, Sahayak Gana (TBMSG) to avoid the lay-monastic distinction.

Dhammayietra. A group of Buddhist social activists in Southeast Asia committed to nonviolence and protection of the environment, such as the Dhammayietra Center for Peace & Nonviolence, P.O. Box 144, Phnom Penh, Cambodia; e-mail: dmy@forum.org.Kh.

eco-karma. Exploring the vastness of human karmic responsibility based on complicity with nuclear proliferation and contamination of the environment.

eco-koans. The dilemma of Buddhists who vow to save all beings while being aware of the vastness of human collusion in despoiling the ecosystem.

ecosattvas. People dedicated to restoring the ecosystem, a term that derives from bodhisattvas.

Esoteric Buddhism. The Buddhist community in Tibet and Mongolia called Tantric or Vajrayana, and in Japan called Tendai and Shingon based on new scriptures which appeared after the Mahayana scriptures, that survive in Chinese and Tibetan, and that encourage the use of new practices that have secret or esoteric levels of meaning expressed in mantras, mudras, and mandalas. These can be misinterpreted by the uninitiated since they go beyond conventional understanding.

expedient means. "Expedient" or "skillful" means to implement compassion in ways that may be unconventional but that are beneficial to other beings based on their effectiveness in getting positive results.

five precepts. The basic five rules for all Buddhists, namely, not killing, not stealing, not lying, not committing sexual misconduct, and not consuming intoxicants.

Friends of the Western Buddhist Order (FWBO). A Buddhist movement founded by Ven. Sangharakshita in the late 1960s in

England that is influential in India among the followers of B.R. Ambedkar and that led to the founding of TBMSG.

Gohonzon. A scroll written by Nichiren that is the object of worship (*honzon*) for Nichiren Buddhists depicting the ten dimensions of life and their non-duality as presented in the Lotus Scripture.

Going for Refuge. The fundamental act that constitutes being a Buddhist, namely, taking refuge in the Buddha, the Dharma (his teachings), and the Sangha (the Buddhist community); also called the Three Jewels or the Three Gems.

human revolution. A term used by Soka Gakkai International to refer to the inner transformation of a person's life and karma once they the embody the practice of chanting "nam-myoho-renge-kyo."

kalyana mitra/mitta. Spiritual friends, a term for the supportive kinship of like-minded people, both monastics and lay, who are committed to similar Buddhist ideals.

Lotus Sutra. A core Mahayana Buddhist scripture that emphasizes the worth of all people as possessing the Buddha nature and the mission of Buddhists to be socially active to help others based on compassion and the sustaining power of eternal Buddhahood.

Mahayana. A term for the Buddhist community in East Asia based on a new scriptural collection that appeared after the death of Gotama Buddha which survives in Chinese and Tibetan and encourages the use of new methods of practice based on the emptiness and interdependency of all things, the compassion of the Buddha, and the equality of practitioners as fellow bodhisattvas.

mandala. A visible picture said to be endowed with Buddhahood that serves as a means for enlightenment and an object of worship.

nirvana. To blow out or remove the ties of karma and the three poisons (ignorance, desire, and hatred) and resulting in bliss and equanimity.

parinirvana. The nirvana of the Buddha at death when his earthly existence is extinguished.

Refuges. A term referring to the Buddha, his Teaching (Dharma), and his Community (sangha) that are the sources of refuge for all Buddhists and collectively called the Three Jewels or Three Refuges.

Sakyadhita. Literally, daughters of the Buddha, the name for the International Association of Buddhist Women, 1143 Piikoi Place, Honolulu, Hawaii, USA 96822.

Sangha. One of the Three Refuges (Buddha, Dhamma, Sangha); the Buddhist community, both monastics and laity.

Sarvodaya Shramadana. Begun in 1958 by A.T. Ariyaratne with some high school student volunteers working in local villages in Sri Lanka, the Sarvodaya Shramadana movement operates on Buddhist and Gandhian principles committed to "the well-being of all" (*sarvodaya*) based on voluntary "energy sharing" (*shramadana*) that has been adopted in over 11,000 villages, making it the largest nonprofit civilian organization in Sri Lanka.

socially engaged Buddhism. A modern movement of Buddhists committed to social reform inspired by the work of Thich Nhat Hanh during the Vietnam War and organized in such groups as the Buddhist Peace Fellowship and the International Network of Engaged Buddhists.

Soka Gakkai International (SGI). Begun in 1930 as a lay Buddhist educational movement for creating value (*soka*) in society based on the teachings of Nichiren (1222-1282) as the Buddha for this age.

sutra. The Sanskrit name for a Buddhist scripture containing the teachings of the Buddha.

TBMSG (Trailokya Bauddha Mahasangha, Sahayak Gana). Literally, "the Association of Friends of the Buddhist Order of the Three Realms," the name of a Buddhist movement in India begun in 1978 under the inspiration of B.R. Ambedkar (1891-1956) and the Friends of the Western Buddhist Order.

Theravada. The Way of the Elders, a term for the Buddhist community in Sri Lanka and Southeast Asia based on the Buddhist scriptures preserved in the Pali language.

Three Jewels/Gems. A term referring to the Buddha, his Teaching (dharma) and his Community (sangha) that are the sources of refuge for all Buddhists and collectively called the Three Jewels or Three Refuges.

Three poisons. Greed, hatred, and ignorance; the core problems that Buddhists work to eradicate.

Three Practices. The practice of morality (sila), meditation (samadhi), and wisdom (prajna) as the foundational practices of Buddhists.

Three Refuges. A term referring to the Buddha, his Teaching (Dharma) and his Community (Sangha) that are the sources of refuge for all Buddhists and collectively called the Three Jewels or Three Refuges.

Three Virtues. A phrase with several Buddhist interpretations, but interpreted by Nichiren as the protection of a ruler, the enlightening capacity of a teacher, and the nurturing role of a parent, or more succinctly as the virtues of wisdom, compassion, and action.

Turning of the Wheel. A metaphor for the teaching activity of the Buddha; the three different phases of Buddhist scriptures are referred to as the three "turnings of the wheel."

Tzu Chi Compassion Foundation. The full title is Fo-chiao Tzu-chi Kung-te hui (Fuojiao Ciji gongde hui), or The Buddhist Compassionate Merit Society; founded in 1966 by Ven. Shih Cheng-yen with the cooperation of a few housewives collecting pennies a day, the organization now has several million volunteer members. It operates a modern hospital, medical school, nursing school, and university in Hua-lian city, Taiwan, as well as gives medical and social relief in over 20 countries around the world.

upasaka (fem., **upasika**). A Sanskrit and Pali name for laity.

Vajrayana. See **Esoteric Buddhism.**

vihara. A peaceful place, a place for religious retreat.

Vinaya. The rules for practice given by the Buddha along with supporting stories and explanations for their existence that are collected in the first section of the Buddhist scriptures; the rules for monks and nuns are summarized into a list from the most serious to the least serious (numbering 200+ for monks and 300+ for nuns) called the *Pratimoksha* and used for recitation twice monthly; vinaya can also apply more broadly to guidelines for any Buddhist practice, monastic or lay.

zazen. Formal sitting meditation.

About the Editor

David W. Chappell is professor and graduate chair of the Department of Religion at the University of Hawaii. He initiated a series of Buddhist-Christian conferences in 1980 and was founding editor of the academic journal *Buddhist-Christian Studies* from 1980-1995. He became the founding director of the Buddhist Studies Program at the University of Hawaii in 1987. In 1988, Professor Chappell was a cofounder of the Society for Buddhist-Christian Studies, and served as its President from 1993-95. He is author of *T'ien-t'ai Buddhism: An Outline of the Four-fold Teachings* (1983), editor of *Buddhist and Taoist Studies*, vols. 1 and 2, and co-editor of *Unity in Diversity: Hawaii's Buddhist Communities* (1997). Currently, he is focusing on Buddhist roles in modern society.

About the Boston Research Center

The Boston Research Center for the 21st Century (BRC), an international peace institute, was established in 1993. Its founder, Daisaku Ikeda, is a Buddhist peace activist and president of Soka Gakkai International (SGI), an association of Buddhist organizations in 128 countries. The Center brings together scholars and activists in dialogue on common values across cultures and religions, seeking in this way to support an evolving global ethic for a peaceful twenty-first century. Human rights, nonviolence, ecological harmony, and economic justice are focal points of the Center's work.

The BRC's programs include a biannual conference series on global ethics, an annual forum on women's leadership for peace, an annual Global Citizen Award, and a series of books on common values which have provided curricular support for university courses in humanities, peace studies, and comparative religion.

BRC publications include the 1998 titles:
- *Subverting Hatred: The Challenge of Nonviolence in Religious Traditions,* Daniel L. Smith-Christopher, editor
- *Abolishing War: Dialogue with Peace Scholars Elise Boulding and Randall Forsberg*

and the 1997-98 three-volume Earth Charter series:
- *Buddhist Perspectives on the Earth Charter*
- *Human Rights, Environmental Law, and the Earth Charter*
- *Women's Views on the Earth Charter*

More information on the Boston Research Center's mission, programs, and publications can be found on the Center's website at www.brc21.org.

About Wisdom

Wisdom Publications, a not-for-profit publisher, is dedicated to making available authentic Buddhist works. We publish translations of the sutras and tantras, commentaries and teachings of past and contemporary Buddhist masters, original works by the world's leading Buddhist scholars, and books exploring East-West themes. We publish our titles with the appreciation of Buddhism as a living philosophy and with the special commitment to preserve and transmit important works from all the major Buddhist traditions.

Wisdom Publications is a non-profit, charitable 501(c)(3) organization affiliated with the Foundation for the Preservation of the Mahayana Tradition (FPMT).

If you would like more information or a copy of our mail-order catalog, please contact us at:

Wisdom Publications
199 Elm Street
Somerville, Massachusetts 02144 USA
Telephone: (617) 776-7416 • Fax: (617) 776-7841
E-mail: info@wisdompubs.org

or visit our website at:
www.wisdompubs.org